Welfare for the Wealthy

Parties, Social Spending, and Inequality in the US

How does political party control of the federal government determine changes to social policy and by extension influence inequality in America? Conventional theories show that the Democratic Party when in power produces more social expenditures and consequently less inequality. *Welfare for the Wealthy* reexamines the relationship between parties and social policy by recognizing the social system as divided and government spending as a choice between public spending and private subsidies. Christopher Faricy argues that both Democrats and Republicans have electoral and policy incentives to increase social spending albeit delivered through different policy mechanisms and targeted towards divergent socioeconomic classes. Faricy using a unique data set of federal tax expenditures shows that Republicans increase social spending through the tax code, which benefits businesses and wealthier workers. In particular, he demonstrates that increases in the level of social tax expenditures are paid for with cuts in discretionary public social spending, which taken together contribute to higher levels of inequality. This analysis has implications for who provides social services, who receives government assistance for social benefits, and income inequality in the United States.

Christopher Faricy is an Assistant Professor of Political Science and Public Policy at The Maxwell School of Citizenship and Public Affairs at Syracuse University. His research has won a number of national awards including the American Political Science Association's 2012 Harold D. Lasswell Award and the Midwestern Political Science Association's 2010 Pi Sigma Alpha Award. His research has appeared in various journals including the *Journal of Politics* and *Political Behavior* and has been financed by The Russell Sage Foundation. His project has also been written about in the *Washington Post*, the *Huffington Post*, and *Mother Jones*.

Welfare for the Wealthy

Parties, Social Spending, and Inequality in the US

CHRISTOPHER G. FARICY

Syracuse University

CAMBRIDGE
UNIVERSITY PRESS

CAMBRIDGE
UNIVERSITY PRESS

32 Avenue of the Americas, New York NY 10013-2473, USA

Cambridge University Press is part of the University of Cambridge.

It furthers the University's mission by disseminating knowledge in the pursuit of
education, learning and research at the highest international levels of excellence.

www.cambridge.org
Information on this title: www.cambridge.org/9781107498402

First published 2015
First paperback edition 2016

A catalogue record for this publication is available from the British Library

Library of Congress Cataloguing in Publication data
Faricy, Christopher G., 1973–
Welfare for the wealthy : parties, social spending, and inequality in the United States /
Christopher G. Faricy.
    pages   cm
Includes bibliographical references and index.
ISBN 978-1-107-10101-2 (hardback)
1. United States – Social policy.   2. Welfare state – United States.
3. Income distribution – United States.   4. Equality – United States.
5. United States – Politics and government.   I. Title.
HN65.F373   2015
306.0973–dc23   2015005320

ISBN 978-1-107-10101-2 Hardback
ISBN 978-1-107-49840-2 Paperback

To my parents
Thank you for everything

Contents

Figures

Tables

Acknowledgments

This book started out seven years ago at the University of North Carolina at Chapel Hill and has been helped along the way by my family, friends, and colleagues. The faculty and graduate students at UNC provided insight, support, and encouragement in getting this project off the ground. Virginia Gray chaired my dissertation committee and provided expert guidance from beginning to end. Virginia knew when to push my writing, knew what aspects of the project needed sharpening, and encouraged me to pursue a book contract. Frank Baumgartner delivered sage advice on the first article to come out of the project and has been extraordinarily helpful and supportive of my early career. Jim Stimson urged me to expand the scope of the project and introduced me to time series analysis. Tom Carsey commented on numerous versions of the dissertation and pushed me to center my argument within the context of existing theories of political parties. I would like to thank Michele Hoyman for her continued friendship and unquestioned support for my career throughout the years. Mike MacKuen, George Rabinowitz, Nate Kelly, John Stephens, and Chris Ellis all provided discerning advice about the project through conversations inside and outside Hamilton Hall. The UNC political science department provided financial support for me to collect data and work on this project during the summer months of graduate school through the Thomas M. Ulhman Award, the James W. Prothro Award, and the American Politics Research Group (APRG). Finally, I'm ever grateful for my friends at UNC who provided emotional support and general good times, including Patrick McHugh, Micah Weinberg, Luke Berchowitz, Joel Winkelman, Heather Sullivan, Ryan Bakker, Patrick Wohlfarth, Peter Enns, Jennifer Weaver, and Jamie Monogan.

This book would not have been possible without the pathbreaking work of Christopher Howard, Jacob Hacker, Suzanne Mettler, Andrea Louise Campbell, Theodore Lowi, Larry Bartels, Martin Gilens, Paul Pierson, Joe Soss, Larry Jacobs, and Theda Skocpol. Their collective work inspired me to pursue a larger project at the intersection of social policy and income inequality. I would also like to thank the staff of the Joint Committee on Taxation for providing copies of early bluebooks that I used to construct my data set and answering questions about data methodology. I have presented various segments of this book at the annual conferences of the America Political Science Association, the Midwestern Political Science Association, and the Western Political Science Association. Additionally, I have received valuable feedback from presentations at the American Politics Research Group at UNC, the Political Methods Workshop at UNC and Duke, The Ford School of Public Policy at the University of Michigan, and the School of Public and International Affairs at the University of Georgia.

The community of faculty and graduate students at The Maxwell School at Syracuse University has been extraordinarily helpful in providing guidance and support for the final stages of the book project. First, I appreciate the feedback I received on latter chapters presented at Political Science Research Workshop (PSRW), the Campbell Institute, and Moynihan Research Group. I received feedback from Len Burman, Matt Cleary, Brian Taylor, Tom Keck, Shana Gadarian, Jon Hanson, Dan McDowell, Sarah Pralle, Quinn Mulroy, Seth Jolly, Kristi Anderson, Hans Schmitz, Gavan Duffy, and Jeff Stonecash. Also, I'd like to thank Taewoo Kang at Washington State University along with Brian Wolfel, Whitney Baillie and Brandon Metroka at Syracuse University for their invaluable work as research assistants.

The anonymous reviewers at Cambridge University Press and elsewhere provided thoughtful comments that markedly improved the organization and substance of the book. Also, I'd like to thank Robert Dressen and the production team at Cambridge University Press for their professionalism in guiding the book through the production stages.

Finally, this book would not have come to fruition without the love and support of my family. My parents have provided encouragement, patience, and unconditional love throughout my life. I'm forever grateful for all the opportunities that their lives and love have brought me. My siblings, Nikki and Peter, have motivated my work in varied but important ways and inspired me more than they will ever know. My nephew, Parker, has taught me the meaning of courage and his experience navigating the medical system has heightened my sense of urgency in studying American social policy. Finally, my lovely and talented wife Lauren has been understanding and sympathetic of all the ups and downs involved in the writing process. Her uncompromising love has nourished me and I'm so blessed to have her and Nathan in my life.

The Politics of Social Policy in America

The fundamental story of political parties and social policy in America has not changed much since 1932. In this familiar narrative, Democrats expand the size of the federal government through increases in social spending that primarily benefit more vulnerable populations (such as the elderly, the working poor, ethnic minorities, and female-headed house-holds) all in an effort to redistribute income and reduce inequality. The Republican Party, on the other hand, cuts social welfare spending in order to reduce the role of the federal government in the economy, which tends to magnify market inequalities. This American political story began with partisan battles over the New Deal, was extended to the Great Society programs, and, most recently, was fought anew over the passage of the Affordable Care Act, otherwise known as Obamacare. In fact it can be argued that the epitome of modern partisan politics is the perpetual conflict between Democrats and Republicans over the proper role of government in financing social benefits and services. However, this simple narrative of Democrats as the party of big government and Republicans as the party of small government is outdated and obscures rather than illuminates the reality of American politics. The traditional account of the partisan politics of social welfare policy is incomplete because it under-counts government social spending, misrepresents who benefits from federal welfare programs, and ignores the role of the Republican Party in expanding the social welfare state. This book sets out to reconstitute our understanding of the relationship between political parties and social policy in the United States by properly conceptualizing the social system as divided between the public and private sectors, and social spending as a choice between public expenditures and private subsidies.

How does the relationship between political parties and social policy change when we recognize the social system as divided and social spending as a choice? The federal government plays a substantial role in funding both public social programs such as Medicare and private social programs such as employment-based health insurance (Hacker 2002, Howard 1997). This fact allows us to theorize about and observe the role of the Republican Party in expanding the scope of the federal government in supporting private social welfare. In this book, I theorize and demonstrate that *both Democrats and Republicans* have increased federal spending for social welfare programs over the last forty years. However, the two parties increase social spending by using different spending tools that subsidize different sectors of the economy, accrue benefits to opposing economic classes, and produce divergent effects on income inequality. There are two welfare states in America: a public one mainly built and maintained by the Democrats and a burgeoning private welfare state primarily supported by the Republican Party as an alternative to programs such as Social Security, Medicare, and Medicaid. My analysis of political party power and changes to funding for public versus private welfare has implications for who provides social services, who receives social benefits, and income inequality in the United States.

Partisan Politics and the Divided American Welfare State

During the summer of 2009, the Democratic and Republican parties engaged in a debate about health care reform surrounding the legislation that later became known as the Affordable Care Act (ACA) or Obamacare. Democrats in Congress, under the leadership of House Speaker Nancy Pelosi, pushed for a reform bill that included a "public option," a provision allowing citizens to buy into a government-run health program that would compete with private insurance plans. In a speech given to the NAACP, Nancy Pelosi argued "we need health care for all Americans, which is a right, not a privilege. And it will have a public option that is necessary to remove the health insurance companies from coming between patients and their doctors" (Pelosi, 7/17/09). Democratic Speaker Pelosi portrays private health insurance companies as a problem with the health care system and then offers the solution of a new public program that would be the equivalent of Medicare for all. This statement goes beyond rank ordering the public and private sectors and accuses private companies of interfering with patient care in a way that requires government intervention into the market. Additionally,

Speaker Pelosi frames health care as a right of citizenship, with the implication that this right should be guaranteed to all people and protected by the federal government. In response to the Democratic demand for a public option, Congressional Republicans pushed back in a public letter sent to President Obama arguing "Washington-run programs undermine market-based competition through their ability to impose price controls and shift costs to other purchasers. Forcing free market plans to compete with these government-run programs would create an unlevel playing field and inevitably doom true competition" (Bacon 2009). In contrast to the Democratic Party, the Republican Senators identify public health care programs as the central problem in the U.S. health care industry and they offer as a solution more competition among health care insurers in the private market. Republicans imply that the federal government has an unfair advantage in the health care market, and public programs are an imminent threat to the free market. The Republican Senators conceptualize health care as a commodity whose quantity and price are determined by the market and thereby imply that a patient's ability to pay should determine the quality of their care. These statements reveal the two parties' opposing preferences for government social programs versus private market solutions. As I argue throughout the book, party conflict over social policy is over more than just whether to raise or lower public spending but rather is a partisan struggle over who deserves federal support for social welfare, how it should be delivered to the public, and the proper ratio of public social spending to subsidies for private welfare programs.

The Divided American Social System

Social policy is defined as any government effort to deliver economic security to citizens through the protection against income loss and the guarantee of a minimum standard of living. This definition allows and even invites us to examine all the ways in which government activity determines social policy outcomes. The United States has a divided social system in that both the public and private sectors provide citizens with benefits and services (Hacker 2002, Howard 1997, 2007).[1] While citizens easily recognize public social programs such as Social Security and Medicare, the federal government also plays an important role in

---

[1] In this book, I use the following terms interchangeably: social welfare, social system, and social welfare state. They all represent the collection of federal programs used to provide citizens basic economic security.

financing and regulating private social programs. The private social system refers to health care, pensions, welfare, education, and other services that citizens receive through their employers or other nongovernment organizations. For example, there are numerous employment-based social programs that receive government subsidies, such as 401k pension plans, employer-sponsored health insurance plans such as HMOs, and private Health Savings Accounts (HSAs), to name a few. The two social systems are financed in different ways by the federal government, provide insurance to different socioeconomic groups, and distribute federal money to divergent economic classes. Therefore, political parties have a choice when it comes to financing popular social goals such as providing health insurance, old-age pensions, or education. A political party can either fund public social programs using traditional government spending, or use federal subsidies to finance businesses, religious institutions, and other nongovernmental organizations in their administration of private social benefits (Surrey 1974, Howard 1997).[2] And while traditional public spending is easily identifiable as money spent by the federal government on programs such as Social Security, Medicare, Medicaid, and Temporary Aid to Needy Families (TANF), government subsidies such as tax expenditures require a more detailed explanation.

The principal subsidy used by the federal government to finance private benefits is formally referred to as a tax expenditure, although most citizens know this type of spending by its informal name – a tax break. Tax expenditures are a formal measure of the revenue lost to the U.S. Treasury from tax breaks such as the deduction for charitable contributions or the home mortgage interest deduction. Budget experts, economists, and policymakers consider targeted tax breaks as being similar to public spending since they are a politically determined use of federal revenue aimed at government-approved activities or groups. This type of spending is comparable to traditional budgetary spending in that it influences the incentives and behaviors of people in private markets and tax expenditure increases ultimately are paid for through higher taxes, lower spending, or increased borrowing. As Republican Representative Paul Ryan explains,

tax expenditures...are similar to government spending – instead of markets directing economic resources to their most efficient uses, the government directs

---

[2] Although there are a few federal tax expenditures that are used to make public social programs like Social Security and Medicare tax free – my arguments and data analysis focus exclusively on tax expenditures for private social benefits and services.

resources to politically favored uses... the key difference is that, with spending, the government collects the money first in the form of taxes from those who earned it, and reallocates the money elsewhere. With tax expenditures, government agrees not to collect the money as long as it is put to a government-approved use. Other tax expenditures literally do take the form of spending through the tax code, because they "return" more money than the taxes owed. (House Report 112–58)

So while some citizens may view tax breaks as a way to reduce their tax burden and get their own money back, political party leaders – who are the main focus of my analysis – view targeted tax breaks or tax expenditures as a way to distribute federal money to their favored constituencies or activities. There is no confusion among policymakers in Washington, D.C. – tax breaks are just government spending by another name and a major component of the American social welfare state.

And although traditional public spending and tax expenditures are both treated as spending for federal budgetary purposes, these two types of social expenditures differ in ways that are crucial for understanding the politics of social policy. First, a tax expenditure program is a type of off-budget spending executed through the tax code, and, therefore, allows policymakers to increase social spending without being accused of explicitly expanding the size of government. American public opinion is paradoxical in that the electorate holds very favorable views toward the government promoting social goals such as affordable health care insurance and greater access to higher education, yet these same citizens hold negative feelings toward the federal government and government spending (Page and Jacobs 2009, Ellis and Stimson 2012). Tax expenditures help federal policymakers support popular policy goals in ways that do not look like expansions of the federal government. Second, a tax expenditure program is the federal government's main policy tool in subsidizing individuals to purchase or consume mainly *private sector* social goods, such as providing exclusions for employee contributions to 401k plans or deductions for a Health Savings Account (HSA). The main beneficiaries of private-sector social benefits are the *providers*, such as banks, financial institutions, and private health care companies, and second, the *recipients* of private welfare, mainly professional, white-collar employees in large companies. Third, social tax expenditures designed as exclusions or deductions provide higher, on average, financial support to wealthier taxpayers than they do the middle or working classes. One of the main reasons that the mass public tolerates public social spending is that they assume it is targeted at assisting more vulnerable populations (e.g., Ellis and Stimson 2012). Social tax expenditures, since they are distributed against a progressive income tax structure, provide the largest financial benefits to citizens who make the most income, and, thereby, are subject to the highest marginal tax rates. The inclusion of tax expenditures alongside budgetary spending fundamentally changes the study of social welfare policy. In the following sections, I highlight just two of these changes to the politics of social policy: first, in measuring the size of the American social welfare state, and second, in determining who benefits from federal welfare programs.

The Size and Composition of the American Social Welfare State

How large is the American social welfare state? The majority of federal spending is directed at financing social programs in the United States. In 2012, the U.S. spent around $2 trillion on public social welfare programs out of a total budget of $3.5 trillion. While this amount is a large proportion of the U.S. budget, it is a relatively small percentage of the country's gross domestic product (GDP) – around 14 percent (Congressional Budget Office 2012). However, the addition of social tax expenditures to traditional spending for public social programs expands both the size of the federal government's involvement in the welfare state and who benefits from social spending. In 2012, the federal government spent around $600 billion through tax subsidy programs used to finance various social benefits and services (Joint Committee on Taxation 2013). If we combine traditional social spending for public programs and social tax expenditures for mainly private welfare, then three out of every four federal dollars are allocated for the provision of social benefits and services in the United States. Moreover, the inclusion of social tax expenditures increases the total amount spent by the federal government on social programs by around 20 percent every year, on average, over the last forty-two years.

How the federal government provides a safety net looks much different when social tax subsidies are properly calculated as part of the total federal budget. Figure 1.1 displays major categories of the 2013 U.S. budget and includes federal tax subsidies (formally known as tax expenditures) as a distinct budget category. In this reconfiguration of the national budget, tax expenditure(s) is the largest independent budget category. The United States spends more on tax expenditures than on Social Security and Medicare combined, and more than on the total defense budget. According to my analysis of the 2012 budget, the United States spent more on tax subsidies for just social welfare programs ($568 billion) than it spent on Medicare ($484 billion) or Medicaid ($415 billion),

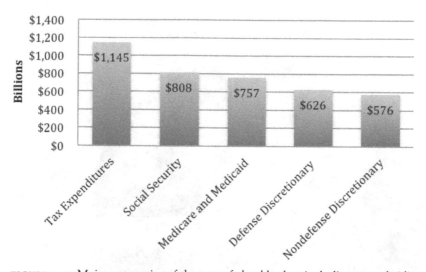

FIGURE 1.1. Major categories of the 2013 federal budget including tax subsidies. *Source:* Author's calculation using CBO and JCT data.

and spent roughly the same amount in the category of Income Security ($579 billion), which includes the *combined* cost of retirement for federal employees, unemployment, food stamps, Supplementary Security Income (SSI), and welfare. Next, for certain social policy areas, such as cash assistance to the poor, the federal government spends more money through tax expenditures than through traditional spending on public programs. For example, one of the largest welfare programs in the United States is the earned income tax credit (EITC), which is run through the tax code and targeted toward the working poor. In 2011, the federal government spent *more than twice* the amount on the EITC (just under $60 billion) as it did on what is commonly thought of as welfare, or TANF – around $26 billion (Joint Committee on Taxation 2012; Congressional Budget Office 2012).

The U.S. budget includes six categories that are explicitly classified for providing social welfare to the public and are as follows: health; income security; Social Security; Medicare; veterans' benefits and services; and education, training, and social services. The public social system is designed to give assistance to the elderly, the unemployed, and the poor. The two categories of Social Security and Medicare represent more than half of the total amount of federal money dedicated to public social programs in the United States. While the primary beneficiaries of Social Security and Medicare are seniors, these two programs are also critical

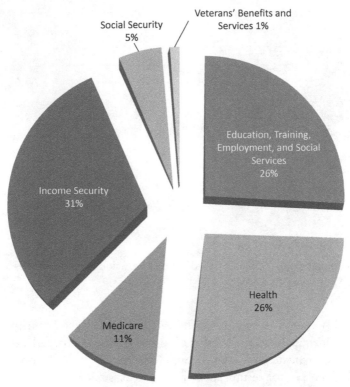

FIGURE 1.2. Tax subsidies for social welfare programs, 2012. *Source:* Author's calculation using JCT data.

in reducing the national poverty rate. The secondary federal public social spending categories such as health; income security; and education, training, and social services mainly provide government support to the working class and poor through programs such as Medicaid, unemployment insurance, food stamps, and welfare. The public system has long been thought to have two tiers: a generous set of core universal programs for seniors and a more miserly set of secondary programs for the poor.

Social tax expenditures, while organized into the same budget categories as public spending, benefit different socioeconomic groups. Figure 1.2 gives a breakdown of six subcategories of social welfare tax expenditures. There are a number of important differences between public social programs and tax subsidies for private social benefits. First, while Social Security and Medicare are the largest public programs, these two categories are minor spending components of the social tax expenditure system. The three largest categories are income security; health; and education, training, employment, and social services, which make up 83 percent of total social tax expenditures. These three budget categories are constituted by the major social programs run through the tax code (e.g., employer-provided pension and health insurance plans) and accrue the lion's share of federal benefits to wealthier professionals in large corporations. While these three budget categories on the private side provide the most benefits to professionals and wealthier households (the most economically secure), on the public side these categories provide assistance to the unemployed and the poor. Next, while the largest programs on the public side are universal social benefits, since any citizen over the age of sixty-five can claim them, on the tax expenditure side the largest programs for employment-based health care and pensions benefit white-collar employees fortunate enough to be offered employment-based benefits from their employer.[3] The inclusion of subsidies for social insurance alongside traditional public benefits results in a large American welfare state; yet, one that is fractured between the elderly and the working poor who rely on public programs while middle- and upper-class professionals receive tax subsidies for employment-based social benefits.

An International Comparison of Social Welfare Systems

The U.S. social welfare system is European in size but not spirit. In the past, comparative studies of social systems have shown that the United States spends less on public social programs than any other major European country (Weir et al. 1988, Organization for Economic Cooperation and Development 2011). Nevertheless, how the American welfare state compares to European systems changes drastically once private social benefits are included in the calculation of social spending. The U.S. private-sector social system is the largest in the world and has rapidly grown over the last thirty years (Adema et al. 2013). In 2009, the United States allocated more than 10 percent of the country's GDP toward the provision and administration of private social benefits and services. The result is that two out of every five dollars spent on social benefits and services in the United States are apportioned through the private market. In Table 1.1, ten countries (including the European average represented by OECD) are compared across three different types of social spending categories in 2007: private, public, and total expenditures (public plus private).

---

[3] Health care insurance rules have changed due to the ACA and will be discussed in greater detail later in Chapters 4 and 7.

TABLE 1.1. *International Comparison of Public versus Private Social Spending as a Percentage of GDP, 2009*

Country	Private		Public		Total	
United States	10.6%	[1]	19.2%	[9]	29.7%	[7]
Italy	2.3	[7]	27.8	[4]	30.1	[5]
Norway	2.3	[7]	23.3	[7]	25.6	[9]
United Kingdom	6.3	[3]	24.1	[6]	30.3	[4]
Spain	0.5	[8]	26	[5]	26.5	[8]
Netherlands	6.7	[2]	23.2	[8]	29.9	[6]
Germany	3.2	[4]	27.8	[4]	30.1	[5]
Denmark	2.9	[6]	30.2	[2]	33.1	[2]
Sweden	3.2	[4]	29.8	[3]	33	[3]
France	3.1	[5]	32.1	[1]	35.2	[1]
OECD average	2.7		22.1		24.8	

Source: Author's arrangement using OECD data.

First, the U.S. spends far and away the most amount of money on private social welfare in the developed world, 10.6 percent of GDP; this is nearly twice as much as the United Kingdom and more than the combined private social systems of France, Sweden, and Germany. In addition, private social spending accounts for 40 percent of *total* U.S. social spending, which again is the highest in the developed world. Conversely, the U.S. is dead last among all advanced industrial countries in the amount of government money dedicated to public programs, at just over 19 percent of GDP – as a comparison, the OECD average is 22.1 percent. In total, the U.S. spends 29.7 percent of GDP on social goods and services, which is around 5 points higher than the European average and similar to Germany, Italy, and the Netherlands. Altogether, the U.S. public welfare state is the smallest, the U.S. private welfare state is the largest, and the combined American social system is above the European average. The inclusion of the private sector not only changes how we think about the U.S. social welfare state in comparative terms but how we understand who benefits from the federal government's role in financing and providing citizens with economic security. The uniqueness of the U.S. social system is not in how much is spent on total benefits and services but rather which groups benefit. While most European-style welfare states distribute assistance disproportionately to the poorest populations, the American social system provides benefits to a wider socioeconomic swath of the electorate with more vulnerable populations generally reliant on the public system while wealthier citizens disproportionately benefit from aid to the private welfare state.

Welfare for the Wealthy: How the Rich Benefit from Federal Social Spending

Ronald Reagan, while running for the Republican presidential nomination in 1976, told the story of a woman from Chicago's South Side who "had eighty names, thirty addresses, twelve Social Security cards and is collecting veterans' benefits on four nonexisting deceased husbands" (Gilliam 1999). This racialized and gendered stereotype of the "Welfare Queen" has become a part of the American lexicon and reflects how the majority of voters, especially white voters, have come to view the recipients of public welfare benefits (Gilens 1999, Kellstedt 2000). Conversely, the private social system in the United States is mainly comprised of employment-based benefits and is supported by federal tax expenditures, which accrue substantial benefits to white, wealthy professionals in corporations. These privileged groups, while receiving substantial federal social benefits and services, are not commonly thought of as welfare recipients. Federal subsidies for private social welfare programs range far and wide, accruing monetary and social insurance benefits to more than sixty percent of working adults and their dependents. These federally supported social benefits and services include, but are not limited to, the following: employer-provided health insurance; employer-provided pensions; student loan interest; deductions for charitable contributions made to schools, hospitals, and religious organizations; contributions to a Keogh plan; contributions to an individual retirement account (IRA) account or Roth IRA; contributions to an employee stock ownership program (ESOP); deductions for college tuition, college fees, student loans, or a university scholarship or fellowship; and HSAs. Contrary to public social programs, many of these benefits are selectively offered by employers and provide the largest financial benefits to the richest recipients.

The majority of social tax expenditure programs are designed to provide the largest benefits to the wealthiest citizens all in the name of government-assisted economic security. For example, President Obama, in a 2011 budget speech, argued, "the tax code is also loaded up with spending on things like itemized deductions. And while I agree with the goals of many of these deductions, like homeownership or charitable giving, we cannot ignore the fact that they provide millionaires an average tax break of $75,000 while doing nothing for the typical middle-class family

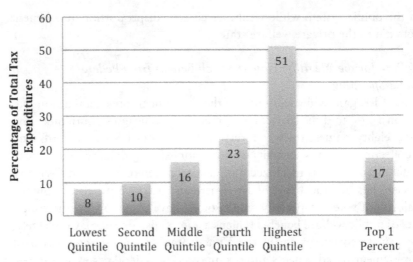

FIGURE 1.3. Share of major federal tax expenditures by income cohort, 2013.
Source: Congressional Budget Office, 2013.

that doesn't itemize" (Obama, 2011a). President Obama's statement
emphasizes that policymakers can choose to finance social benefits either
through tax expenditures (by allowing citizens who use government-
approved private social services to write smaller checks to the government) or through traditional spending (by writing a check to citizens or
directly providing social insurance or services). The primary difference
between social tax expenditure programs and programs such as Medicaid, direct student loan programs, public housing, and food stamps is
who benefits. Since the beneficiaries of public social programs are well
documented (see Campbell 2003, Soss 1999, Howard 2007), in the following sections, I expose the primary recipients of tax subsidies and the
private social programs they finance.

The majority of tax expenditure programs are upside-down subsidies that are of more value to wealthier taxpayers than they are to
middle- and working-class citizens. Since the federal income tax has a
progressive structure, tax expenditure programs formulated as deductions or exclusions reduce the progressivity of the tax system. Tax expenditures regressively distribute income by reducing tax rates more for
those who pay higher marginal rates than for households with lower
marginal rates. So while most public programs give higher benefits to
poorer recipients many social tax expenditure programs provide more
money to richer taxpayers. Figure 1.3 shows the income distribution of

TABLE 1.2. *Distribution of Tax Expenditure Benefits for Private Pension Benefits, 2015*

Income Cohort	Percent Share of Total Tax Benefits
Lowest Quintile	0.6
Second Quintile	3.5
Middle Quintile	9.5
Fourth Quintile	18.7
Top Quintile	67.6
Top Quintile Breakdown	
80–90th	18
90–95th	15.5
95–99th	23.6
Top 1 Percent	10.4

Source: Tax Policy Center, T13–0265 Tax Benefit of Certain Retirement Savings Incentives (PVA).

a large sample of tax expenditure programs from the federal government in 2013. In the figure, the horizontal axis displays the share of total tax expenditure benefits for each income quintile from the lowest, on the left, to the highest, on the right, and on the far right showing the accruement of benefits to the top one percent. The vertical axis shows the share of total tax expenditures ranging from 0 to 60 percent. The overall relationship between income, and total tax expenditure benefits is clear – the higher a household's income, the more benefits it receives from federal tax expenditure programs. The lowest two income cohorts receive only 8 and 10 percent of total tax expenditure benefits, respectively. The middle class does not fare much better, accruing just 16 percent of total tax expenditures. However, the wealthiest families (the top 20% of income earners) received over half (51%) of the total tax benefits from the federal government. These households that made on average $188,000 in 2013 received a larger share of tax benefits than the bottom 80 percent of American households. The top 1 percent of income earners (average income over $700,000) received 16 percent of the total benefits from federal tax expenditures, which is more than the entire middle class.

The federal government heavily subsidizes employment-based pension benefits through tax expenditure programs. Table 1.2 displays the distributional effects aggregated across four major tax expenditure programs for private retirement accounts that include the following:

employment-based IRAs, employment-based defined-benefit plans, employment-based defined-contribution plans, and deductions for self-employed retirement plans. In 2015, these four programs cost the federal government $127 billion. The rows in the table are organized by income cohort, and the column shows the percent share of the total tax expenditure programs by income cohort and groups within the top income quintile. The top income quintile (the wealthiest 20 percent of households) received 68 percent of the total benefits directed at private pensions or $86 billion just for this one year. The wealthiest households accrued *three times* the amount of benefits for private pensions as compared to the bottom 80 percent of American families. These programs are regressively distributive even when accounting for how much of the federal government's revenue comes from the top twenty percent of income earners. Moreover, the wealthiest one percent of households received more of the federal tax benefits (10.4%) for private pensions than did the entire middle class (9.5%). Altogether, high-income Americans benefit twice over from federal tax expenditures for private welfare: once, in the form of subsidized social benefits, and second, with lower effective income tax rates. All total, the vast majority of social tax expenditure programs are welfare for the wealthy.

A Theory of Political Parties and the Divided Social System

This book recasts our understanding of the relationship between political parties and social policy by offering a new theoretical argument that builds on research from political institutions, political behavior, comparative politics, and public policy. In bringing together these disparate lines of research, I construct a more inclusive and accurate representation of the choice that political parties face in constructing social policy: the choice of altering the social spending ratio more toward financing public benefits or in the direction of subsidizing private programs. The political choice between traditional spending for public programs and subsidies for private benefits is more than just a mechanical choice over different policy tools. This choice reflects the two political parties' divergent electoral calculations along with their philosophical differences about the proper balance between public and private power in society.

How does politics, in general, and political party power, specifically, change the role of the federal government in financially supporting the public or private side of the divided social welfare state? And what are the consequences of these policy choices for income inequality in America? There are a number of plausible theories that could characterize the relationship between political party control of the federal government and changes to the divided social system. One possibility is the Democratic Party supports all types of social spending regardless of how it is delivered and who benefits from it, and conversely, the Republican Party, the party of small government, opposes all forms of government social spending. If this is true then when Democrats take power there should be increases in both traditional social spending for public programs and social tax expenditures for private benefits, which would benefit the rich and the poor and everyone in between. In addition, there would be no relationship between changes in social spending and income inequality because the two forms of spending (traditional public and tax expenditures) would cancel each other out by distributing federal revenues both up and down the income ladder. A second possibility is that Democrats, over time, support subsidies for private welfare and Republicans, when in the majority, increase direct spending for public programs. In this scenario, Democratic social spending could potentially drive up the level of income inequality and Republicans would reduce inequality through their spending patterns when in office. This is the most unlikely scenario. A third possibility is that both Democrats and Republicans increase both traditional social spending and social tax expenditures, and therefore, there is no observable difference between Democrats and Republicans when it comes to annual changes in social spending. In this case, the two parties might not at all discriminate based on spending type, so that both parties – when in power – increase any and all spending in order to gain favor with the largest number of potential voters. As with the first situation, if both types of social spending rise there would be no observable impact between social expenditures and changes in income inequality.

A fourth possibility is that both political parties prefer to increase social spending when in power but choose different spending tools, with one party favoring traditional social spending for public programs and the other selecting social tax expenditures for private welfare. In this situation, not only would the two parties show clear preferences for one type of spending over another, but they would also trade off an increase in one spending mechanism with a decrease in the other. We might expect that Democrats, for electoral and ideological reasons, would increase traditional public spending at the expense of tax subsidies for private welfare and Republicans would raise the level of social tax expenditures

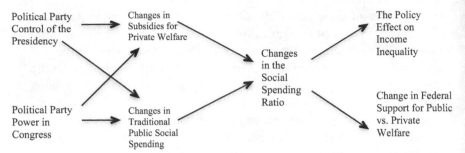

FIGURE 1.4. A dynamic model of political parties and the divided social system.

for private benefits while lowering spending on public programs. These partisan trade offs of social spending would have the potential to impact the level of income inequality. For example, a Republican increase in tax subsidies for private benefits and a corresponding decrease in public spending would result in federal money being moved from programs that assist the poor to subsidies that accrue money to the rich and thereby contribute to a higher level of income inequality. While arguments could be made for any one of these possibilities, I argue that the last scenario is the most common in modern American politics.

The theoretical relationship between political parties and the divided social system is represented by the following arguments. First, a vast majority of the American public, even a majority of conservatives and Republicans, prefers an active role for the federal government in providing a social safety net (Page and Jacobs 2009, Ellis and Stimson 2012). Therefore, the boundaries of mass public opinion do not allow a campaign strategy for Republicans that includes cuts to government social spending while providing voters nothing in return. Second, the two political parties, when in the majority and operating under the constraints of public opinion, design social policy in a way that increases federal social spending for their core constituencies while paying for this increase with cuts to government benefits that accrue to the opposing party's voters. Specifically (and as modeled in Figure 1.4.), a political party in power will substitute traditional spending for public social programs with subsidies for private social benefits (or vice versa). In addition, the two political parties design long-run social policy in ways that adhere to their party members' ideology and preferences for government distribution. While political parties are concerned with getting their members reelected and keeping power they also care about how government power is utilized for policymaking. In particular, a party in power wants to move federal policy in the ideological direction of their elite membership (legislators, activists, and donors) over the long run. For Democrats, and their liberal base, this means crafting public policy to foster greater societal equality in one part through the public administration of benefits, and in a second part, through taking income from the very wealthy and redistributing it down the income ladder. The Republican Party designs public policy, for their highly conservative supporters, in ways that use federal money to subsidize businesses and private enterprise while distributing federal money up toward wealthier families. And while both parties change the ratio of social spending for electoral and ideological reasons, Democrats are most concerned with who receives federal benefits while Republicans are more motivated to change the ideological direction of federal policy.

The model I will use throughout the book, Figure 1.4, represents my theoretical argument on the relationship between political parties and changes to the divided social welfare state. I expect that Democratic and Republican Party control of both the executive and legislative branches will produce opposing changes to social spending, and by extension, the level of income inequality. I examine both branches of government since the annual budget process and tax legislation involve the coordination of political parties across Congress and the White House. Next, I expect that political party control of the federal government will produce changes in three types of social spending: traditional public expenditures, subsidies for private welfare, and a ratio of the two. I use mandatory and discretionary social expenditures to represent traditional public spending and tax expenditures to represent federal subsidies for private welfare. The social expenditure ratio is the annual level of social tax expenditures as a proportion of aggregate federal social spending or social tax expenditures plus discretionary social spending. I expect that as Republicans gain more power in the federal government there will be increases in tax subsidies for private welfare benefits and decreases in discretionary public spending. When federal money is transferred from traditional public social programs to subsidies for private welfare then government support for social insurance is moved from programs that assist the working class and minorities to the upper-middle class and wealthy. Additionally, the relocation of federal money from welfare programs that progressively distribute money to social tax expenditure programs that regressively distribute federal revenue to the wealthy should increase the level of income inequality in the United States. Consequently, the implications of this argument are that changes to political party control of government and by extension social policy influence which sector of the economy receives more government assistance for administering social programs (public bureaucracies or private businesses), which citizens receive increased government support for social benefits (working/lower-middle class or upper-middle/rich), and the level of income inequality in America.

An Outline of the Book

In Chapter 2, I review the extant literature on the politics of social policy and pay particular attention to the recent slate of studies on the divided social state. Next, I introduce my theoretical argument on the partisan politics of the divided social system. The argument rests on three particulars. I first argue that widespread voter support for federal social programs places pressure on *both* political parties to use government power to provide citizens with social benefits and services. Second, I argue that a political party in power substitutes one type of social spending for another so as to distribute federal money and benefits to its electorally important constituencies and away from the other party. The party in power's electoral coalition and ideological makeup determine the type of social spending trade off that occurs. The differences in the two parties' socioeconomic electoral coalitions align nicely with who disproportionately benefits from the public versus the private side of the divided social system – so moving federal support from one side to the other is a form of distributive politics. Next, I argue that a party in power will design social policy in a manner that reflects the members' ideological leanings and preferences for the distribution of federal money. The electoral and ideological goals of the parties complement and reinforce one another. Finally, the parties' social spending choices produce distributive effects, which in turn impact the level and direction of income inequality.

In Chapter 3, I reevaluate the existing wisdom on political parties and changes to social policy in America. In particular, I reexamine the relationship between Democratic Party control and increased government spending for public programs. Although groups associated with the Democratic Party's electoral coalition benefit the most from public social spending the latest reforms to national welfare and Medicare confuse rather than clarify the conventional theory of the Democratic Party and expansions of the federal social welfare state. Next, I discuss in detail the data and methods that will be employed throughout the book. This section includes an explanation of the new data set on federal tax expenditures used to represent government subsidies and a discussion of the error correction model (ECM) used in the time series analysis. I examine the relationship between Democratic Party power and higher social spending for public programs. Democratic control of the White House results in higher levels of discretionary social spending and total public social spending (discretionary plus mandatory). Second, I test the relationship between political party control of government and social expenditures using a new measurement of total government social spending, which combines traditional public spending and tax expenditures. My results provide no statistically conclusive evidence for Democratic control of government and higher levels of aggregate social spending. These results confirm my suspicion that social policy is best understood as a political choice between direct spending for public benefits and tax expenditures for private programs (and not as a simple choice of just raising or lowering all federal spending).

In Chapter 4, I begin building a framework for studying the politics of the divided social state through an examination of tax expenditures and the private social system. First, I define and explain the significance of the private American social welfare state. In particular, I chart the recent growth of private social spending and compare private social expenditures in the United States to other advanced nations' spending patterns. Next, I argue that groups more commonly associated with the Republicans' electoral coalition disproportionately benefit from private sector social benefits and services. I then pivot to exploring the distinctive role that federal tax expenditures play in the American private welfare state. The government influences the private social state in many ways but none more pervasively than through federal tax expenditure programs. I first describe the concept of tax expenditures and examine how this policy instrument relates to federal government efforts at subsidizing and privatizing social benefits. Second, I show the growth of federal tax expenditures over time and describe their development in four social policy areas: health care, pensions, welfare, and education. Next, I use a new data set and empirically test how changes to the amount of social tax expenditures influence private sector spending on social benefits. My analysis shows that federal increases to the amount of social tax subsidies correspond to higher business spending on employee social benefits. Therefore, the federal government not only influences social policy directly through changes in public spending but also indirectly through changes in tax expenditures, which in turn determines the amount of private social spending in America.

Chapter 5 directly tests the theory of political parties and the divided social system. First, I explain how the Republican Party has used social tax expenditures as part of a larger strategy to privatize social programs. In the dynamic analysis of the theory, I find evidence that increased Republican control of the federal government correlates with increases to the annual level of tax expenditures for private social programs in both the short and the long term. In addition, increased Republican Party control results in higher ratios of social tax expenditures to total social spending. The major implication of these results is that both political parties increase social spending when in office, just using different modalities of federal spending that accrue benefits to politically and economically divergent populations. In addition, I examine alternative explanations to partisanship for changes to the modality of federal social spending. First, I examine the relationship between party leader ideology and changes in social spending and find that more conservative Republicans produce larger changes in the level of social tax expenditures. Next, I test the idea that increases to social tax expenditures are a function of divided government and find no evidence for this claim. Finally, I evaluate political party polarization alongside Republican control of the federal government in determining changes in social spending and show that both party control and polarization drive increases in the social expenditure ratio. The implications of these results is that as the national Republican Party has become more conservative over time there has been a corresponding increase in the level of social tax expenditures and a greater substitution of tax expenditures at the expense of discretionary social spending for public benefits.

In Chapter 6, I change my analysis from studying the partisan causes of social spending to their policy effects. In particular, I examine how the ratio of social tax expenditures to total social spending influences the level of income inequality in the United States. Previously, I argued that political parties use social policy to distribute both social and financial benefits toward their constituencies and away from the opposing party's supporters. Since public social spending and tax expenditures distribute federal money in opposing directions, I expect to find that higher levels of the ratio of tax expenditures to total spending correlate with increases in national income inequality. My analysis reveals that increases in the social expenditure ratio correspond to higher levels of income inequality in both the short and the long term, even when controlling for political and economic factors. The implication of these findings is that changes in social policy influence economic security not only through access to social insurance but also through changes in the level of national income inequality. Social spending has always been associated with efforts aimed at reducing inequality. I demonstrate, here, that social spending through the tax code contributes to the historically large income gap between the rich and the poor.

Finally, in Chapter 7, I explain how my analysis here challenges existing ideas about party politics, who benefits from federal welfare, and the role of public policy in addressing income inequality. I examine the implications of the partisan theory of the divided welfare state for studies of social welfare and public policy. I argue that the analysis here demonstrates how Republican presidents use tax policy and cuts in spending to increase the level of income inequality. Next, I use the partisan theory of the divided social system to explain the critical differences between the ACA and the Republican "Ryan" Plan. Finally, I explain how making tax expenditures part of the formal budget process and linking taxes with specific spending programs would improve the politics of social policy.

2

The Partisan Politics of the Divided U.S. Social Welfare State

Conservative advisor Bill Kristol penned a now-famous memo to Republicans about defeating the Clinton health care bill in 1993 that discusses the relationship between social policy and electoral politics. Kristol argued

> its passage (Clinton's health care reform) in the short run will do nothing to hurt (and everything to help) Democratic electoral prospects in 1996. But the long-term political effects of a successful Clinton health care bill will be even worse – much worse. It will relegitimize middle-class dependence for "security" on government spending and regulation. It will revive the reputation of the party that spends and regulates, the Democrats, as the generous protector of middle-class interests. And it will at the same time strike a punishing blow against Republican claims to defend the middle class by restraining government. Kristol 1993.

There are a number of important questions that arise from the Kristol memo. How do electoral considerations influence a political party's strategy on social welfare policy? How can a political party in power target a socioeconomic class of voters with social benefits? How do party leaders balance short- and long-run considerations when designing social policy? And if Republicans believe that the Democratic Party benefits at the ballot box from increased social spending then why wouldn't the Republican Party try to distribute social benefits too? In this chapter, I introduce a partisan theory of the divided social welfare state in America. My theoretical argument examines the electoral and political motivations of both the Democratic and Republican parties in crafting social welfare policy.

In the following sections, I review the extant literature on the divided social system. In particular, I highlight recent studies from policy scholars on how the different characteristics of public versus private social welfare influence political changes to social policy over time. This line of literature foreshadows how Republicans and Democrats differentiate their approaches to the divided social system. Next, I provide a broad sketch of my party-centered theory of the divided social system. First, I consider *why* the major political parties would have different approaches to the divided social welfare state. I argue that the opposing electoral coalitions and member ideology of the Democratic and Republican parties create different incentives for favoring one type of spending versus another. Second, I examine *how* the two political parties distribute social benefits through the selection and substitution of policy tools across the divided social welfare state. I argue that Democrats in power increase government spending for public social programs and offset the costs through reductions in private subsidies, while Republican Party control results in an overall increase of federal subsidies for private social programs at the expense of traditional spending for public social welfare.

A Divided U.S. Social System

The fundamental dividing line between the Democratic Party and Republican Party is over the role of the federal government in the economy. As applied to social policy, the Democratic Party has continually expanded social welfare programs through increases in government spending while the Republican Party has limited social programs through spending cuts. This resilient relationship between political parties and changes to social spending has been found across time (McCarty et al. 2006), across levels of government (Fellowes and Rowe 2004), and across countries (Blais et al. 1993, 1996, Huber and Stephens 2001).[1] While these relationships are certainly true, most empirical research does not take into account many of the assorted policy tools used to finance social policy such as tax expenditures, grants, and loans. These forms of off-budget spending have all grown more popular in recent decades and constitute an increasing percentage of total federal spending. Most importantly, many of these policy instruments are used to subsidize private sector organizations and businesses, especially those that provide and administer social programs. The inclusion of government subsidies for private welfare allows us to observe modern partisan conflict through the study of the politics of the divided American welfare state.

---

[1] Across countries, leftist parties produce more social spending and rightist parties produce less.

This study builds off a long line of work examining the role of the federal government in creating and perpetuating the divided American welfare state (see Gitterman 2010, Hacker 2002, Howard 1997, 2007, Mettler 2007, Morgan and Campbell 2011, Titmuss 1965). There are a number of recurring themes in the public policy literature on the divided social system that are relevant for the analysis in this book. First, the federal government is heavily involved in the financing, regulation, administration, and provision of both private and public social programs. As an example, Esping-Andersen (1990) in *The Three Worlds of Welfare Capitalism* argues that international comparisons of social welfare need to account for the private sector and studies that only examine public social programs are incomplete and inadequate. He develops the concept of welfare-state regimes, which represents a social welfare state as being compromised by the state, the private market, and the family. In creating social welfare state regime types, Esping-Andersen categorizes the United States as a liberal welfare state (liberal in the classic sense). A liberal welfare state is exemplified by the dominance of private organizations in providing benefits and services and therefore limiting the federal government to a secondary role of providing means-tested benefits to the poor and dependents. A number of more recent studies such as Hacker (2002), Howard (1997, 2007), and Mettler (2007) show that the United States spends more on private social benefits than any other industrialized country in the world.

While the private welfare system is substantial in the United States, its size and scope are determined by the interaction between public and private programs. The seminal work on the American divided social system is Jacob Hacker's *The Divided Welfare State* (2002). Hacker argues that the early development of a private health care system in the United States hindered future political efforts to create a universal, government-run public health insurance program. More recently, Morgan and Campbell (2011) show that the provision of private prescription drug benefits through Medicare Part D resulted in a lower demand among seniors for a publicly provided drug plan. Hacker (2002) contends that the United States' early adoption of a Social Security program allowed public retirement benefits the necessary time and space to develop, in part, due to the lack of an established private pension system. He goes on to show that future efforts at developing private retirement plans had to contend with both the elderly constituency built by public pensions and the bureaucracy (the Social Security Administration) charged with administering the program and protecting its policy turf. For example, President Reagan failed in his efforts to privatize Social Security, which resulted in the elderly becoming more politically active, and relatedly, the AARP growing in number and lobbying strength (Campbell 2003). These studies demonstrate that path dependency, policy feedback, and organized interests determine changes to the divided social system, and that a trade off exists between the government's promotion of private welfare benefits and public demand for government-administered social programs. In this book, I formally examine the role of political party power in moving federal money from one side of the divide to the other and expect that a party in the majority can alter the balance and path of the divided social system despite existing policy constraints.

Additionally, policy studies of the divided welfare state demonstrate how different the politics of private social welfare can be from the politics of public social policy. The major American public social programs were created during periods of unified party control, with large Democratic majorities, and a liberal public mood. An early and important work on private social welfare is *The Hidden Welfare State* (1997) by Christopher Howard. Howard (1997) shows that a number of new social tax expenditure programs for private welfare were created during periods of divided government, during an era of political party polarization and without the constraint of mass public opinion. Suzanne Mettler (2007) argues and demonstrates that the mass public is largely unaware of welfare benefits provided through social tax expenditure programs and that this interferes with the accountability between the public and policymakers. The result is that interest groups can protect and perpetuate social tax expenditures out of the eye of the public. Relatedly, Morgan and Campbell (2011) demonstrate the important role of interest groups and Congress in facilitating the creation and expansion of private social benefits. The implications from this line of work are that unified party control is not a condition necessary for the expansion of subsidies for private welfare, public opinion may be less of an influence on social tax expenditures than it is on public benefits, and different political actors are important for the formation of private as opposed to public social programs. In Chapter 5, I systematically examine the influence of political party control of the federal government, divided government, and political polarization on the growth of social tax expenditures for private programs.

The most important distinction between social tax expenditures for private programs and public social spending is who benefits. Scholars (Hacker 2002, Howard 1997, Mettler 2011, Surrey 1974, Titmuss 1965)

have argued that tax expenditures for social programs benefit populations different from those helped by public social welfare. In particular, Howard finds that most tax expenditures are targeted to assist the
provision of employment-based social benefits, and the employees who
are most likely to be offered these benefits work in large corporations
and earn high incomes. Howard (1997), Hacker (2002), and Mettler
(2011) all argue that most tax expenditures for private social programs
are designed to distribute more federal money up the income ladder
to wealthier households and offer little to no benefit for poor families
(except for the EITC). This form of welfare for the wealthy stands in
stark contrast to the function of most public programs that either directly
offer more assistance to the poor and unemployed or provide a large
benefit-to-cost ratio to the working poor through program design (e.g.,
Social Security). In addition, this line of work highlights that not only
do wealthier citizens benefit from social tax expenditures but so too do
the *private providers* of social welfare goods (such as large banks, private HMOs, and private drug companies, to name a few). Businesses
that offer employee social insurance benefit from tax-free compensation
and providers receive annual government subsidies worth hundreds of
billions for their investment and insurance products. In Chapter 6, I evaluate how changes to social tax expenditures correspond to changes in the
level of income inequality. I expect that given the regressive distribution
effects of tax expenditures, an increase in social tax expenditures will
cause higher levels of inequality. In total, the public policy literature has
improved our understanding of the politics of social policy by including
in their analysis federal tax expenditures that finance private social benefits and services alongside traditional social spending. And although some
of the more recent work (see Howard 2007 and Morgan and Campbell
2011) suggests a role for political parties in the creation of and changes
to the divided social system, the exact motivations and mechanisms that
Democrats and Republicans use to shape the divided social state are as
of now unexamined.

A Theory of Political Parties and the Divided Social State

My theory of political parties and the divided social welfare state works at
the nexus of research from American politics and public policy. Political
parties have both the political motivations and the institutional capabilities to craft social policy as a means to distribute government benefits to
their constituencies and move federal policy in the ideological direction

of their members. My theoretical argument employs the following line of logic. First, the mass public, including a majority of self-identified Republicans, has continually called upon the federal government for higher levels of social spending. Therefore, a political party in power that is concerned about its electoral fortunes must respond to this public pressure with increased social spending or risk losing power. Second, a political party, operating under the constraints of public opinion, distributes government social benefits to its core constituencies and offsets this increase, in part, by taking away federal money from the opposing party's voters. This policy strategy looks different for Democrats and Republicans since each political party's electoral constituency is sorted out on one side of the divided welfare state or the other. The socioeconomic groups that rely on public social programs have traditionally aligned themselves with the Democratic Party while the socioeconomic groups that benefit from private social welfare are more likely to identify with the Republican Party. The Democratic Party when in power will increase public social spending at the expense of subsidies for private welfare as a means to target government benefits to their core voters and move policy in a liberal direction. Conversely, Republicans in the majority will raise the level of subsidies for private welfare while cutting public expenditures so as to distribute social benefits to their loyalists while moving federal policy in a conservative direction. While both parties are motivated by electoral and ideological goals, Democrats are more concerned with using social policy to distribute benefits to their constituencies and Republicans are primarily motivated to use social welfare as a mechanism to shift the ideological direction of the federal government. The implications of this theoretical argument are that which political party controls federal power determines, in part, who administers social services, who receives federal money for social benefits, and the balance between public and private power in the United States.

Why Political Parties Distribute Social Welfare Benefits

Why would both political parties, and not just the Democratic Party, distribute social welfare benefits to voters? Social programs such as health insurance, pensions, and education are widely popular with the American public (Ellis and Stimson 2012, Page and Jacobs 2009). It is generally recognized that citizens who self-identify as liberals and those who align themselves with the Democratic Party are supportive of increased federal social spending, especially toward programs that assist more vulnerable populations such as the elderly and the poor (Jacoby 2000, Lewis-Beck 2009). In addition, various studies demonstrate that citizens who classify egalitarianism as the most important American political value also favor more government spending on redistributive social programs (Feldman 1988, Jacoby 2006). The New Deal and Great Society programs targeted electorally important groups such as unions, urbanites, minorities, farmers, and the working poor. These two periods of social welfare expansion helped create the modern Democratic Party's coalition of unions, women, minorities, liberals, the working class, and educated suburbanites. As a result, traditional theories of political party power and social policy claim that the Democratic Party has an electoral incentive to support and expand social welfare programs.

The Republican Party faces a different political challenge concerning social policy. While ardent conservatives do not favor higher social spending, there is a *majority* of self-declared conservatives and self-identified Republicans who do support a greater role for the federal government in the provision of social welfare (Page and Jacobs 2009, Ellis and Stimson 2012). For example, Ellis and Stimson (2012) find that even though more of the electorate has identified as conservative over time, this ideological change has not been coupled with any measurable decline in public support for spending on social programs – a liberal position. A majority of the public during the period of their study consistently preferred more federal government spending on a variety of social programs. Most importantly for this study, the authors demonstrate that more than 50 percent of self-declared conservatives prefer higher levels of federal social spending for specific goals such as education or specific programs such as Social Security (Ellis and Stimson 2012). In addition, Ellis and Stimson (2012) find that approximately 40 percent of the total American electorate represents a belief system they describe as symbolically conservative and operationally liberal. These are survey respondents who identify with the political label conservative yet consistently prefer more federal spending on social programs. They find that, over time, there are *more than twice* as many self-identified conservatives who take liberal positions on federal social spending than there are consistent conservatives who match their ideology with policy preferences for a smaller federal government. Page and Jacobs (2009), similarly to the previous study, conducted a national survey and found that a plurality of American citizens fall under the category of conservative egalitarians. These are survey respondents who identify as ideological conservatives yet support federal government involvement in a large number of social programs. For example, Page and

Jacobs (2009) find that a clear majority of Republicans (80 percent and 60 percent, respectively) support the federal government's involvement in "spending whatever is necessary to ensure that all children have really good public schools" and that "Washington ought to see to it that everyone who wants to work can find a job." The cumulative result of these studies is that many Republican voters, despite the public perception of favoring smaller government, demand more federal spending on popular social programs and goals.

There are a number of implications from these studies that are relevant to theorizing about political parties and the divided social system. First, a vast majority of the electorate at any one point in time over the last forty years has supported increased federal involvement and spending for the provision of social benefits and services. The overwhelming support for government spending on social programs, from Democrats to Republicans to political independents, means that there is no viable electoral strategy that would allow a political party to simply cut federal social spending without offering the public – in return – some government support for social programs. Second, a majority of citizens who identify as conservatives and a majority of Republicans prefer more federal spending on a range of social goals including health care, pensions, and assistance to the poor. Therefore, traditional theories of social policy claiming that the Republican Party has an electoral incentive to reduce federal social spending do not recognize the real constraints of public opinion on political party behavior. However, if we recognize that different policy instruments can be used to finance either the public or private social system, it becomes easier to see how Republicans could support federal subsidies for private social welfare while still claiming support for small government. The Republican Party's support of tax subsidies for private welfare, in particular, allows party members to thread the ideological needle of supporting less government spending in the abstract (a position favored by their supporters, who are consistent conservatives) while in reality subsidizing popular social goals demanded by the mass public (a position that appeals to conflicted conservatives and a majority of the electorate). In the following section, I describe the theory of distributive politics and how it maps onto the partisan politics of the divided welfare state.

The Distributive Politics of the Divided Social State
A political party in power has different options for distributing social welfare benefits to its electoral constituencies. First, a party can widely

and indiscriminately distribute universal social benefits to the whole electorate. The political effect of this strategy would be to not only help the party's voters but also give benefits to independents and voters from the other party. These types of social spending programs are by their nature very expensive and hard to get through Congress unless the party in power has unified control of the federal government. Second, a political party in the majority could target swing voters with increased social benefits and services. A swing voter is usually a citizen who consistently votes but does not have a stable partisan identification. This political strategy of persuasion could be used if the party in power has a large number of members in swing districts or swing states. A third possibility is for a political party, in the majority, to direct social spending toward its core constituencies and pay for this spending increase through cuts to programs that benefit the opposing party's voters. A party that operates along these lines would be using social spending as a means to mobilize its supporters to get out and vote in the next election while taking away government benefits from voters who, in a polarized environment, are already lost to the opposing party. I contend that a political party in power will mobilize its core voters with social benefits while paying for this increased spending with reductions in subsidies for other types of social welfare.

Distributive politics is an institutional commitment by political parties to aid incumbents in delivering tangible and traceable benefits to their constituencies or congressional districts. According to the core voter model of distributive politics, a political party interested in vote maximization will distribute government goods and services to their major voting blocs (Cox and McCubbins 1986). Cox and McCubbins (1986) define core voters in two ways: first, as voters who have strong preferences for one party over another, and second, as voters who can be directly identified and targeted with government benefits. The authors argue that a political party in power designs public policy, in part, as a means to mobilize latent partisans to vote. The most prized (and least costly) voter for a political party is one who already agrees with the party on policy issues and has an elastic probability of voting, which is conditional on targeted spending toward his or her group. A political party practicing distributive politics is either "rewarding loyalists" or "turnout buying," depending on a voter's probability of voting (Nichter 2008). The core voter distributive politics model posits that a party in power makes payments to electoral groups to sustain their coalition over a long period of time. A political party in power will take the low-risk strategy of overinvesting in its core supporters as a way to maximize votes but also offering policies that reflect the ideology of the median member of the governing coalition. The transfer of social welfare benefits and services to core voters increases the likelihood of their turnout, sends signals to other constituencies about which groups they are politically aligned with, and deters primary challengers.

As an example, the budgetary process allows a political party, in the majority, to narrowly target direct spending for public projects or services back to its party supporters. Numerous studies demonstrate that the constituencies in districts of the majority party have been disproportionately favored in the distribution of all types of direct spending such as defense dollars (Carsey and Rundquist 1999), transportation funding (Lee 2000), and federal grants (Levitt and Snyder 1995). Levitt and Snyder (1995) conclude that political parties are better skilled at targeting specific types of voters and not as adept at directing money to individual member districts. They find "that Democratic control of both the House and Senate over most of the post-war period has allowed Democrats to fashion a portfolio of spending programs that disproportionately benefit their constituents. It appears that parties in the United States can, given enough time, target types of voters, but they cannot easily target individual districts" (p. 961). I argue here that a political party in the majority uses changes in social spending to target socioeconomic groups within its electoral coalition as opposed to targeting social benefits by district.

The Electoral Connection and the Divided Welfare State

The political and economic polarization of voters has allowed a political party to target core constituencies by moving federal money from one side of the divided social system to the other. The Democratic Party's socioeconomic electoral coalition relies more on public social benefits and the Republican Party's socioeconomic voting core benefits more from private social programs. I argue, here, that the Democratic Party favors the use of direct spending for public social programs, in part, because the public social welfare state disproportionately benefits the working class, racial minorities, ethnic minorities, and women. These same groups are central to the Democratic Party's electoral coalition and benefit twice over from public welfare: once, from their reliance on the insurance and services provided by public programs, and again, from the progressive redistributive effects. These policy features help explain why the Democratic Party has historically favored the addition and expansion of direct social spending for public programs (more on this argument in Chapter 3). Conversely, federal tax expenditures subsidize wealthier citizens in procuring social insurance, benefit financial institutions and private health care companies in offering their products, and lower the costs for large businesses that offer fringe benefits to their employees as a form of wages. For example, the reigning conservative view on investment income is that it should not be taxed (or taxed at very low levels), and therefore, the Republican Party has proposed a steady stream of tax deductions and exclusions for health savings accounts, retirement savings accounts, education savings accounts, and even unemployment savings accounts. These federal subsidies not only serve as a form of government assistance to banks and financial firms for their various investment products but reward wealthier households that have enough disposable income to save, and, therefore, purchase these accounts. Consequently and contrary to existing theories of social policy, both Democrats and Republicans can help their members by using social welfare spending to distribute government goods and services to important voting communities.

Democrats and Republicans have developed distinct and divergent socioeconomic core constituencies (McCarty, Poole and Rosenthal 2006, Gelman 2008, Stonecash and Mariani 2000, Gimpel and Schuknecht 2001, Stonecash et al. 2003). Specifically, the working class and minorities have become more Democratic while wealthier whites have become more aligned with the Republican Party over time (Stonecash 2000, McCarty et al. 2006). The top income quartile was only marginally more likely to identify with the Republican Party in 1956, but in 2000, those in the top income quartile were more than two and half times as likely to vote for the Republican Party as the lowest income quartile (McCarty et al. 2006). Stonecash (2000) finds a steady increase in support for the Democratic Party among the working class between 1952 and 1996. In this study, he showed that socioeconomic differences in voting started in the 1970s and have grown larger over time. The increase in class divisions between the two political parties is valid both inside and outside the South and whether you isolate white voters or examine all voters (Bartels 2008, Nadeau and Stanley 1993, Nadeau et al. 2004).[2] However, the link between class and Presidential vote can change depending upon the

---

[2] Nadeau et al. (2004) show that partisan polarization based on income class started in the 1970s and has only become stronger over time, even among Southern Whites. In fact, Nadeau et al. (2004) find that the class partisan link among Southern Whites to be stronger than that among non-Southern Whites. The wealthy have continually supported the Republican Party and this individual level correlation grew stronger over the course of this study (Bartels 2008, McCarty et al. 2006).

level of analysis. Gelman (2008) finds a strong relationship between class and partisan voting in poorer states (that also are more conservative) yet little correlation between class and Presidential vote in richer and more Democratic states. In addition to these class cleavages, the Civil Rights legislation of the 1960s sparked an exodus of white Southern voters from the Democratic to the Republican Party. The Democratic Party became more likely than the Republican Party to support aid for racial minorities and, therefore, racial policy developed as an important characteristic dividing the two parties (Carmines and Stimson 1989). The major implication of these studies is that as voters have sorted themselves out socioeconomically over time then it would follow that the two political parties use social policy as a means to move federal money either up or down the income ladder.

In addition to the partisan divergence of socioeconomic voters, economic interest groups have also selected into one of the two political party coalitions (Grossmann and Dominguez 2009, Koger et al. 2009, Heaney et al. 2012). Grossmann and Dominguez (2009) find that during primary elections unions make up the majority of groups in the Democratic coalition while corporations are the dominant constituency for Republicans. These same patterns of support with unions overwhelmingly favoring Democrats and businesses and corporations supporting Republicans were found when they examined the mentions of interest groups between Democratic and Republican legislators from the Congressional Record. The union and business divide is not only found in electoral support but also through financial network analysis of the two political parties. The patterns of interest group support reinforce the class divisions found in the partisan identification and presidential voting of individual citizens. It is not just that working class citizens have become increasingly Democratic but that unions are uniformly Democratic, which provides even more political incentive for the Democratic Party to implement policies that redistribute federal money down the income ladder. Conversely, wealthier households and corporations have the same broad financial interests in distributing money to the rich.

There are a number of industries, which are represented by special interests, that benefit from social tax subsidies by having their services or products subsidized so that their customers do not pay the full cost of using private social welfare. In the following section, I examine campaign donation patterns across relevant industries that have a financial

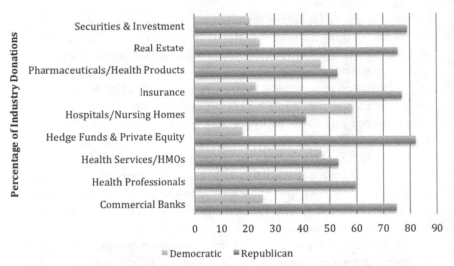

FIGURE 2.1. Industry PAC donations in the 2012 presidential election. *Source:* Author's compilation using data from The Center for Responsive Politics.

stake in federal social spending during the 2012 Presidential election. In a Presidential election won by a Democratic incumbent, we might expect that most groups would be strategic and risk adverse by donating heavily to the Democrats. Yet the data in Figure 2.1 show that even in a Presidential election won by an incumbent Democratic President more social welfare industries donated to the Republican Party. The skewed distribution of campaign donations toward the Republican Party is a function, in part, of their efforts to subsidize businesses and private organizations in their provision of social welfare. First, banks, private equity firms, and investment houses all benefit from the numerous social tax expenditures that subsidize citizens in purchasing private retirement accounts. These financial institutions sell 401k(s) and 403b(s) to self-employed individuals and businesses with employment-based retirement programs. Figure 2.1 shows that financial institutions disproportionately (on average a 75%/25% split) gave to Mitt Romney and the Republicans in 2012. Second, private hospitals, pharmaceutical companies, health insurance companies, and businesses that provide health services have financial incentives to support the addition and extension of tax expenditures for health care. In 2012, although the health care industries lean Republican, there is a more even split between Democratic and Republican donations. The passage and implementation of Obamacare are probably the most likely explanations for the split campaign donations. Next, real estate companies benefit from the tax expenditures that assist homeowners with their mortgage payments and associated taxes. Again, the real estate industry donated three times more to the Republican Party than to the Democratic Party in 2012. Overall, the patterns here provide some evidence that those industries that benefit from social tax expenditures reward the Republican Party with campaign donations at election time.

While both parties are concerned about the electoral ramifications of changing social policy, I expect Democrats to be more concerned over who benefits from social welfare spending rather than how they benefit. First, the major economic interest group within the Democratic Party has a vested interest in employment-based social benefits and services (Gottschalk 2000, Hacker 2002). Unions wanting to attract members, trying to counter the power of business owners, and frustrated with national failures to achieve universal health care and other benefits turned to encouraging policymakers to pass and grow subsidies for employment-based plans. So while more liberal Democrats may have strong preferences for government-run programs they have also had to balance the interests of American union members. Second, Democratic voters favor government spending on vulnerable populations but also have reported lower levels of trust in the federal government over time (e.g., Hetherington 2001). In addition, Democratic voters demonstrate more concern over which socioeconomic groups are assisted through spending and less concern over how government benefits are delivered (Faricy and Ellis 2014). Finally, the Democratic Party is more of a network of special interest groups who make demands on the federal government for specific public goods, including social welfare (Grossmann and Hopkins 2014). Therefore, in a hyperpolarized political environment and during periods of divided government the Democratic Party is more willing to compromise on the delivery mechanism of federal funds and less willing to negotiate about who receives social benefits. A countervailing factor is that the Democratic Party has issue ownership of public social programs. I expect that the Democrats' priorities are primarily to protect and, when they can, expand the major public social programs and secondarily to add new benefits through public programs if they can or through private subsidies if they must.

In conclusion, although Republicans and Democrats are compelled by the constraints of mass public opinion to spend on social programs they can choose how to design social expenditures and by extension who benefits. The socioeconomic sorting across the divided social state allows each political party to target the types of voters that are at the core of its respective electoral coalitions by changing the balance of direct spending for public programs versus tax expenditures for private welfare. A political party in power by trading off types of social spending improves its members' chances at reelection while taking away resources that benefit the minority party's constituency.

Member Preferences for Social Policy

While political party members construct public policy to distribute benefits for reelection, they are also concerned with making a personal contribution to changing the ideological direction of federal policy over the long run. There are a number of factors that motivate a policymaker to use social programs as a means to move the ideological direction of federal policy. First, party members in government have become more ideologically extreme over the years (McCarty et al. 2000, 2006). An implication of political polarization is that as ideologically extreme members replace moderate legislators then the long-run ideological direction of federal policy becomes more of an institutional goal for the two national parties. In addition, political party members find themselves representing more similar districts as polarization has intensified over the years. The realignment of the South and other demographic movements have resulted in electoral constituencies that are increasingly similar for members of the same party and different across the two political parties (Jacobson 2005, Abramowitz and Saunders 2006, Theriault 2008). There is evidence from studies on polarization that political parties are driving voters to ideological extreme positions, and that in turn ideological voters are increasingly self-selecting into one of the two parties (Carmines and Stimson 1989, Zaller 1992, Abramowitz and Saunders 1998, Layman and Carsey 2002). The homogenization of districts has also resulted in legislators increasingly being more concerned about losing their seats due to a primary opponent than to the opposing party in a general election (Brady et al. 2007, McGhee et al. 2014). The result of these trends is that legislators face less of a trade off between working on legislation for their district and working on ideological-driven bills. In essence, the legislative goals of members, their party leaders, and the districts have become more closely aligned so that working to protect and move forward an ideological agenda has become itself a type of "pork."

Second, political party elites have polarized in ways that make it easier for party leaders to coordinate members around an ideological agenda. The theory of "conditional party government" ties together electoral and party member polarization in explaining partisan policymaking (Rohde 1991, Aldrich and Rohde 1998, 2000). Aldrich and Rohde argue that while a political party has both electoral and policy goals, party members are primarily concerned with reelection. Therefore, the uniformity of a political party's electoral constituency determines how willing individual members are to turn over power to political party leaders to enforce party line votes. In contrast, when members' interests within a party do not line up, the individual members are more likely to retain power in order to meet the specific needs of their district. One of the characteristics of party polarization is that members' constituencies are more socioeconomically and politically homogenous across congressional districts (Jacobson 2001, 2005). The authority given to party leaders from their membership provides the necessary carrots and sticks (such as campaign money and committee seats) that result in more party line votes and greater party polarization. As applied here, the core constituencies for both Democrats and Republicans have sorted themselves out so that parties do not need to make large economic trade offs when constructing economic and tax policy (Abramowitz and Saunders 1998, 2000, 2006, Jacobson 2001, 2005, Layman and Carsey 2002, Stonecash et al. 2003, Brewer 2005).

So while party members have the incentives and capacities to pass ideological agendas, what does liberal versus conservative social policy look like? A policy's ideological bent is a function of who benefits, how it is delivered, and who administers the benefits or services. Direct spending for public social programs and tax expenditures for private welfare represent opposing political philosophies. Liberal policy makers promote the use of government activity and social spending to correct for market failures that undermine equality. Direct spending for public programs can be thought of as a liberal policy since the combined effects are to target vulnerable populations with social insurance, progressively redistribute federal money, and use federal government administration to ensure equal opportunity for citizens in gaining economic security. Conservative policy makers promote the idea that the private market is superior to any other system in creating an environment and incentive structure that fosters individual economic freedom. Therefore, social tax expenditures can be considered an example of conservative public policy since the combined effects are to subsidize businesses in their efforts to provide social goods and services, regressively distribute money to wealthier citizens (or job creators), and bypass public bureaucratic administration through off-budget spending. Specifically, the Democratic Party wants to move federal policy in a liberal direction at the expense of conservative benefits and Republicans desire to move federal policy in a conservative direction while reducing the impact of liberal programs.

Is there evidence that Republicans and Democrats demonstrate divergent preferences for public versus private forms of social welfare? Table 2.1 compares the positions of the two political parties across three social policy issues (pensions, health care, and education) using the 1980 party platforms. I used the 1980 election since it is often singled out as a bellwether for the rise of the conservative movement within the Republican Party. And since party platforms are not binding nor are they highly reported on by the media, they might better reflect the sincere preferences of party elites. As indicated by the policy positions in the platform, the Republican Party supports tax subsidies for each and every single social issue and also emphasizes the private market in discussing the provision of pensions and health care. In fact, the Republican preference for tax subsidies in 1980 was also included in other policy areas not in the table such as welfare, disability assistance, housing, and energy. Notice that the Republican platform does not directly attack Social Security and Medicare but instead offers up positive alternatives such as a private retirement initiative that uses tax exemptions and exclusions and in discussing health care they refer to patients as "health care customers" who can be assisted by tax and financial incentives. Democrats, in comparison, continually make arguments for the importance of public social programs in providing citizens economic security. In 1980, Democrats portrayed themselves as the creators and protectors of Social Security, calling the largest government social program "a covenant" with the elderly and declare their goal of bringing people "a government-run universal health care program." In these sections, there is no shying away from the Democratic Party's full-throated support of a more active federal government as a way to bring about greater equality through increased spending.

While both political parties are determined to change the ideological direction of federal policy, this is a more important goal for Republicans than it is for Democrats for the following reasons. First, the Republican Party has moved further to the ideological right than the Democratic Party has moved to the left (McCarty et al. 2013). The simple fact is that

TABLE 2.1. *A Comparison of Political Party Platforms on Social Spending, 1980*

Social Issue	Republican Party	Democratic Party
Old Age Pensions	"We propose to assist families, and individuals of all ages, to meet the needs of the elderly, primarily through vigorous private initiative. Only new tax exemptions and incentives can make it possible for many families to afford to care for their older members at home."	"The Democratic Party will oppose any effort to tamper with the Social Security system by cutting or taxing benefits as a violation of the contract the American government has made with its people. We hereby make a covenant with the elderly of America that as we have kept the Social Security trust fund sound and solvent in the past, we shall keep it sound and solvent in the years ahead."
Health Care	"As consumers of health care, individual Americans and their families should be able to make their own choices about health care protection. We propose to assist them in so doing through tax and financial incentives."	"The answer to runaway medical costs is not, as Republicans propose, to pour money into a wasteful and inefficient system. The answer is not to cut back on benefits for the elderly and eligibility for the poor. The answer is to enact a comprehensive, universal national health insurance plan."
Education	"We are dismayed that the Carter Administration cruelly reneged on promises made during the 1976 campaign. Wielding the threat of his veto, Mr. Carter led the fight against Republican attempts to make tuition tax credits a reality."	"We must begin to think of federal expenditures as capital investments, favoring those which are productive and which reduce future costs. In this context, education must be one of our highest priorities. Education is also the indispensable prerequisite for effective democracy. Federal aid to education has increased by 73 percent – the greatest income increase in such a short period in our history."

Source: Author's excerpts from *The American Presidency Project* (John T. Woolley and Gerhard Peters at the University of California, Santa Barbara).

the Republican Party's median member has become more conservative over time, pulling the party's legislative agenda to the far right of the ideological spectrum. As conservative members have replaced moderate members within the Republican Party, the implementation of a conservative agenda has become the main motivation for more and more members. Second, the Democratic Party owns the issues of Social Security and Medicare while Republicans own the issues of privatization and lowering taxes (Petrocik 1996, Egan 2013). The Republican Party only wins on social policy if public trust is shaken in the viability of the major public programs and voters seek out private solutions for economic security. Republican campaign tacticians such as Lee Atwater understand full well that the Republican Party is advantaged when people blame the federal government for society's problems and seek government solutions that rely on the private market. Lee Atwater remarked about the Republicans' strategy in the 1980 election,

we were able to make the establishment, insofar as it is bad, the government. In other words, big government was the enemy, not big business. If the people are thinking that the problem is that taxes are too high and government interferes too much then we are doing our jobs. But if they get to the point where they say the real problem is that rich people aren't paying taxes, that Republicans are protecting the realtors and so forth, then I think the Democrats are going to be in pretty good shape. Edsall and Edsall 1991.

Finally, the Republican Party is mainly a network of conservative interest groups not interested in policy compromise (Grossmann and Hopkins 2014). Grossmann and Hopkins (2014) found that Republican voters prefer legislators who stick to their conservative principles to those who compromise to get policy passed. As long as legislative compromise on social welfare issues expands the scope of the federal government, then Republican voters have incentive to reject even small expansions of public programs. In turn, the main conservative interests that support the Republican Party, such as fiscal conservatives, Chamber of Commerce Republicans, and religious groups, can all be brought together to support subsidies for the private administration of social programs. Tax subsidies for private social welfare lower the level of federal revenues that can be used for future government spending, subsidize business interests, and in some cases provide federal money to religious groups in providing social assistance. The implication of this line of logic is that Republicans are primarily motivated to move social services to the private sector and, therefore, have a strong preference for private subsidies over public spending.

How Political Parties Distribute Social Welfare Benefits

How do the two political parties distribute benefits and services to their respective electoral constituencies in a way that adheres to their members' dominant ideologies? In the following sections, I examine the role of policy tools in allowing political parties to select the delivery mechanism of social funding to particular groups in society. The study of policy tools or policy instrument choice is integral to understanding the politics of the divided social state. A public policy instrument is defined as "a method through which government seeks a policy objective" (Salamon 2002, p. 29).[3] As was previously discussed, the mass electorate has polarized in ways that make distributing benefits across the divided social system politically possible. First, partisan voters have polarized economically over the decades with more working-class citizens casting votes for the Democratic Party and wealthier voters aligning themselves with the Republican Party. Next, poorer and more vulnerable populations are served by the public system, and wealthier citizens are enrolled in the private system, resulting in different socioeconomic preferences for public versus private welfare. Therefore, the political-economic polarization of voters fits well with the socioeconomic bifurcation of the divided social welfare state. All total, Democrats distribute benefits to their constituencies through increasing direct spending for public social programs while Republicans target their supporters by raising tax expenditures for private welfare.

There are many different mechanisms the government uses to create public policy. Previous studies on the relationship between political parties and social policy focus exclusively on changes to one policy instrument: budgetary spending for public programs. Yet the last forty years has witnessed a tremendous growth in the diversity of policy instruments used by the federal government to provide social benefits and services. These tools include traditional spending, tax expenditures, grants, regulations, loan guarantees, government corporations, and loans (Hacker 2002, Howard 1997, Kettl 1997, Salamon 2002). The selection of the

---

[3] Another definition of policy instruments is any "technique by which government authorities wield their power in attempting to ensure support and effect social change" (Bemelmans-Videc et al. 1998).

right combination of policy tools is one of the most complex and important decisions made by political parties in strategic legislative planning. One study argues "what makes the use of different (policy) instruments so significant is that each instrument has its own distinctive procedures, its own network of organizational relationships, its own skill requirements – in short its own political economy" (Salamon 1989). So while political parties might agree on broad policy goals, such as providing income security to citizens or national defense, they often disagree over the means or policy instruments.

Although there are numerous policy instruments that are important for social policy, I choose to focus on just two, direct spending and tax expenditures, for the following reasons. First, direct spending and tax expenditures are the two largest categories of government spending for federal social programs that together summed to $2.87 trillion in 2010. In order to place this value in context, total U.S. budget expenditures in 2010 were listed at $3.7 trillion. Second, direct spending and tax expenditures represent opposing political economies. Direct spending is a tangible method of equalizing disparities caused by market economies both by using government administration to counter private businesses and by progressively redistributing federal income to poorer citizens. On the other hand, tax expenditures appeal to conservatives as a policy means to subsidize the private market to perform public services and regressively distribute income toward wealthier individuals.[4] Finally, direct spending and tax expenditures are passed and expanded using different policy processes in the legislature. Specifically, tax expenditures have to pass through fewer veto points in the legislative process, are not subject to annual review, and function as a form of entitlement spending. The important political and policy differences between direct spending and tax expenditures influence the opposing approaches to social policy of the Democratic and Republican parties.

There are numerous studies showing Democratic Party control of the federal government produces higher levels of traditional spending (e.g., Levitt and Synder 1995). However, there are more recent studies that have found evidence of the Republican Party increasing government expenditures by using policy tools outside of the annual budget process. Bickers and Stein (1996, 2000) demonstrate that in periods of Republican

---

[4] I use the term "distribute" when discussing tax expenditures since although they distribute more money to the wealthy, it is uncertain whether collectively all social tax expenditures are redistributive.

control of government, there are increases in contingent liabilities, a type of policy instrument that includes direct loans, guaranteed loans, and federal insurance programs. These types of spending programs under-write risks for individuals and groups by guaranteeing that the federal treasury repays any loss. Most importantly, contingent liabilities benefit core Republican constituencies including small businesses, farmers, and entrepreneurial businesses. In addition, Faricy (2011) found that Repub-lican control over the U.S. Congress resulted in higher levels of social tax expenditures to direct social spending. When Republicans increase social tax expenditures at the expense of direct social spending, federal finan-cial support for social welfare shifts from the middle and working classes to wealthier households (Ellis and Faricy 2011). Not only do political parties in government produce different patterns of policy tool usage but also recent survey experiments show that partisan voters reveal different preferences for traditional spending versus tax expenditures.

Republican and Democratic voters have opposing preferences for *how* social spending is delivered and *who* benefits. One recent study con-ducted a simple experiment that asked voters whether they supported different social programs. They described these programs either as tax deduction or as direct payments from the government. Additionally, they also either described each program as beneficial to the wealthy or did not include this information. The study finds that Republican and Democratic respondents differed in their level of support for social policy designed as a public spending program versus those framed as a tax expendi-ture program (Faricy and Ellis 2014). First, Republican respondents were more likely to favor social tax expenditure programs as compared with those citizens who identified as Democrats.[5] Next, Democratic respon-dents were less supportive of social tax expenditure programs once they were informed the benefits disproportionately accrue to wealthier house-holds. Interestingly, this additional information on the regressive dis-tributive effects of social tax expenditures did not diminish Republican respondents' support for tax subsidies. Therefore, Republican respon-dents favored social programs delivered through the tax code and were not bothered by more benefits going to the rich. Democratic respon-dents were less supportive of private subsidies and responded negatively to social programs that distribute money to the rich. These findings are

---

[5] Although a majority of the public (when partisans are not separated out) favors social tax expenditures over direct public social spending. Faricy and Ellis (2014) examine responses by both party and ideology and find that party and ideology produce similar results.

similar to other studies that find ideological differences in support for tax expenditures and direct spending (Haselswerdt and Bartels 2013).

At the beginning of this chapter, I argued that Democrats and Republicans desire to use the power of the federal government to distribute social benefits to their loyal electorates in ways that reflect the membership's governing ideology. Here, I explained how the sorting by income across the divided social welfare state allows a party in power to select a delivery mechanism that targets federal funding. If this theoretical argument is correct, then there should be observable differences between Democrats and Republicans in their use of direct spending for public programs and tax expenditures for private benefits.

Conclusion

The most common narrative about American politics is that Democrats, when elected, will seek to expand social welfare while Republicans, in power, counteract government growth through reductions in social spending. My theoretical argument alters this idea by arguing that both Democrats and Republicans have incentives to use the federal government to expand social welfare, albeit through different delivery mechanisms that utilize different sectors of the economy, reward opposing partisan constituencies, and produce divergent income distribution effects. I argue that Democrats and Republicans use social policy, in general, and social spending, in particular, to distribute benefits to voters and to tilt the direction of overall federal policy in their preferred direction. The two political parties can accomplish these goals due to the sorting out of partisans across the divided social system and through the selection and trade off of public spending and tax subsidies. The result is that the party in power can determine which side of the divide receives increased federal funds (and which side loses), who receives more government support for social insurance (and who loses), and the balance of public versus private power in the delivery and administration of social benefits and services.

While my goal is to explain the electoral and policy motivations behind the observed relationship between party control and spending, there are limits to my argument. First, I am arguing that Democrats and Republicans have preferences for social spending types and trade one type of spending for another. I am not arguing that Democrats will only pursue public spending, and Republicans will only increase tax expenditures. In fact, there are numerous examples of the Democratic Party supporting expansions of the EITC, although Democratic support for social tax expenditure programs has been almost exclusively for the creation and expansion of refundable tax credits for the working poor (the one type of tax expenditure that does not regressively distribute federal money). Second, a fact of the policy process is that a party's preferences are not always mapped onto policy outcomes. This could be due to intraparty negotiations, interparty negotiations, divided government, policy path dependency, interest group influence, and the power of the budget committees. However, even with these constraints I expect to observe noticeable differences between Democrats and Republicans in their patterns of social spending. Next, my theoretical argument is meant to explain partisan behavior at the federal level over the last forty-two years of this study. While I believe that the theoretical argument presented here can travel across different countries and time periods, it is not tested on different levels of government or across a particularly long time period. Finally, my theoretical argument is about the motivations behind party behavior and my tests are of the relationship between party control and spending patterns.

In the next chapters, I test the different components of the theoretical argument laid out here. In Chapter 3, I empirically test the relationship between Democratic Party power and changes to public social spending. I first examine one of the counterhypotheses that the Democratic Party favors social spending in all its forms and has no preferences for public social spending. Next, I examine if Democratic Party control of the federal government results in higher levels of public social spending from 1970 to 2012. I expect to find, as have previous studies, that Democrats in power increase public social spending. Chapter 4 discusses the role of social tax expenditures in subsidizing the private social system and why the particular characteristics of both would appeal to the Republican Party. In Chapter 5, I test the relationship between Republican Party control of government and changes to social tax expenditures both as a stand-alone category and a ratio to total social spending. If my theoretical argument is correct, then Republican control of the government should result in higher levels of social tax expenditures and a higher proportion of tax expenditures to aggregate social spending. I also test other political factors (such as polarization and divided government) alongside Republican Party control to ensure that it is partisanship and not institutional factors that determines changes in social tax expenditures. In Chapter 6, I explore how changes in the modality of social spending influence corresponding changes in the level of income inequality. The totality of these empirical tests provides supporting evidence to my theoretical argument that changes to political party power do not change the total amount spent on social programs but rather how the federal government finances social welfare and who benefits.

3

Political Parties and Public Social Spending

Testing the Conventional Wisdom

How does political party control of the federal government determine changes to public social programs in America? Extant research reveals a consistent relationship across time between Democratic Party control of government and higher levels of social welfare spending (Cooper and Bombardier 1968, Mayhew 1991, Cox and McCubbins 1993). Since the 1930s, the main dividing line between the Democratic and Republican parties has been over the size of the federal government, in general, and the size of the American social welfare state, in particular. The New Deal era saw the formation of a national Social Security program, welfare for single mothers and their children, assistance to farmers, and an extensive jobs program. President Franklin D. Roosevelt established a coalition of support for these social programs comprised of urbanites, labor unions, the working class, minorities, liberals, farmers, and Southerners. This "New Deal" coalition dominated politics for over thirty years and was only interrupted by the election of a Republican war hero, Dwight Eisenhower. The Republican Party formed a countercoalition during the New Deal era comprised of industrialists, businesses, and the wealthy, who united through their opposition to the continued expansion of federal social programs and their desire to promote pro-business policies. While the two political parties' electoral coalitions have evolved over time (especially on racial and social issues), the partisan socioeconomic cleavages remain to this day. The relative stability of the two parties' electoral coalitions is related to the equally persistent narrative of national social policy. This obstinate description of American politics claims that Democrats always expand public social spending as a means to build upon and protect their New Deal/Great Society voting coalition and Republicans consistently reduce federal social spending (with the indirect aim of lowering the amount of federal taxes needed to finance government) in the service of private businesses and their wealthier constituency.

In this chapter, I review and test the traditional relationship between political parties and public social expenditures in the United States. First, I review the existing relationship between political parties and social policy with particular emphasis on changes to public programs during the course of this study. I examine who benefits from public social programs and how this matters for understanding the partisan politics of social policy. In recent decades it has not been politics as usual, as a Democratic administration campaigned on and ended federal welfare as an entitlement program while unified Republican control of government resulted in the largest expansion of Medicare benefits for seniors since 1965. These counterintuitive changes to public social policy expose some weaknesses in the existing partisan narrative of social policy and point to some new ways of understanding the relationship between political parties and social policy in the United States. Second, I describe the data and time series analysis used to test the dynamic relationship between political party control of the federal government and changes in social spending. These methods are repeated throughout the book for all the major analyses. If the conventional wisdom still holds, there will be a clear correlation across time between Democratic Party power and increased social spending for public programs. I find some evidence for the relationship between Democratic Party control of the government and higher levels of federal social spending on public benefits. In particular, Democratic presidents produce first-year increases to both total and discretionary social spending. There is, however, no statistical relationship between a Democratic Congress and increased social expenditures. Finally, I test the relationship between Democratic Party power and changes to all federal social spending both public expenditures and subsidies for private welfare. If the partisan politics of social policy is merely about the overall level of social spending and not about how it is delivered and who benefits, then there should be an observable correlation between Democratic Party control of government and increases to aggregate social spending. I find no clear evidence that Democrats indiscriminately increase all forms of social spending when in power. The lack of a clear empirical relationship between political party power and social spending calls into question our understanding of the politics of social policy and presents an opportunity to theorize about the relationship between political parties and the divided social welfare state.

The Democratic Party and Higher Public Social Spending

The Democratic Party's expansion of public social welfare programs has assisted groups that are part of its electoral coalition. In the following sections, I examine the political conditions that have resulted in the growth of public social welfare programs. The historical expectation is that only unified Democratic Party control allows the passage of large-scale social policy change. However, while unified Democratic control of the federal government produced the Affordable Care Act, there were other changes to national social programs that occurred under other partisan arrangements such as divided government and unified Republican power. The key to understanding recent social policy changes under Democratic leadership is understanding who benefits. In the previous chapter, I argued that the explicit and implicit distributive effects of social programs determine partisan changes to social spending. Democratic support of both means-tested and universal public social programs is driven by their desire to redistribute national income to the working poor. The Democratic Party's recent political strategy has been to fiercely protect and, where it can, expand the scope of Social Security, Medicare, and Medicaid while building smaller, supplementary benefits to help the working class through the public sector if possible but using private subsidies if the political environment dictates such.

U.S. policymaking is best characterized as a process that oscillates between periods of stability in which there are small, incremental changes to policy and periods of sizeable change during which policy outcomes are drastically altered (Baumgartner and Jones 1993). Baumgartner and Jones argue that human information-processing capabilities are limited. Policymakers are bombarded with information and as a result they must prioritize some issues over others when setting the national policy agenda. Additionally, political institutions are often designed to discourage an immediate, proportional response to every incoming demand or signal for change, so policies are stable most of the time. However, large social policy changes can and do occur from time to time. When those issues that were once ignored or paid little attention win the attention of the policymakers (either because signals for change are too strong to ignore or because weak to moderate signals accumulate over time and reach a threshold), changes occur and do so rapidly to correct previously accumulated errors and thus catch up with the political reality (Jones and Baumgartner 2005, 2012). This characterization of public policy certainly applies to public social welfare programs.

The American public welfare state has been built primarily during short periods of rapid expansion such as the New Deal era, the Great Society period, and the recent passage of the Affordable Care Act. These periods of dramatic policy change occurred under the following conditions: Democratic Party control of the presidency, large Democratic majorities in Congress, and a liberal public mood. For example, President Johnson used a liberal shift in public opinion and a large Democratic majority in the legislature to create the Great Society programs that attempted to improve the economic security of the urban and rural poor and politically breathe new life into the Democratic Party's "New Deal" coalition. The Great Society programs included a food stamp program; loans and grants for low-income housing, schools, transportation, and infrastructure, along with cash assistance to the poor; and the creation of Medicare and Medicaid. The decades after the passage of Medicare saw only incremental changes to the public social system such as the Supplemental Security Income Program, Adoption Assistance and Foster Care, Child Care Block Grant, and the State Children's Health Insurance Program (SCHIP).[1] The period of this study, from 1970 to 2012, begins after the implementation of Medicare and ends after passage (but before the full implementation) of the Affordable Care Act.

An examination of only the public side of the divided social system reveals a system with two tiers: a first tier of robust and generous programs targeted toward the elderly and a second tier of more stringent and less generous programs aimed at the poor (Skocpol 1988).[2] Over the last forty years, federal social programs aimed directly at the working class suffered from direct attacks or neglect while old-age assistance programs expanded their reach and increased in generosity. These patterns of policy change were the result of changes in the pace and distribution of economic growth, the social construction of target groups, changes to society and the economy that resulted in program drift, and political polarization. For example, the elderly, a group viewed positively by the public and with strong organizational support, experienced expansions to their assistance

---

[1] My period of study begins in 1970 and ends in 2012 due to the constrictions of overlapping data sets. The data on federal spending for public programs is from the policy agendas project running from 1947 to 2012 and the federal tax expenditure data ranges between 1969 and 2012. Therefore, for the purposes of comparing the two modalities of federal social spending I examine the period from 1969 to 2012.

[2] Although as Howard (2007) argues, if you include both public and private programs (e.g., EITC) then programs for the poor can be considered more generous.

programs while federal welfare that disproportionately helps the poor and minorities, groups viewed less positively and with weak formal organizations, suffered significant federal cuts (Schneider and Ingram 1993). In the following section, I review changes to public social programs aimed at nonelderly populations.

Some of the primary public social programs aimed at poverty assistance, such as welfare, food stamps, and the minimum wage, were reduced in size and scope by direct policy actions or policy neglect (Hacker 2004). President Johnson's Great Society era soon gave way to a period, starting in the 1970s, of slower economic growth and increased scrutiny of public social spending (Skocpol 1988). As evidenced by the failed social reforms of the Carter administration, social welfare advocates were now fighting on two fronts: to expand the unfinished policies of the previous decades (e.g., universal health care) while at the same time defending the established social programs of the New Deal and Great Society eras. The Reagan administration proposed budgets that attempted to cut tens of billions of dollars from the Great Society programs through stricter eligibility requirements and decreased benefits (Slessarev 1988). An example is that after twenty years of substantial growth, food assistance programs were cut during the Reagan administration through stricter eligibility requirements (Giertz and Sullivan 1986). Later in this chapter, I discuss the major changes made to the federal welfare program that included ending its status as a federal entitlement program, capping lifetime benefits, adding new work requirements, and decreasing the generosity of program benefits through devolution.

A number of public social policies have failed to be updated in ways that align with changes to the economy and labor force (Hacker and Pierson 2010). The major form of government neglect is captured through the idea of policy drift, which occurs when social services and benefits remain stagnant while inflation and changing labor markets erode the extent and generosity of social insurance (Hacker 2004). For example, the minimum wage is a federal benefit whose value has been eroded both by market changes and inflation. The last time the federal minimum wage was updated to a higher rate in 2009. The real value of the minimum wage, as adjusted for inflation, continually decreased between 1969 and 2009. One study found that the real value of the minimum wage fell by over twenty percent between 1967 and 2010 (Autor, Manning, and Smith 2010). Correspondingly, more lower-skilled workers have been pushed into minimum wage jobs by the transfer of unionized manufacturing jobs overseas and the increase in service-sector positions. In addition, the rise of the service sector economy and decline of unions (whose employers offer worker benefits at low rates) reduced the number of workers who were offered and enrolled in employment-based health care insurance and private pension plans. The federal government did not alter existing programs to address this trend, and many of these workers went without insurance or had to pay premium prices on the individual market. These forms of policy neglect and inaction coupled with the elimination of federal welfare as an entitlement added up to fewer public social benefits and services for America's nonelderly poor.[3]

Contrary to federal welfare and the minimum wage, entitlement programs such as Social Security and Medicare added supplementary programs, increased their eligibility to cover more populations, expanded their monetary generosity, and had their payments tied to inflation (Mettler 2007). During the 1960s, increasing Social Security benefits became a popular campaign tactic employed by both political parties in their fight for the elderly's vote. The Nixon administration working with a Democratic Congress passed new Social Security Amendments in 1972, which created the Supplementary Security Insurance (SSI) program. The SSI program served as an income assistance program for the elderly poor, blind, and disabled. In 1975, Social Security benefits became tied to inflation, and replacement rates increased for the working- and middle-class elderly. While President Reagan was successful in cutting smaller means-tested programs, his efforts to reduce Social Security benefits largely failed (Teles 2007). President Reagan signed into law changes that allowed federal employees to transfer into the Social Security program in exchange for harsher penalties for program fraud and abuse. In fact, the attempts at reforming Social Security politically activated many low-income senior citizens, which in turn made future reform efforts politically dangerous (Campbell 2003). In 1996, President Clinton expanded Social Security through raising the earnings limits in exchange for Congress eliminating access to Social Security based on drug addiction or alcoholism. President George W. Bush was also unsuccessful in transforming Social Security into a system of investments for private retirement programs in 2005. The multiple unsuccessful

---

[3] This trend was expected to expand the Medicaid program, adding the elderly and disabled, pregnant women, and treatment of certain cancers. However, it should be mentioned that a conservative bloc on the Supreme Court (along with Breyer and Kagan) struck down the Obamacare Medicaid expansion.

efforts to reduce the largest federal social welfare programs, Social Security and Medicare, have led many scholars to conclude that the U.S. social welfare state was resilient in a period of international social policy retrenchment while European countries were drastically reducing their social expenditures and services (Huber and Stephens 2001, Pierson 1996). The whole of these changes expanded the generosity and scope of Social Security.

Once Medicare passed in 1965, the complexity and inflationary incentive structure of the program resulted in steady cost increases to the federal government. During the 1970s, the Kennedy-Mills bill, the Long-Ribicoff bill, and President Nixon's Comprehensive Health Insurance Plan (CHIP) all failed in extending the benefit of Medicare to nonelderly populations. The only successful reforms in the 1970s came in the form of federal legislation that was used to subsidize private health maintenance organizations (HMOs), which will be discussed in greater detail in the next chapter on private social welfare. One shift for Medicare during this period was bureaucratic, when the administration of the program was moved from the SSA to the new Health Care Financing Administration (HCFA) in 1977. This shift removed federal workers from working directly with the elderly and laid the foundation for future legislation that attempted to privatize the program (Olson 2010). By the time of the election of President Reagan in 1980, Medicare was the fastest growing federal program and was targeted for cuts in Reagan's 1981 budget. As part of its overall strategy to shrink the federal government, the Reagan administration restructured and reduced the reimbursement fees given to hospitals and physicians that provided Medicare (Marmor 2000, Weaver 2000). The national mood shift to fiscal conservatism along with the growing and expected future costs of Medicare displaced any serious agenda of universal health care reform in the 1980s. The 1990s saw few changes to the Medicare program since the Clinton administration's primary focus was on creating some form of universal coverage that controlled health care costs for the nonelderly (Oberlander 2003). In 1997, the Clinton administration and Republicans in Congress agreed to Medicare reforms as part of the Balanced Budget Act. These included both market-based reforms such as the addition of Medicare Plus Choice and traditional reforms that restructured the fee system to hospitals and doctors. The largest expansion of Medicare occurred under President Bush and is discussed in detail in the next section. In 2012, Republican Mitt Romney ran unsuccessfully for president, promising to overhaul the Medicare program into a voucher program that would assist seniors in purchasing private health insurance coverage. The sum of the enacted policy changes kept the basic promise of Social Security and Medicare in place for older Americans.

The Democratic Party's Electoral Coalition and Public Social Programs

The Democratic Party's electoral coalition is primarily constituted of demographic groups that benefit in one way or another from federal public social programs. The programs of the New Deal firmly established the Democratic Party as the party of the urban working class. The New Deal electoral coalition dominated federal politics for decades and helped establish a long-running Democratic majority. President Johnson built upon the coalition by recognizing the intersection of race and poverty. Johnson's war on poverty included race-based programs as a means to assuage poverty and was designed to add African-Americans into the Democrats' electoral coalition. The continued efforts of the Democratic Party to court the urban working class, women, and minorities is reflected in the stability of the socioeconomic components of the New Deal coalition today. Recent studies show that blacks, Latinos, women, the working class, and union members have consistently identified with and voted for the Democratic Party since the 1950s (Knuckey 2013, Zingher 2014). In the following sections, I demonstrate how the most loyal groups in the Democratic electoral coalition disproportionately benefit from the design of major public social programs.

The steadfast support of the Democratic Party for Social Security and Medicare is about both courting the elderly vote and protecting large public programs with skewed progressive distributive effects. The two largest and most generous public social programs, Social Security and Medicare, are federal entitlements directed at the elderly. These two programs alone accounted for more than $1.4 trillion of federal spending in 2012. The elderly have become an important voting group that has swung back and forth between supporting Democratic and Republican candidates for president. The activism of seniors and the electoral impact of the AARP have resulted in both parties continually courting favor with America's elderly through expanding Social Security and Medicare (Campbell 2003). Yet even programs targeted at the elderly are designed to provide greater replacement rate benefits to lower-income participants. Since these public programs provide a higher benefit-to-cost ratio for working class seniors, they indirectly provide greater assistance to groups more likely to have lower lifetime earnings, such as minorities and women.

TABLE 3.1. *Social Security as a Source of Retirement Income by Race and Gender, 2012*

	Social Security Is 90% or Higher of All Income	Social Security Is 50% or Higher of All Income
Black	49%	74%
Latino	55%	77%
White	35%	65%
Unmarried Women	49%	77%
Unmarried Men	40%	67%

Source: Reno, Virginia P. and Elisa A. Walker. 2013. National Academy of Social Insurance.

For example, Social Security has been found to generate more benefits per taxes paid for women than for men (Social Security Administration 1999). Additionally, women are more likely to be helped out of poverty by Social Security and claim more money from the Social Security Survivors and Disability programs. Table 3.1 demonstrates the importance of Social Security to women and minority populations, both as a major source of retirement income and as a protection from falling below the poverty line.

The economic benefit of Social Security and Medicare to the working class, minorities, and women helps explain why even when the elderly vote for Republican candidates – the Democratic Party still has an electoral incentive to protect these public social programs. First, Social Security is a much more important source of retirement income for blacks and Latinos than it is for older whites. As shown above, half of racial minorities (Latinos and blacks) used Social Security payments for more than 90 percent of their income as compared to only 35 percent of whites. These racial disparities are mirrored in the second column, which measures the proportion of a group that uses Social Security for more than half of their income. In contrast, elderly whites tend to rely more on assets and private pensions as a source of their retirement income. For example, one study reports that 69 percent of white retirees receive a portion of their income from assets and capital as compared with only 33 percent of retired blacks and 29 percent of retired Latinos (Social Security Administration 2000). As evidenced in the bottom rows in Table 3.1, women are more reliant on Social Security for their retirement income (whether measured as 50% or 90% of total income) as compared with men. If Supplementary Security Income (SSI) is included in the calculations than the gender disparity within Social

TABLE 3.2. *Medicare Beneficiaries by Race, Income, and Health Condition,*
2010

	Fair/Poor Health Status	Poverty Rate (200% of poverty line)	Medicare Only	Employee Plan or Medigap	Medicaid and Medicare
Black	43%	65%	23%	32%	35%
Latino	46%	66%	25%	27%	27%
White	26%	41%	10%	67%	11%

Source: Kaiser Family Foundation, Disparities in Health and Health Care, 2010.

Security benefits widens. Another way to measure the importance of Social Security to different populations is to determine what the poverty level would be for each racial and ethnic group with and without Social Security. According to the Social Security Administration, the poverty rates would go up for every demographic group and Latinos and blacks would experience a threefold increase in the percent of impoverished retirees. Altogether, since blacks and Latinos have higher relative poverty rates compared to whites, the redistributive structure of Social Security helps more minority populations stay above the poverty line.

Medicare, again targeted at older citizens, provides a substantial amount of medical and financial security to elderly minorities and the working class. Racial and ethnic minorities over the age of sixty-five are more likely to suffer from illnesses and live in poverty than elderly whites. Therefore, minority populations are more likely to use government health care coverage and have less ability to pay for supplementary health care insurance out of pocket. As Table 3.2 indicates, elderly racial minorities report a poor or fair health condition nearly twice as much as older white respondents. In addition and as observed in the second column, a vast majority of racial minorities using Medicare have an income that is near the federal poverty line compared to whites, which would activate low-income supplements. Next, racial minorities are also more likely to rely soley on Medicare for health care coverage compared to whites. Approximately one out of four black and Latino elderly Americans has no additional medical coverage outside Medicare, as compared to only 10 percent of all whites sixty-five years of age and older. Correspondingly, two out of three elderly whites have employment-based retirement benefits or Medigap, compared to only one out of three blacks and one out of four Latinos. These differences in supplemental health care insurance result in higher out-of-pocket spending for minorities and poorer populations. Additionally, blacks and Latinos over sixty-five more often use Medicaid to supplement Medicare than do their white counterparts. Altogether, elderly minorities are more likely to use health care insurance, not have access to private insurance, and have to rely on both Medicare and Medicaid coverage. So although the direct target population for Medicare and Social Security is the elderly, it is no secret to policymakers that these programs disproportionately assist the working class, women, and racial minorities.

Public social programs aimed at providing income security to the poor and unemployed are also more likely to assist the working class, racial and ethnic minorities, and women. There are a number of federal programs designed to assuage poverty, such as the Temporary Assistance to Needy Families (TANF), Medicaid, and food stamps. These programs accrue benefits to populations historically hit hardest by poverty, such as households headed by single females, blacks, and Hispanics. In 2010, four million more women were below the poverty line than men (Bureau of Labor and Statistics 2011). In addition, households that are headed by a single adult are more likely to be headed by women, and these single female-headed families have a greater likelihood of falling below the poverty line. In 2010, 34 percent of single female-headed households were poor, compared to 17.3 percent of single male-headed households, and only 7.6 percent of married couples with families (Bureau of Labor and Statistics 2010). In addition to gender, there are clear racial and ethnic differences in the current poverty levels. In 2010, only around 10 percent of whites (non-Hispanic) were considered poor, compared to 27.4 percent of blacks and 26.6 percent of Hispanics. Next, unemployment insurance is more likely to provide financial assistance to working class populations and racial and ethnic minorities (U.S. Department of Labor 2010). In conclusion, the public social welfare state, created during periods of unified Democratic control of government, assists not only the poor and elderly but also other demographic groups that are electorally important for the Democratic Party. Therefore, I expect the Democrats when in power to increase public social spending but more importantly to use federal programs to distribute funds to the working class.

Partisan Politics and Modern Social Welfare: Challenges to the Conventional Wisdom

The established relationship between the Democratic Party and public social programs has been challenged recently by major changes to the structure of the American public social system. This study begins after a decades-long period known as the era of easy money. The period after World War II and up until the early 1970s was characterized by significant and sustained economic growth that allowed policymakers to expand public benefits while reducing marginal rates or keeping the level of taxation constant. The 1970s brought about structural changes both economically and politically that altered the political calculations of financing the American public welfare state. First, the reactions to the growth of government and the Civil Rights Movement injected racial attitudes into national politics in ways that affected public support for welfare policy. Gilens (1999) has shown that citizens are misinformed about welfare recipients. In particular, the media overrepresents African-Americans as being the face of poverty. These images and stories bleed into public attitudes about work ethic and deservingness and, therefore, many whites perceive welfare as a "black" program and thereby report lower support for welfare spending. These spurious linkages also influence citizens' perception of the deservingness of welfare recipients and the efficiency of government welfare programs (Gilens 1999, Soss et al. 2003). Second, slower economic growth over the last forty years has resulted in more of an explicit and visible trade off between higher social spending and increased deficits and debts. It has been easier for the political party out of power to portray new and increased federal social spending as being fiscally irresponsible and contributing to the rising national debt. Third, the period under study witnessed a rise in political polarization, as the Republican Party became much more conservative and Democratic Party more liberal (Poole and Rosenthal 1993, 2001). The rise of polarization in the 1970s moved the pivotal legislative position from the chamber median (ideologically moderate) to the more ideologically extreme majority party median (Aldrich and Rohde 2000). In the eyes of the electorate, the Democrats "own" the policy issues of Social Security, Medicare, and protecting other popular public social welfare programs (Egan 2013). The Democrats' ownership of public social welfare programs along with polarization has increased the politicization of federal funding for public social welfare programs.

The restructuring of traditional welfare under a Democratic administration and the expansion of Medicare under unified Republican control of the federal government provide the most glaring examples of exceptions to the conventional wisdom of parties and social policy. The American social welfare state has experienced periods of incrementalism and dramatic change over the last forty years. There are two instances of social policy change that underscore the limitations of the current partisan theory of social policy. The first is the transformation of federal welfare from AFDC to TANF under the Clinton administration. This change in welfare, which was spearheaded by a Democratic president and shaped by a Republican legislature, captures some of the recent political pressures on the American social welfare state. President Clinton promised to end welfare, in an attempt to rebrand the national Democratic Party by appealing to suburban whites through reforming an unpopular, broken, and racially charged government program (Marmor 2000). The second case of Medicare Part D examines how unified Republican control of the federal government produced the largest expansion of Medicare in the program's history. The creation of Medicare Part D diverged from previous Democratic changes to Medicare in that it relied heavily on setting up a marketplace for private health organizations and used federal subsidies for private drug companies (Morgan and Campbell 2011). These unusual social policy changes confound the conventional wisdom of parties and social policy and in turn suggest ideas for a new theoretical framework for understanding the politics of social spending.

The Peculiar Politics of TANF

While running for president, Democratic candidate Bill Clinton declared that if elected he "would end welfare as we know it." Why would a Democratic presidential candidate propose curtailing benefits to welfare? And what does the transformation of welfare from AFDC to TANF tell us about the relationship between political parties and social policy? The passage of TANF was brought about by a shift to divided government, party polarization, and changes to mass public opinion on the efficacy and efficiency of welfare. In 1996, President Clinton signed into practice the Personal Responsibility Work Reconciliation Act (PRWORA). This law was the most wide-ranging set of welfare reforms of the last forty years. The new law replaced the Aid to Families with Dependent Children (AFDC), a government entitlement, with Temporary Assistance to Needy Families (TANF), a block grant program to the states. The stated goals of TANF were to provide assistance that kept children in their own homes, prepare people for work and marriage, reduce unmarried pregnancies, and encourage more two-parent families. The shift from AFDC to TANF represents both policy downsizing, which reduced the federal government's responsibility, and devolution that transferred more power over the program's administration and benefits to the state level. The law was created with a tone of paternalism and a goal of benefit deterrence. For example, TANF gave the states a large amount of discretion over both the eligibility for and the generosity of benefits (Weaver 2000).

In the early 1990s, AFDC was under serious political pressure due to a number of problems, including a recent spike in caseloads, anemic incentives to enter the labor market, reported fraud and abuse, its potential impact on marriage, and the focus on children as opposed to adults. These various flows of negative policy feedback were combined with the increased racialization of welfare to produce anti-spending attitudes (Gilens 1999). As Gilens (1999) has demonstrated, the white American public has developed a distorted view of blacks and poverty in America that has produced an attitudinal connection between race and deservingness that in turn spilled over into reduced support for "welfare" programs. Some Democratic leaders, including Clinton, wanted to move the party toward the ideological center by divorcing the Democratic Party brand from the unquestioned support of unpopular poverty programs (Judis and Teixeria 2002). The political calculation was that if welfare could be tied to work incentives then the public's attitude would change toward the program and its recipients in ways that would make future government social spending more palatable to voters. Additionally, in the early part of President Clinton's first term his moderate proposal for welfare reform was crowded out of the policy agenda by a focus on the budget deficit and health care reform. The legislative agenda was set for serious welfare reform once Republicans took over the House of Representatives and the Senate with sweeping victories in the 1994 midterm elections. The new Republican leadership promised to pass a "Contract with America" during their first hundred days in office, which included a conservative proposal for welfare reform. On the other side of the aisle, President Clinton's reform proposal upset the party's liberal coalition both in the electorate and Congress. For example, public union groups were concerned that the new work requirements would increase competition for their jobs while liberal advocacy groups and the Congressional Black Caucus criticized the administration's proposals as being too punitive toward the working poor, especially single mothers (Weaver 2000). President Clinton won the 1992 presidential election by running as a New Democrat, which entailed moderating the party's positions on issues such as welfare, and then once in office put this theory into practice by triangulating his policy positions between those of conservative Republicans and liberal Democrats in Congress. The combination of increased party polarization, especially a more conservative Republican Party, along with divided government produced welfare reform that was to the center-right of the Democratic Party's median member.

In June of 1994, President Clinton sent a proposal to Congress that was not voted on because Republicans were counting on picking up more seats in the midterm election and moderate to conservative Democrats were afraid of how voting for welfare reform would play with their constituents. In November of 1994, the Republican Party won control of Congress for the first time since 1947–48, and, by extension, won control of the welfare reform agenda. The 1994 midterm elections resulted in political party polarization being felt in the legislative process. The election injected a large number of conservative Republicans, eager for welfare reform, into the House of Representatives at the expense of moderate Democrats and Republicans, resulting in the two parties being further apart in their preferences for welfare reform legislation. In the Senate, presidential hopeful Republican Robert Dole had to pass a bill through a moderate Senate that would also have a chance in the more conservative House. After the House and Senate both passed welfare reform measures, President Clinton vetoed the first two versions out of conference committee, since the first bill cut Medicaid and Medicare and the second bill reduced federal spending on food stamps and school lunch programs. The upcoming 1996 election put pressure on Republicans in the legislature to decouple welfare reform from cuts to popular health care programs, and once a bill was passed by Congress that focused exclusively on welfare reform President Clinton, feeling his reelection pressures, signed the bill into law.

The transformation of welfare from AFDC to TANF handed over to the states the ability to determine eligibility requirements, which types of recipients are exempt from the new work requirements, and the generosity of the cash benefits. The federal government reduced the scope of welfare spending by ending the entitlement for cash assistance and capping the lifetime benefits at five years. The result has been that fewer households have received less generous cash assistance from welfare. There have been no measurable effects between welfare reform and changes in the national poverty level. The pursuit of welfare reform by President Clinton reflected the Democratic Party's efforts to be nationally competitive in presidential elections by appealing to suburban voters at the expense of less politically active and poorer citizens. Additionally, Larry Summers, Secretary of the Treasury under Clinton, successfully made the argument that moving poverty assistance off the budget to the tax code would be more effective and politically sustainable (Steuerle and Carasso

2000). The TANF reform showed that Democrats were willing to reduce spending on a public program as long as assistance to the poor is funded elsewhere. The most recent evidence is that President Clinton's theory of progressive revisionism, where linking welfare to work would pave the way for future public spending, has not resulted in the mass public being more supportive of public welfare spending nor has it deracialized the perceptions of welfare (Soss and Schram 2003).

The Partisan Politics of Medicare Part D

In 2003, the Republican Party, having control over the presidency and Congress, created a new prescription drug program for Medicare that would cost around $400 billion over the next ten years. Why was the largest expansion of Medicare passed during a period of unified Republican control of the federal government? And what does this mean for the conventional wisdom concerning political parties and social spending? The conservative revolution in national politics, signified by the election of President Ronald Reagan, sought not only to scale back government activism and social programs, but more ambitiously to transform America's federal entitlement programs into a private social welfare state (Teles 2007). The most successful Republican attempt at the privatization of a public social program, to date, is the passage of Medicare Part D. During the 2000 election, Governor Bush proposed reforming Medicare so that seniors were given federal subsidies to purchase prescription drugs from private health companies. In the summer prior to the midterm elections of 2002, the Republican-controlled House of Representatives passed a prescription drug bill that would apply universally to seniors, use private health companies to administer the benefits, and cost hundreds of billions over decades. This bill did not make it through the Democratically controlled Senate. In the run up to the 2004 election, Republicans in the legislature were pushing to revisit the prescription drug plan as an integral part of the party's overall strategy for reelection. Republican leaders had calculated that passing a prescription drug plan that utilized private health and drug companies would have the dual electoral advantage of taking away a potential policy idea from the Democratic Party while laying the groundwork for privatizing other parts of the Medicare program in the future (Morgan and Campbell 2011). Although support from relevant interest groups and conservative legislators was lukewarm at times during the process, the final passage of the Medicare Prescription Drug, Improvement, and Modernization Act (MMA) was signed into law by President Bush in late 2003.

The traditional theory of political parties and social policy cannot explain why Republicans spent political capital to expand Medicare. However, my theoretical argument takes into account federal subsidies for the private sector and can therefore help shine some light on why the Republican Party initiated, worked for, and ultimately passed a new social welfare entitlement program. First, a new tax expenditure program for a health savings account (HSA) was used as a sweetener to get more conservative Republicans to vote for the final passage of the MMA (Oberlander 2007). The more conservative Republican legislators in Congress were initially not thrilled with the idea of being part of a process that would create a new federal entitlement, something many of these members had been fighting against their whole political careers. These conservative members signed on to Medicare Part D when new tax subsidies were added to allow workers who are enrolled in high-deductible health care plans (used by the wealthy) to subsidize a portion of their costs. Not surprisingly, recent studies show that wealthier workers in large companies are more likely to use HSAs (Kaiser Family Foundation 2010). Conservative legislators found spending through the tax code to be more acceptable than public spending, even if the public spending was allocated to private companies. Second, the MMA was sold to conservative legislators as a positive step to the ultimate goal of completely privatizing the Medicare program. The MMA's reliance on pharmaceutical companies and private health providers built off of the Republicans' success in passing Medicare Advantage six years earlier, which offered seniors a chance to buy health insurance from a private provider. In addition, the MMA was an opportunity for the Republican Party to demonstrate to voters that it could craft a social policy that did more than cut public benefits but instead offered a reliable private alternative for social benefits to voters (Morgan and Campbell 2011). The MMA is particularly instructive about the new politics of social policy. The Republican Party actively pursued legislation that utilized government funds to promote a private option for prescription drugs.

The partisan politics of social policy is complex and messy and cannot be captured by the simple idea that Democrats always expand and that Republicans always reduce federal spending for social programs. There are political incentives for both political parties to increase federal social spending. The Republican Party both with welfare reform and MMA wanted to demonstrate to voters that it could provide publicly demanded economic security through private, market-based social programs. In contrast, Democrats during a time of policy retrenchment and economic austerity had to protect the previous gains made to Social Security and Medicare while trying to find new methods to address poverty that were electorally and politically sustainable over time. These recent trends in partisan politics complicate the traditional empirical relationship between Democratic Party control of the federal government and more expansive social policy.

Is the example of TANF typical of the post-Great Society period and, if so, is there still an observable relationship between Democratic Party power and higher public social spending? Even given the evolving complexities to the politics of social policy, I expect to find that Democrats in power will have increased government spending on public programs on average more than Republicans over the last forty-two years. Democrats spent most of the last forty years protecting the gains made previously to Social Security, Medicare, and Medicaid and taking advantage of any opportunities to incrementally add expanded eligibility or greater generosity to existing public social programs. Conversely, Republicans have sought opportunities to scale back the public welfare state while using tax subsidies to grow a parallel private social welfare system that one day may compete with (and possibly overtake) the public system. While TANF and MMA are exceptions to the rules, these two programs, by themselves, will not negate a forty-year relationship between political party power and changes to public social spending. In the next section, I discuss the data and methods that will be employed to examine the full and dynamic relationship between political party control and changes in the modality and degree of social spending in America.

Measuring Political Party Dynamics and Public Social Spending

I now pivot to explaining the formal test of the relationship between political party control of the federal government and changes to social policy. In measuring the relationship between political parties and traditional social spending, I use Democratic Party power in both the executive and legislative branches since extant theoretical arguments predict that Democratic control results in increased expenditures for public social welfare. The period of study ranges from 1970 to 2012. This forty-two-year period represents the overlap between the data set on traditional social spending and the new federal data set for tax expenditures.[4] I employ two

---

[4] Although tax expenditure data from the Joint Committee on Taxation began in 1967, the equation used for calculating revenue loss from tax breaks was experimented with

measurements of federal budgetary public spending: one that focuses on annual changes to discretionary social spending and the other representing yearly changes to total federal social spending for public social welfare (discretionary plus mandatory). I expect that a shift to greater Democratic power will produce a positive and statistically significant increase in both discretionary and total public social spending in both the short and the long run.

I begin by examining the partisan causes of changes in federal spending for public social programs. There are six budget categories used to represent federal spending for public social welfare: education; training, employment and social services; health; Medicare; income security; Social Security and railroad retirement; and veterans' benefits and services.[5] These categories include all the major public programs, including Social Security, Medicare, Medicaid, unemployment insurance, food stamps, and TANF, as well as tens of other smaller programs that are less well known, such as medical research grants.[6] I test two types of public social spending: first, total public social spending, which includes both discretionary and mandatory spending, and second, just discretionary social spending, which is determined annually by Congress and the President. In measuring both types of direct spending, I use appropriations spending data for social welfare from the Policy Agendas Project developed by Jones, True, and Baumgartner.[7] I use the Policy Agendas Project coding to separate out discretionary from mandatory social spending. The two social spending variables are adjusted for annual changes to inflation and per capita to account for any increases in spending that are attributable

---

for the first few years and began to stabilize around 1970. The appropriations data from the Policy Agendas Project ends in 2012 resulting in a time period of the study from 1970 to 2012.

[5] While there is some disagreement over what categories constitute social welfare, the categories used here are standard across comparative welfare state studies. The only category used in this grouping that may be questioned by some scholars is education. However, the federal government categorizes education as a social welfare policy along with training and social services, and changes to education spending move together with other spending changes in health care, welfare, and pensions. I decided not to use housing as a category since the politics of this policy does not correlate as closely with the other categories. However, since some scholars do include housing as a component of social welfare, I run some of the later analysis with housing and include the results in the Appendix.

[6] I list the specific public programs within each subcategory that make up public social spending in the Appendix.

[7] Wlezien and Soroka (2003) argue that scholars studying social welfare spending should use appropriations spending, since these bills mandate the amount of budget authority to an issue area while direct outlays often lag behind the appropriations decision.

to population growth or overall price levels. The first variable in the model measures total direct social spending that includes mandatory social spending, which is, by definition, outside the annual appropriations process and directed toward popular programs such as Social Security and Medicare. The second dependent variable is discretionary social spending, which is altered during the annual appropriations process. I expect Democratic Party power to produce more significant changes to discretionary social spending.

Measurement of Political Party and Economic Influences on Social Expenditures

The main independent variables of interest measure Democratic Party control of government. The first variable is control of the executive branch, which is represented by a dummy variable that is coded one for a year with a Democratic president and zero for a year with a Republican executive. The second variable is Democratic Party power in the legislature, which is represented by a value of two for unified Democratic control, one for a split Congress (e.g., Democrats control the House and Republicans control the Senate), and zero for unified Republican control of the legislature. I expect that increases in Democratic Party strength in government will correspond to higher levels of direct spending for public programs. A switch from a Republican to a Democratic president should result in more significant changes to public spending than Democrats gaining one more chamber in the legislature.

Moreover, I expect that changes to political party control will result in changes to public social spending even when accounting for economic and demographic factors. I use different sets of control variables for the two models since the factors that influence mandatory social spending do not influence changes in discretionary social expenditures. The first economic control variable is the annual change in national unemployment. An increase in unemployment, which signals a weakening economy, should influence an increase in social spending. A rise in the national unemployment level triggers spending on the joint federal–state unemployment insurance program and will likely create upward pressure on federal spending under Democratic administrations. Next, a rise in the overall price level also impacts both types of spending, but in the opposite direction. As inflation creeps up, the federal government could decide to slash direct social spending in order to bring price levels back down. I use these control variables for all the models in this chapter. Finally, I include a variable for changes to the gross domestic product (GDP) since the federal government may choose to spend more on social programs in years when revenues are higher at the federal treasury.

In addition to economic controls, I include demographic variables to control for the societal effects on mandatory social expenditures. As the population ages, there are automatic increases in mandatory social spending that stem from Social Security and Medicare. Therefore, I include a variable for the percentage of the population that is elderly and able to collect from these large public social programs. Next, certain public programs aimed at the poor, such as Medicaid coverage, are determined, in part, by the number of families below the poverty line. A variable for the percentage of families that fall below the poverty line is added to account for Medicaid and other government spending aimed at reducing poverty. Altogether, these variables will help determine if changes in political party power in government affect social spending once economic and demographic factors are taken into consideration. In the second model, testing the relationship between party control and changes to discretionary social spending, I only export over the poverty and inflation measures as potential influences on federal spending. The majority of discretionary programs provide assistance to the poor and a party concerned about short-term inflation can always cut discretionary spending. In the next section, I explain how the conventional relationship between Democratic Party control and social spending will be dynamically tested using time series analysis.

Testing the Partisan Dynamics of Social Spending Using Time Series Analysis: An Error Correction Model

I use an error correction model (ECM) since the relationship between political party control and social spending will have both short- and long-run effects. ECMs are a form of time series analysis appropriate to utilize when a dependent variable responds to independent variables in the short term and maintains a long-term equilibrium level with these same variables. There are a number of theoretical and statistical reasons for my choice of an ECM. First, this model properly represents my theoretical argument that political parties in power create social policy for both a short-run electoral advantage and as a means to influence the long-run ideological direction of public policy. Next, a change in political party control produces an immediate impact in spending that will be represented in the budget and tax bills for that following year, but since many of the spending increases involve entitlements or spread spending changes out over a number of years, the full effects will not be evident all at once. Finally, this model is consistent with the economic and demographic control variables, which are expected to impact government spending immediately (such as in changes to the number of families below the poverty level or the percentage of the population that can legally collect Social Security and Medicare) and create additional effects that are experienced over time.

Specifically, I estimate the short- and long-run effects of political party changes in government on social spending using a single equation method. I utilize the single equation method over the next best alternative, the two-step estimator (Engle and Granger 1987), for a number of practical reasons. First, the single equation estimator model is the better method when dealing with smaller sample sizes and not one of the following models has a group of observations over 42 (De Boef and Granato 1999). Second, a single equation ECM applies to both integrated and stationary time-series data since the dependent variable takes on its past values and those of the independent variable (De Boef and Granato 1999, De Boef and Keele 2008). Federal spending data, both public spending and tax expenditures, can be considered integrated data given that yearly estimates take into account the previous fiscal year's expenditures for each budget category.[8]

---

[8] ECMs are a method to control for a dependent variable that has a deterministic trend, such as government spending, that may increase over time due to nothing more than growth in the population. I control for the time trend by constructing the dependent variable as per capita spending, but the additional control of the ECM assists in avoiding the production of spurious results and false inferences. All of this being said, the data for all four dependent variables can be treated as an integrated time series. First, both discretionary and direct social spending are a function of the budget process that is determined by the previous year's estimates and therefore is a strictly cumulative process. Next, annual changes in social tax expenditures (Chapters 5 and 6) are produced by changes to the tax code and therefore cannot be mean reverting. The social expenditure ratio is composed of the previous two spending data sets, both of which are non-mean reverting. The numerator value is a function of the annual value of social tax expenditures. The denominator is a function of the annual value of aggregate social expenditures, which is public spending plus social tax expenditures. In order to check the validity of theoretically integrated data, I ran multiple augmented Dickey–Fuller (ADF) tests with a constant, a time trend, and one lag for the four variables: annual direct discretionary social spending, annual total public social spending, annual social tax expenditures, and the social spending ratio. Not one of these measures reported a negative value less than -3.50, so the null hypothesis of a unit root cannot be rejected. Although the number of observations is relatively small for all four models, these results confirm the theoretical argument for an integrated time series.

The single-equation ECM is as follows:

$$\Delta Y_t = \alpha + \alpha_1 Y_{t-1} + \beta_1 \Delta X_t + \beta_2 X_{t-1} + \varepsilon_t$$

In this equation, changes in the dependent variable Y are a function of short-run changes in the independent variable X as well as the separation from a long-run equilibrium between X and Y, which is determined by the error correction rate. For each independent variable X, there are two estimates of the population parameters: β_1 for the differenced variable and β_2 for the lagged level of the independent variable. The estimator β_1 produces an estimate of the immediate change in the dependent variable (the annual change in social spending) in the short term, from a shock in the independent variable. For example, as we change from a Democratic to Republican president the next budget should produce a decrease in traditional expenditures for public social programs. It is crucial to note that this "short-run" effect is not ephemeral but simply the effect that occurs in the immediate period. The β_2 estimator is part of the "long-run" effect of X on Y or what is commonly referred to as the error correction section of the model. β_2's impact on the dependent variable does not happen in the near term but rather the effects are spread out in each period over a set range of time. An example of this is that as Republican power in Congress increases after a midterm election (a shock to the composition of the legislature) the long-run equilibrium level of government spending and the composition of the U.S. Congress will change so that the level diverges from the previous equilibrium and this change corrects over time. β_2 alone does not provide the long-run impact, and must be combined with α_1, the error correction rate, to determine the actual size of the long-term effect. The long-run multiplier is computed by dividing β_2 by α_1 to derive the complete long-term impact of a tremor or shock to X on Y through the error correction rate. In addition to determining the long-term impact on the dependent variable, α_1 produces information on how fast a disturbance from the long-run equilibrium is expunged. The error correction estimator, or α_1, can be translated as the proportion of the equilibrium disturbance that will be eliminated in each time period starting with the time period $t + 1$. In conclusion, ECMs provide the necessary framework to determine how increases in political party strength in government influence both short- and long-run changes to social spending. Next, I present the results of the test between Democratic Party control of the federal government and changes to both total public social spending and discretionary public social spending.

Democratic Party Control and Public Social Spending, 1970–2012

Democratic presidents produce immediate increases in public social spending while Democratic control of the Congress has no observable impact on social spending changes. In Table 3.3, in the first column, I report the results of the relationship between Democratic Party control and changes in total public social spending (mandatory and discretionary), and in the second column I reveal the relationship between Democratic Party control and changes to only discretionary social spending. In the first model, a change from a Republican to Democratic president correlates with higher levels of social spending in the short term and although the long-term coefficient is signed in the right direction, it is not statistically significant (as measured by both the long-term coefficient and the multiplier). The Democratic increase of more than $200 million in public social spending is 5 percent of the average total over this period. This finding reiterates other studies that show Democratic executives increasing spending soon after they enter office (Bartels 2008, Hibbs 1987). There is no clear relationship between Democratic control of the legislature and higher levels of social spending. And although Democratic control of both the White House and Congress are positively signed with long-term social spending increases, these coefficients report too much variance to rise to the level of significance. All three Democratic presidents during this study promised more federal spending during their campaigns, were elected after long periods of Republican control of the White House, and initially governed with the mass public reporting a high level of liberal policy mood. These conditions resulted in Democrats, soon after taking office, injecting more federal money into schools, social services, and job training. For example, during their honeymoon periods, President Obama passed the stimulus package that included funding for education and the ACA, and President Clinton enacted legislation that supported childhood immunization, expanded Head Start, started AmeriCorps, and increased education funding.

The inclusion of economic and demographic controls adds explanatory power to the base model. As the economy grows, the federal government spends more on social programs in both the short and the long term. This result falls in line with the idea that the government will take increased revenue from growth and turn around and spend it on popular programs. There is some evidence from the negatively signed coefficients (although not significant) that the federal government reacts to inflationary pressures by cutting back on traditional public social spending. Surprisingly,

TABLE 3.3. *Democratic Party Control and Public Social Spending, 1970–2012*

Independent Variable	Total Public	Discretionary
Short-Term Effects		
Δ Democratic President	207.8**	145.8**
	(78.59)	(52.54)
Δ Democratic Congress	−36.00	−17.73
	(50.39)	(36.15)
Δ Unemployment	68.45*	
	(49.16)	
Δ Inflation	−10.59	−28.22**
	(17.76)	(10.81)
Δ Poverty Rate	−32.36	69.66*
	99.87	(43.25)
Δ GDP	.235**	
	(.081)	
Δ Elderly	−242.2	
	(283.1)	
Long-Term Effects		
Democratic President$_{t-1}$	28.11	28.61
	(67.33)	(42.59)
Democratic Congress$_{t-1}$	37.78	−6.81
	(40.40)	(24.37)
Unemployment$_{t-1}$	78.79**	
	(40.11)	
Inflation$_{t-1}$	−3.35	−15.37*
	(17.77)	(9.49)
Poverty Rate$_{t-1}$	−94.12	−41.47**
	(48.83)	(18.98)
GDP$_{t-1}$	.357***	
	(.090)	
Elderly$_{t-1}$	124.8**	
	(66.39)	
Error Correction Rate		
Social Spending$_{t-1}$	−.713***	−.305**
	(.179)	(.117)
Constant	−781.6	609.5**
	(635.8)	(210)
Long-Run Multiplier		
Democratic President	39.37	93.57
	(89.70)	(128)
Democratic Congress	52.91	−22.28
	(54.34)	(80.37)
Adjusted R^2	.591	.311

N = 42 for all columns. ***p<.001,**p<.05, *p<.10 One-tailed tests; Standard errors in parentheses.

the number of American households below the poverty line correlated with less government spending on public social programs, although again the coefficients were not statistically significant from zero. While federal social spending does not respond to the poverty level, it does react as expected to an increase in the national unemployment rate. A one-unit increase in the national unemployment rate causes an increase in spending for public social programs in both the short and the long run (of roughly 1 and 2 percent, respectively, of the overall spending average). Finally, the increase of citizens over the age of sixty-five is the largest contributing factor to federal social spending in the long term – a growth of over 3 percent. This finding is not surprising given the increasingly larger proportion of social spending allocated to mandatory programs for the elderly such as Social Security and Medicare. Overall, Democratic presidents, a growing economy, the number of elderly people, and increases in the unemployment rate drive up total public social expenditures.

It is possible that the traditional relationship between political party control and changes to federal social spending becomes stronger when mandatory spending is subtracted from the analysis. The logic here is simple; a political party in power can manipulate discretionary spending through the annual appropriations process in ways that they cannot change mandatory spending (without changing the laws governing these programs). In the second model (second column), I test the association between Democratic Party control and yearly changes to discretionary social spending for public programs. Again, I find evidence that increased Democratic Party power produces higher annual levels of discretionary social expenditures for public welfare programs even when controlling for economic and demographic factors. A switch to a Democratic president results in a positive and statistically significant spending change in the short run of over $145 million or 41 percent of the average yearly discretionary social spending change. As predicted, this is a higher increase than the previous correlation between Democratic control and total public spending (41% compared to 5%). The long-run relationship between a Democratic presidency and spending is signed in the right direction but not significant. Democratic power in the legislature is negatively signed with social expenditures in both the short and the long run but not statistically significant from zero. Again, the federal government responds to inflationary pressures with cuts to discretionary social spending in both the short and the long term. In this model, the federal government – in the short run – counteracts an increase in poverty with more discretionary social spending. However, this short-term increase in social spending is negated by a long-term decrease in social spending due to increases in household poverty.

In brief, a newly elected Democratic president immediately increases direct social spending for public programs even when controlling for economic and demographic factors. These results show that even after the Great Society era and during a period of social welfare retrenchment the Democratic Party raises the level of spending for public welfare. Although the legislature is not statistically significant in the models, it is important to note that all three modern Democratic presidents, Jimmy Carter, Bill Clinton, and Barack Obama, enjoyed a Democratic Congress their first two years in office and took power after at least eight years of Republican control of the presidency.

There are two potential reasons why Democratic Party control of the legislature does not correspond to even higher levels of federal social spending in the two models. First, the rise in the level of mandatory spending, specifically Medicare and Social Security, over time has lessened the relationship between political party control and annual changes to public social spending. Political parties have less of the budget to manipulate, as Social Security and Medicare have become larger shares of federal social spending and the national budget. For example, mandatory spending was 26 percent of the national budget in 1962 but 57 percent in 2013, a 31-point increase in just over fifty years. Second, the time period in this study starts after the last large federal expansion of social spending as part of President Johnson's Great Society program. This forty-two-year period was a time when the Democratic Party was looking to protect the federal programs established during the New Deal and Great Society eras. Democrats spent their legislative efforts fighting both retrenchment and privatization efforts by the Republican Party and did not have the public support for any more large expansions of the public welfare state.[9] Even under these difficult political trends, a Democratic president with unified

---

[9] I also split apart the data into two periods, 1970–1992 and 1993–2012, to determine if the relationship between Democratic Party power and total social spending was stronger at the beginning of the time period. The regression results showed that Democratic control was negatively signed and not statistically significant even in the earlier period of 1970–1992, so the results here are not a byproduct of just the first two decades. My analysis in earlier drafts of this manuscript of total public spending from 1970-2009 also produced null results. Therefore, it is quite possible that the significant relationship between Democratic Party control and positive changes to total public spending are a function of the stimulus and the ACA. However, it is important to note that all the models of discretionary public spending and Democratic Party control have shown a positive and significant relationship even when the analysis was limited to 1970–2009.

control of the federal government and some degree of public approval can raise short-term social expenditures for public programs.

An Alternative Test of the Democratic Party and Higher Social Spending

The previous analysis showed that Democratic presidents produce higher levels of public social spending in the short run. Yet, a full analysis of the relationship between political party control of the federal government and social policy must take into account both public social spending and subsidies for private social welfare. The conventional wisdom on political parties and social policy argues that there is a clear division between Democrats and Republicans over the issue of government spending on social policy. Democrats, when in power, increase federal spending for social programs while Republicans cut back on social welfare spending. If this relationship is true beyond just public social programs then we should observe Democrats supporting all forms of federal funding for social programs, including government subsidies for private welfare that accrue benefits to the rich.

In this section, I test the relationship between Democratic Party control of the federal government and yearly changes to aggregate social spending. Since social policy properly defined is any government effort at providing economic security to citizens, this surely includes both direct spending on public programs and the hundreds of billions of dollars directed through the federal tax code to private providers of social welfare. It is possible that the Democratic Party favors not just public spending but any form of social spending (even tax subsidies aimed at the private sector) and Republicans want smaller government regardless of how the money is delivered, who benefits from it, or how popular the social goal. If this relationship is true, then Democratic Party control of the White House and Congress should produce clear increases to an aggregate measure of federal social expenditures (public spending plus tax subsidies). In order to test this idea, I introduce a unique measure of aggregate federal social spending that is a product of both annual spending for public social benefits and tax expenditures for private social welfare. I use a new data set for social tax expenditures from the nonpartisan Congressional Joint Committee on Taxation (JCT).[10] I combine the tax expenditure data with the

---

[10] I go into greater detail about the measurement of tax expenditures in the next chapter.

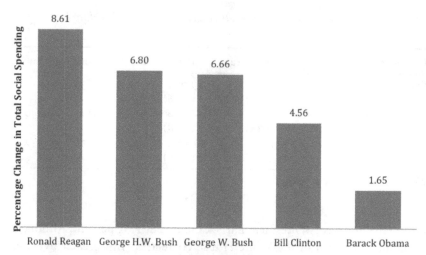

FIGURE 3.1. Change in total social spending by president, 1980–2012. *Source:* Data from the Policy Agendas Project and Joint Committee of Taxation (JCT) with author's calculation.

traditional budgetary data for public social programs from the Office of Management and Budget via the Policy Agendas Project. If the main division in American politics is over the total amount of government spending (as opposed to the type of spending), then Democratic Party control of the executive and legislative branches should conclusively correlate with higher levels of aggregate federal social spending.

Before conducting statistical tests of party control and aggregate social spending, I start by presenting descriptive statistics on the relationship between political party power and changes to aggregate federal social spending. Figure 3.1 presents the relationship between political party control of the presidency and the average percent change in aggregate social spending. Surprisingly, it is Republican presidents and not Democratic ones that produce larger changes in social spending. I have organized the graph by placing the president with the largest change on the far left of the horizontal axis and the smallest change on the far right. The largest average growth in social spending, 8.6 percent, occurred during the 1980s under President Ronald Reagan. In fact, Ronald Reagan produced nearly twice as much growth as compared to the highest spending Democrat, Bill Clinton. After President Reagan, the next two highest averages were under George H.W. Bush and George W. Bush at 6.8 and 6.6 percent respectively. The smallest average increase in social spending came

TABLE 3.4. *Percent Change in Annual Aggregate Social Spending by Political Party, 1970–2012*

Chamber	Democratic	Republican	T Score	P Value
Presidency	.056	.094	1.63	0.110
	(.013)	(.016)		
House of Representatives	.097	.046	−2.11	0.040
	(.015)	(.008)		
Senate	.089	.067	−0.93	0.352
	(.019)	(.007)		

Note: Standard Errors in parentheses.

during the first term of President Barack Obama at 1.65 percent. Although Republican control of the White House correlates with greater average increases in aggregate social spending, these tests cannot determine if the partisan differences here are statistically significant across control of the federal government.

I now turn to evaluate partisan changes to total social spending using a difference of means test between Republican and Democratic Party control across the executive branch, the House of Representatives, and the Senate. If traditional theories of partisanship and social spending are correct, then Democratic Party control will be associated with higher aggregate social welfare expenditures across all three chambers. In these tests, I used dummy variables for Republican control of the presidency, the House of Representatives, and the Senate. In addition to the difference of means tests, I ran an analysis of variance (ANOVA) to account for possible interaction effects of the three governing units (executive, house, and senate) and consider the influence of divided governmental control on changes in total social spending – these results are in the Appendix.[11]

In Table 3.4, I present results from three difference of means tests of partisan control and total social spending. These results reveal an uncertain relationship between political party control of government and changes to aggregate federal social spending. The first row shows that Republican presidents nearly doubled the social spending of Democratic

---

[11] I additionally ran an ANOVA with partisanship as a scaled variable in order to account for interaction effects. The scaled variable ranges from three equating to total Democratic control, two and one as divided control, and zero as total Republican control. Again, there was no statistical difference between the two political parties. These results are discussed in the Appendix.

ones, 0.094 to 0.056. However, this difference of means is not statistically significant so therefore we cannot rule out an undefined relationship between party and spending. In contrast, Democratic control of the House of Representatives produced more than twice the increase in total social spending and is statistically significant from zero. Finally, the small co-efficient gap and variance between Democratic and Republican control of the Senate produces an unspecified relationship between party control and social spending. The totality of the results here is decidedly mixed and assuredly does not show a clear relationship between Democratic Party control over the federal government and increased aggregate social spending.

These results call into question the persistent idea that there is a clear difference between the two political parties in the level of federal spending and the size of government. If there was ever going to be an observable partisan difference over levels of federal spending then it should be evident in the area of social policy over the last forty-two years. If the major division between the two political parties is not based in the overall level of federal financing, then what is the partisan fault line when it comes to social policy? I have argued and expect to demonstrate in the next two chapters that the major division between Republicans and Democrats is over using the federal government to finance a favorable ratio of public welfare programs to private social benefits.

Conclusion

This chapter reexamined the established relationship between the Democratic Party and changes to social policy. My analysis found that Democratic Party control of the White House resulted in higher levels of social spending on public programs over the last forty-two year period. There is plenty of evidence from actual changes to legislation that the Democratic Party has both protected and increased the generosity of social entitlement programs over the years (Hacker 2002, Howard 2007, Mettler 2011). However, the relationship between political party control and annual changes to total social spending for public programs has lessened as there has been a rise in the number of elderly Americans and by extension mandatory social spending. These results provide some evidence that the escalation of entitlement spending has crowded out the previously strong relationship between Democrats and higher social spending. However, Democratic presidents are particularly adept at increasing discretionary public social spending in the short term. These programs disproportionately target the working class, an important constituency in the Democratic Party's coalition. It is important to note, however, that discretionary social expenditures are a small and shrinking part of the overall U.S. budget. For example, in 2008 discretionary social spending was approximately 5 percent of total federal social expenditures.

In this chapter, I tested the relationship between political party power and changes to aggregate social spending (public spending plus tax expenditures) to determine if Democratic Party control produced increases to federal spending on social programs regardless of how it is delivered or who benefits from the program. I found that Republican presidents increased aggregate social spending more than Democratic presidents.[12] In contrast, Democratic control of the House of Representatives produced higher aggregate social spending and there was no statistically conclusive relationship between party and social spending in the Senate. In total, there is no empirically clear relationship between political party control of the federal government and aggregate social spending, leading me to conclude that the main partisan difference is not over the overall level of social spending but, in turn, how federal money is allocated and who benefits.

In the next chapter, I begin to build a foundation for examining the relationship between political parties and the divided social welfare state by examining federal tax expenditures and the private social system in America. The American private welfare state is the largest in the world and has grown substantially over the last four decades. I explain how applying the concept of policy tools allows us to study the myriad ways in which the federal government finances social policy, especially in the private sector. The addition of tax expenditures and private social welfare to the overall analysis of social policy provides a political rationale for Republican Party government activism. Tax expenditures depart from traditional public social spending in who benefits, how they pass through the legislature, and the political opportunities they present to Republicans versus Democrats. Finally, I examine the association between social tax expenditures and changes in private social spending in the United States.

---

[12] This study is not the first analysis to find that Republicans increase social spending (see Browning 1986).

Appendix to Chapter 3

Political Parties and Total Social Spending, ANOVA Bonferroni 1970–2012

	Unified Republican Control	Republican Control of One Unit	Republican Control of Two Units
Democratic Control of One Unit	−.001 (1.00)		
Democratic Control of Two Units	.024 (1.00)	.025 (1.00)	
Unified Democratic Control	.014 (1.00)	.015 (1.00)	−.010 (1.00)

N = 42, Standard errors in parentheses.

This test accounts for the possible effects of divided government on partisan differences in social spending. None of the differences here are close to statistically significant as evidenced by the uniform p-values of one across all the conditions. For example, we would expect the largest difference in aggregate social spending to be between unified Democratic control and unified Republican control, yet the difference is only 0.014 and not statistically significant from zero. These results provide further evidence that the partisan differences over social policy are not purely about the level of aggregate federal funding.

Federal Public Social Programs

Education, Training, Employment, and Social Services
Elementary, Secondary, and Vocational Education
Financial assistance from the federal government
Occupational, vocational, and adult education
Education for disadvantaged
Special education
Indian education programs
Impact aid

Higher Education
Student financial assistance for higher education
Family education loan program
Other higher education support

Research and General Education Aids
Research and general education aids
The Smithsonian Institute
The Library of Congress
The Institute of Education Sciences
Public broadcasting
State formula grants for libraries

Training and Employment
Payments to states under the Job Training Partnership Act (JTPA)
The Comprehensive Employment and Training Act (CETA)
The Workforce Investment Act of 1998 (WIA)
Federally funded state employment services
Adult and youth training grants
Dislocated worker training grants
The Jobs Corp

Other Labor Services
Bureau of Labor Statistics
Employment Standards Administration
Labor Management Standards

Department of Labor Administration

Social Services
Block grants for social and community services
Rehabilitation services
Aging services programs
Children and family services

Health

Health Care Services
Health care for Native Americans, coal mine retirees, and merchant seamen
Programs for substance abuse and mental health services
Block grants for maternal and child health
Grants for Human Immunodeficiency Virus
Public health preparedness
Project BioShield
Medicaid

Health Research and Training
National Institutes of Health (NIH)

Consumer and Occupational Health and Safety
The Food and Drug Administration (FDA)
Occupational Safety and Health Review Commission (OSHA)
Consumer Product Safety Commission

Medicare
Part A, Hospital Insurance (HI)
Part B, Supplementary Medical Insurance (SMI)
Part D, Medicare Prescription Drugs (D)
Administrative costs

Income Security
General Retirement and Disability Insurance (excluding social security)
Railroad worker retirement
Special benefits for disabled coal miners
Net transactions of the Pension Benefit Guaranty Corporation (PBGC)

Federal Employee Retirement and Disability
Unemployment Compensation
Unemployment Insurance (UI)

Food and Nutrition Assistance
Food stamps
Supplements for Women, Infants, and Children (WIC)
Child nutrition and special milk programs

Other Income Security
Supplemental Security Income (SSI)
Temporary Assistance for Needy Families (TANF)

Social Security
Old Age, Survivors Insurance (OASI)
Disability Insurance (DI)
Program administration

Veterans Benefits and Services

Income Security for Veterans
Disability compensation
The administration of veterans' pensions
Burial benefits
Life insurance

Veterans' Education, Training, and Rehabilitation
Vocational rehabilitation benefits
GI Bill

Hospital and Medical Care for Veterans
Medical research
Medical care
Hospital services
Medical facility construction

Veterans' Housing
Guaranteed housing loan program

Other Veterans' Benefits and Services
Veterans' cemeteries
Administrative expenses

4

Government Subsidies and the Private American Social System

The Special Case of Tax Expenditures

A family sitting down to prepare their annual tax return can select from a large menu of federal government tax subsidies for social benefits and services. For example, taxpayers can claim the following tax expenditures for social welfare: exemptions for dependents such as children or elderly parents, exclusions of their contributions to employer-based health insurance and pension plans, deductions for college tuition and fees and interest on student loans, additional deductions for IRAs, deductions for health care savings accounts, the child tax credit, education credits, or the earned income tax credit (to name a few). These various tax exclusions, deductions, and credits all share one thing in common: politicians designed them as a means to provide people income security through the subsidization of private social programs or activities.[1]

The majority of empirical research on political parties and social policy has focused exclusively on how the government funds public social programs. In ignoring private-sector social benefits and the government subsidies that finance them, scholars have excluded a significant amount of government activity from their research and the means through which most American citizens receive social benefits and services. Here, I begin to develop a framework for studying the politics of the divided

---

[1] It is important to note that a couple of tax expenditure programs are used to increase the generosity of both Social Security and Medicare. Currently, Social Security benefits are fully or partially excluded from a taxpayer's gross income. Higher income taxpayers can exclude around 85 percent of Social Security payments. Similarly, Medicare benefits are excluded from federal taxation. Taxpayers are allowed to deduct the amount over and including their contributions to Medicare A, B, and D.

social state. In particular, I address the following questions in this chapter: what constitutes the private social welfare state? Who benefits from private benefits and services, and how large is the private system? I show that private social spending has grown at a faster rate than public spending, that the United States spends more on private social welfare than any other industrialized democracy in the world, and that the citizens who enroll in private social programs are different from the populations normally associated with public assistance. The second half of the chapter focuses on explaining the role of tax expenditures in financing and promoting private alternatives to public social programs. I document the rise of social tax expenditures over time and discuss their regressive distributive effects. I detail their use and historical development in the provision of health care, pensions, welfare, and education. Finally, I empirically examine the relationship between the two, to determine if increases in federal tax subsidies for social welfare produce corresponding increases in private social spending in the United States. My analysis indicates that there is a statistically significant relationship between the rise of social tax expenditures and increases in business spending on private social benefits. The implication of these results is that the federal government affects economic security not only through changes in direct spending for public social programs but also through changes in federal tax subsidies for private welfare benefits.

The Private Social System in the United States

My goal in this part of the chapter is to situate private social programs within the context of the politics of American social policy. In this study, the private social system refers to health care, pensions, welfare, education, and other services citizens receive through their employers or other nongovernment organizations.[2] The majority of private social benefits are offered voluntarily by businesses and subsidized by the federal government through tax expenditures. These subsidies provide tax incentives for businesses to offer and individuals to purchase social benefits from private companies – through, for example, contributions to 401k plans, or employer-based health care insurance. In this section, I examine the characteristics of the private social system with a particular focus on

---

[2] While I emphasize employment-based social benefits, my analysis includes the federal government's subsidization of purchases of individual social insurance and religious and nonprofit social services.

how private social benefits have grown over time as a form of worker compensation for U.S. businesses.

The study of federal financing for private social welfare programs is politically important for a number of reasons. The majority of American citizens (especially among the nonelderly) receive health care insurance and pension benefits through the private social system. In 2012, more than 170 million nonelderly citizens received health insurance through their employers or their partners' employer-sponsored health care plans, which is close to four times the amount of people who received insurance from Medicare in the same year (Smith and Medalia 2014). The large group of citizens enrolled in private social programs is not evenly distributed throughout the population. In particular, recipients of federally subsidized social benefits tend to be wealthier, less racially diverse, and professionals working in larger corporations. I document, here, changes to public versus private health care coverage and who benefits from employment-based pensions in the United States.

Second, private social spending represents a large amount of activity in the U.S. economy.[3] According to a recent Organisation for Economic Co-operation and Development (OECD) study, private social spending accounted for 10 percent of all American economic activity and this percentage has grown over time (Organisation for Economic Co-operation and Development 2012). In order to put the size of the private social system in perspective, it accounts for roughly the same percentage of gross domestic product as the manufacturing sector in the United States (Bureau of Economic Analysis 2010). The federal government through the use of regulations and subsidies has played a critical role in growing the private side of the divided social welfare state. The U.S. Treasury Department estimates that the federal government spent more than $600 billion on tax subsidies alone for social welfare in 2012. In order to put this figure in perspective, the U.S. government spent $550 billion on Medicare in the same year. I chart the size and growth of the private social spending in two ways: through comparisons to public-sector social spending, and through comparisons of private social spending in other countries. For all these reasons and more, the inclusion of government financing for private social services is crucial in studying the politics of American social

---

[3] According to data from the Employee Benefit Research Institute (EBRI), around 60 percent of the nonelderly population receives health insurance through their employer or their spouse's employer (Employee Benefit Research Institute 2010).

policy. The federal government has contributed in many ways to the United States having the largest and fastest growing private social system in the world.

The Private Social State: Employment-Based Social Benefits and Services

My analysis of the private social system focuses primarily on employment-related social benefits and services. These programs constitute around 96 percent of total private-sector social expenditures (Social Security Administration 2005).[4] The administration and provision of employee social benefits involve the coordination of the government, businesses, and individual employees. Employers voluntarily offer any number of private social welfare programs to their employees such as health care insurance (now mandated by the Affordable Care Act [ACA]), old-age pensions, life insurance, long-term disability, education and training, childcare, legal assistance, travel reimbursements, paid sick leave, vacations, and maternity leave. These private social programs serve the same public interest as government programs, which is to assuage economic risk by providing basic income security through social insurance and services.[5] While businesses offer assorted social benefits, by far the largest and most important are the employment-based programs for health care insurance and retirement savings. The United States has a predominately private health care system since most Americans receive health insurance through their employment (or spouse's employment). For example, employer-sponsored health care insurance represents 91 percent of all private insurance and 71 percent of the total health care insurance market (Employee Benefit Research Institute 2009). Not only are the majority of citizens enrolled in employment-based plans, but these workers also receive – by extension – the federal subsidies that accompany private

---

[4] Although I include spending data on nonprofit and voluntary social services and benefits, I do not theorize about these organizations since they represent such a small percentage of total private spending.

[5] It is difficult to draw a clear line between public and private social benefits since many private organizations rely on government grants, subsidies, and loans while some public programs use private administration to deliver social benefits to citizens. Yet, employment-based benefits are safely considered an example of private welfare. Businesses offer these programs, they use private health care and financial companies to administer and provide benefits, and rely heavily on employer and employee contributions (Hacker 2002).

health insurance. In the following sections, I describe employment-based health care insurance and pension plans and how they have grown as a proportion of worker compensation over time.

Businesses voluntarily provide health insurance to employees that ranges from acute hospital visits to full coverage including dental and eye care. Modern employment-based health benefits have a number of basic features. One, these plans use a variety of private administrators such as commercial insurance programs, Blue Cross and Blue Shield plans, self-insured plans administered by third-party administrators (TPAs), or multiple employer welfare arrangements (MEWAs). In 2008, 98 percent of Americans with employer-based plans were enrolled in some form of managed health care. The majority of these plans are represented by health maintenance organizations (HMOs) and preferred provider organizations (PPOs). A managed care system arranges for and finances medical services using provider payment methods with a select network of providers. Second, almost all employment-based health care plans require the employee to share in the costs of coverage. These cost features include premiums, deductibles, coinsurance, copayments, and maximum caps on benefits. Recent studies show that businesses have been raising the level of employee contributions as a means to keep up with increased health care costs and to move some of the risk from the employer to employee (Employee Benefit Research Institute 2012, Hacker 2004). And although nondiscrimination rules apply to health insurance plans offered through employers, these rules do not apply to employment-based cafeteria plans purchased from third parties or part-time employees. This feature permits higher-income employees and union members to purchase "Cadillac" insurance plans with substantially higher quality benefits and services that are not subject to tax.

As with health care insurance, employers can choose to provide savings and private pension plans to employees for retirement. There are two main types of employer-based retirement plans: defined contribution (DC) plans, typified by 401k and 403b pensions, and defined benefit (DB) plans, also known as traditional pension plans. Defined contribution and defined benefit plans differ across a number of important factors. Under a DC plan, employer contributions are based on a predetermined formula. Employers and employees both make contributions and these are placed in individual accounts on behalf of each participant. Conversely, DB plans typically are funded by the company and do not always require participants to contribute. The DB payments are held in one trust on behalf of all participants, and these contributions are subject to federal funding rules and regulations. The overwhelming majority of individuals receiving DC benefits assume all of the investment risk for their accounts. On the other hand, DB pension plans spread the risk by having participants receive a specific benefit amount calculated from a specific formula, usually based on average salary and years of service, regardless of the investment performance of the plan's assets (Hacker 2006). Next, DC and DB plans diverge in how they pay out monetary benefits to participants. DC plans commonly pay out benefits in a lump sum and the employee is responsible for managing this money so that it lasts the rest of his or her lifetime. In contrast, DB plans are required to offer life annuities, a certain amount paid out regularly over time, for as long as the beneficiary lives and thus does away with the need to manage financial assets during retirement. There has been a recent movement by employers to offer more DC plans since they cost less and place more risk for asset management on the employees (Hacker 2004). The number of private-sector workers participating in a DB pension decreased from 30.1 million in 1980 to 19.9 million in 2006, while workers enrolled in a DC plan increased from 18.9 million in 1980 to 65.8 million in 2006 – an increase of around 250 percent (Employee Benefit Research Institute 2010).

Employment-based social benefits and services are treated as a form of income for the employee and as a business cost for the employer. The federal government provides financial assistance to businesses through the tax code by making both employer and employee contributions to private and public social programs tax free using targeted tax breaks. In exchange for company benefits, employees are often expected to provide matching contributions to employer-provided social insurance and benefits through payroll deductions. For example, employment-based pension plans do not count employee contributions to IRAs as formal wages, and the accrued financial benefits of retirement plans are not taxed until the retiree deducts the benefits.[6] Additionally, taxes on benefits for employers are based on net income, and fringe benefit costs are subtracted from revenues along with all other business costs. For example, contributions to retirement savings programs, medical premiums, and payments are

---

[6] Employers provide savings and private pension plans to employees for retirement as well as for Social Security and these plans are integrated. In addition, some plans (e.g., Roth) allow workers to contribute after-tax dollars to retirement plans.

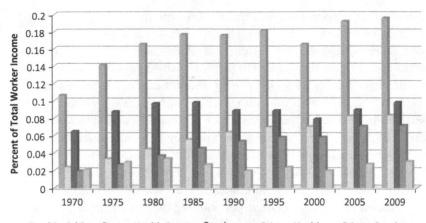

FIGURE 4.1. Employer social spending as a percentage of total worker compensation, 1970–2009. *Source:* Author's compilation using data from the Employee Benefit Research Institute (EBRI).

excluded in calculating an employee's annual gross income and, therefore, can be deducted as a business expense by employers.[7] Economic studies have found that a substitution effect exists between wage and nonwage income. The substitution effect occurs when employers increase employee social benefits at the expense of salary so that total worker compensation remains flat over time. While the majority of studies have the substitution effect at a one-to-one ratio or higher, exactly how much income a worker gives up in order to gain more employment-based social benefits is a subject of scholarly dispute (Woodbury 1983, Gruber and Krueger 1991, Gruber 1994, Baicker and Chandra 2006). The government subsidization of private social welfare through the tax code hides the full cost of benefits to workers and has contributed to increased private social spending over time.

Over the last forty years, businesses have nearly doubled their spending on employment-based social benefits as a form of worker compensation. Figure 4.1 shows employer social spending as a percentage of total worker compensation (wages and salary plus employment-based

---

[7] Employees pay no income or taxes on contributions to health insurance made by their employers. This tax exclusion applies equally to employees who participate in cafeteria health insurance plans and those who participate in flexible account plans.

benefits) across five categories on the horizontal axis from left to right: total social benefits (payments to public and private programs), health care spending (payments to Medicare and private insurance), private health insurance contributions, pensions (payments to Social Security plus private pensions), and private pension contributions. The data are displayed in five-year periods from 1970 through 2009. The bar on the far left in Figure 4.1 shows that business spending on total social benefits and services doubled over thirty-nine years. Employer social spending accounted for around 10 percent of an employee's compensation package in 1970 but grew to nearly 20 percent of total worker compensation by 2009. The overall trend is that employment-based social benefits have nearly doubled as a proportion of worker compensation and this increase has been driven almost entirely by the increasing cost of private health care insurance.

There are a number of important trends to note in Figure 4.1. First, employment-based social benefits now represent close to two out of every five dollars in worker compensation. Second, health care spending quadrupled during this period from 2 percent to 8 percent of total worker compensation. This steep rise in health care spending is driven almost entirely by payments to *private* health care insurance (not Medicare), since business spending on private health care increased sevenfold and also represents nearly 90 percent of the total employer spending on health care benefits. In fact, the increase in health care contributions is mostly responsible for the overall increase in total social benefits as a proportion of worker compensation. Next, employment-based pensions only increased by about a third, and between 1975 and 2009 employer spending on private pension programs, as a proportion of total compensation, increased by less than one percent. Interestingly, even with the rise in health care costs, employment-based spending on retirement accounts was slightly larger than spending on health care insurance. In total, employer spending on social benefits has gone up as a proportion of a worker's total compensation. However, it is important to note that the increase in business social spending has not resulted in more workers being covered by private insurance or businesses shouldering more of the social insurance risk compared to workers. In fact, as business social spending has gone up fewer workers as a percentage of the labor force have been covered and more risk has been transferred to the individual employee (Employee Benefit Research Institute 2012).

TABLE 4.1. *Sources of Health Insurance Coverage for the Nonelderly Population, 1996–2008*

	1996	2000	2004	2008
Total	100%	100%	100%	100%
Employer-based	64.8	68.4	63.1	61.1
Own name	33.3	34.6	32.0	31.4
Dependent	31.5	33.8	31.1	29.7
Individual	16.8	16.0	17.5	16.7
Public	16.2	14.6	17.7	19.4
Medicare	2.0	2.2	2.5	2.9
Medicaid	12.2	10.7	13.6	14.9
Tricare/CHAMPVA	2.9	2.8	2.9	3.0
No Health Insurance	16.4	15.6	16.9	17.4

Source: Paul Fronstin, Employee Benefit Research Institute, Sources of Health Insurance and Characteristics of the Uninsured.

Who Benefits from Private Social Insurance?

A majority of American workers rely on employment-based health care insurance and enroll in an employment-based retirement program. Table 4.1 shows the change in health care insurance coverage for nonelderly Americans between 1996 and 2008 (in four-year increments). The overall trend line has been a small shift of the population from the private health care system to public health care programs due to both structural (aging population) and economic changes (the beginning of the Great Recession). During this period, 64.5 percent of the nonelderly population was, on average, covered under employer-sponsored health care insurance. Between 2000 and 2008 there was a loss of employer-based health insurance from 64.8 to 61.1 percent and this slack was taken up by increases to Medicaid and citizens who just went without insurance. In 2008, 51 million people or 19.4 percent of the nonelderly population were covered under public programs; note that the private health care system covers three times the population of the public system. The public health care system (excluding Medicare) includes the more than 39 million people who participated in Medicaid or the State Children's Health Insurance Program (SCHIP) and the 7.8 million citizens who received health benefits through Tricare of Civilian Health and Medical Program of the Department of Veterans Affairs (CHAMPVA). From 1996 to 2008, the percentage of the nonelderly population on public health care increased 3.2 percent and this increase was caused mainly by a rise in poor households qualifying for Medicaid. The other category that caught people coming off of private insurance was the percentage of the public without any health care insurance, which went up by one percent. Recent studies and reports show that the data here are part of a larger trend of the decline of employment-based health care insurance from the 1980s (Enthoven and Fuchs 2006). In fact, one study estimates that there has been a 15 percentage point reduction in employment-based health care insurance even for full-time employees (Enthoven and Fuchs 2006).

As America grows older, more people have invested and relied on private pension plans for retirement income. In 2008, more than 101 million people were enrolled in employment-based pension plans (Employee Benefit Research Institute 2009). In 2010, around 21 percent of elderly Americans received at least some income from either traditional employment-based retirement plans or IRAs (Employee Benefit Research Institute 2011). While private pensions have been growing over the years, they currently represent only the third most popular source of retirement income behind Social Security and personal assets. The complementary role that private pensions serve as an income source for people over sixty-five is evidence for the importance of Social Security as the major source of retirement income (Hacker 2002). In total, a large number of American citizens rely on employment-based social benefits for their health care insurance and as part of a comprehensive plan for retirement savings. Nevertheless, the citizens who rely on private social welfare are not equally distributed throughout the adult population.

How do the recipients of private welfare compare with those of traditional public social programs? We know from the last chapter that the two groups that benefit most from public social welfare programs are the elderly (Social Security, Medicare) and the poor (Medicaid, TANF, food stamps). In addition, I discussed how certain groups, such as single female-headed households, the working class, and racial and ethnic minorities disproportionately benefit from public programs due to their higher-than-average probability of falling below the poverty line (Soss 1999, Kelly 2009). The aforementioned groups all disproportionately identify as Democrats in surveys and historically have voted for the Democratic Party in national elections. Therefore, scholars have connected the Democrats' support for higher social spending with their electoral incentives to use government as a means to assist their loyal voting blocs. In this study, the inclusion of private social programs in defining the American welfare state expands and complicates our understanding of who benefits from federal social spending and the politics of social welfare.

A government welfare recipient, "taker," or "welfare queen" requires only two criteria: first, the citizen has to receive financial support from the government, and second, that money must be for the purpose of obtaining social benefits or using social services. The typical recipient of private social welfare is a white, wealthy professional earning a higher-than-average income in a large company. Noticeably, these characteristics are contrary to those of the people commonly identified as "welfare queens." These differences between public and private beneficiaries are important for both politics and policy. The demographic characteristics of private welfare recipients align closely with the demographic features of the average Republican voter. Therefore, if the Democratic Party supports higher levels of public spending because of who receives federal social benefits it only makes sense that the Republican Party would favor government subsidies for private social welfare given that the modal recipient is a white, male professional in a large corporation. In the following sections, I examine more closely the demographic characteristics of private social welfare recipients.

The Beneficiaries of Private Pensions

The main beneficiaries of federally subsidized private social welfare are workers who both are offered and enroll in employment-sponsored social programs. There are meaningful differences in the distribution of employment-based health care insurance and pension benefits across income, race, occupation, and company size. Table 4.2 provides the characteristics of workers who are offered and participate in employment-based pensions.[8] The modal enrollee of a private pension program is a white professional with an advanced college degree earning a high salary in a large corporation. In contrast, Social Security, as shown in the previous chapter, allocates more on-average benefits to women and is a more important source of retirement income for the working class and minorities.

The trend in the table is clear for every category of socioeconomic status; employee pension participation skews toward wealthy professionals indicated by multiple measures of socioeconomic class such as

---

[8] Although I only report on employment-based pensions, employment-based health care statistics report nearly identical results (Employee Benefit Research Institute 2010, Kaiser Family Foundation 2010).

TABLE 4.2. *Who is Offered and Participates in Private Pension Plans, 2012*

Characteristic	Offered (Percent)	Enrolled (Percent)
Race/Ethnicity		
White	52.4	43.3
Black	48.4	36.9
Hispanic	33.1	24.4
Education		
No HS Diploma	20.9	12
HS Diploma	42.4	32.8
Some College	47.6	36.7
BA	59.4	51.2
Graduate	67.4	61.4
Salary		
$10,000 or <	21.3	6.6
$10,000–19,999	28.1	14.6
$20,000 29,999	41.9	30.5
$30,000–39,999	53.6	45.0
$40,000–49,999	62.4	55.5
$50,000–74,999	68.1	63.0
$75,000 or >	70.4	67
Occupation		
Management and financial	57.1	51.2
Professional	64	55.1
Service	30.8	21
Construction	32.8	27.1
Transportation	42.4	31.9
Employer Size		
10 or <	14.0	11.2
10–49	29.7	22.7
50–99	44.1	34.5
100–499	54.2	42.7
500–999	59.2	47.3
1,000 or more	64.9	51.3

Source: Craig Copeland, Employee Benefit Research Institute, Employment-Based Retirement Plan.
Participation: Geographic Differences and Trends, 2013.

education level, income, and occupation. First, white workers are nearly twice as likely to be enrolled in employer-based retirement plans as compared to Latino employees. The next category in Table 4.2 shows differences across educational level. A worker with a graduate degree is five times more likely to enroll in an employment-based pension plan as compared with a worker without a high school degree. Second, the disparity between the lowest and highest levels of income is even greater than education level. A high-income worker is ten times more likely to be offered a company pension as compared to the lowest paid workers. In fact, only 6 percent of low-income workers are enrolled in pension plans. The socioeconomic differences evident in the above income comparisons are reinforced by occupational differences where more than half of white-collar professionals are offered pensions while less than one out of three construction and service workers are given the opportunity to save for retirement. Finally, an employee in a large company or corporation is much more likely to be offered and to enroll in company pensions than workers at smaller firms. This discrepancy is in part due to the fact that larger firms can spread more risk among their employees and therefore receive a lower per unit cost for social insurance. Altogether, the portrait of a private social welfare beneficiary is that of a white, full-time professional who earns a high income in a large corporation.

The characteristics of private welfare beneficiaries correspond nicely to the characteristics of citizens who are more likely to identify with the Republican Party. The majority of men have increasingly identified with the Republican Party, resulting in a gender gap. This trend is especially pronounced among white men (Box-Steffensmeier et al. 2004). For example, in the 2012 presidential election white men voted for Republican Mitt Romney by a 2 to 1 margin. Next, wealthier citizens, who are highly enrolled in these plans, have increasingly identified with the Republican Party and voted for Republican presidential candidates over the years (Stonecash 2000, McCarty et al. 2000). Again using the 2012 presidential election exit polls as an example, voters making more than $100,000 a year voted for Republican Mitt Romney by a ten-point margin (New York Times 2012). Finally, wealthier professionals with a college degree have trended toward the Republican Party over the last forty years (Stonecash 2000). In the 2012 election, voters with no high school degree broke by 2 to 1 margins for President Obama while voters with at least a bachelor's degree voted more for Mitt Romney. All total and in contrast to public social programs, the characteristics of those who are enrolled in employment-based health care and pension programs align well with the characteristics of Republican voters. And as discussed in Chapter 3, not only are the recipients more likely to be Republican, but also the private providers and businesses that benefit from these subsidies are loyal Republican donors. The next section examines the relative size of the

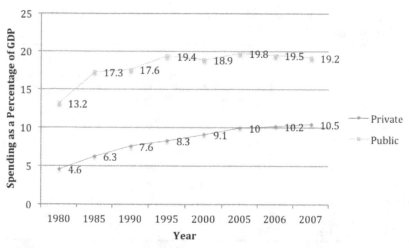

FIGURE 4.2. The growth of private versus public social welfare in the United States, 1980–2007. *Source:* Author's compilation using OECD data.

private social welfare state in comparison to both public social spending and private social expenditures in other rich countries.

Private Social Welfare Spending in the United States

The U.S. private social system is not just large as measured by the number of citizens who rely on it for health care, pensions, and other services but it is also sizeable as a proportion of the total economy. The American private social system is the largest in the world and has been growing rapidly over the past forty years. Private social welfare spending has increased in the U.S., whether measured in comparison to public social spending over time or internationally. First, the private social system in the United States has grown at a faster pace than the public social state. Figure 4.2 shows the change in private social expenditures, spending by businesses and voluntary organizations, and public social spending as a percent of gross domestic product (GDP) from 1980 to 2007. While both types of social spending have increased over the last three decades, private social spending has grown at a faster rate than public social expenditures. Private social expenditures more than doubled during this period from 4.6 percent of GDP in 1980 to 10.5 percent of GDP in 2007. In 1980, private social spending was just over one-third the size of the public welfare state but since 2005 private social spending has annually accounted for *over one-half of total public social spending.* Overall, private social spending has increased both as a portion of U.S. economic activity and as

TABLE 4.3. *Private Social Spending as a Percentage of GDP and Total Social Spending, 2007*

	Pensions	Disability	Health	Other	Total	% of All Social Spending
United States	4.3	0.5	5.6	0	10.5	39.3
Canada	4.1	0	1.3	0	5.4	24.1
France	0.2	0.6	1.4	0.7	2.9	9.3
Germany	0.8	1.0	1.0	0	2.8	10.1
Japan	3.3	0.2	0.2	0	3.5	16.2
Mexico	0	0	0.2	0	0.2	2.9
Sweden	2.1	0.7	0	0.1	2.9	9.5
Switzerland	5.3	1.1	1.0	0.8	8.2	30.1
Great Britain	4.5	0.4	0.1	0.8	5.8	22.0

Source: Author's compilation using data from Table I.3 Composition of private social spending in Adema, Fron, and Ladaique. 2011. "Is the European Welfare State Really More Expensive?" *OECD Working Paper 124.*

part of the nation's total social welfare expenditures (public plus private). The accelerated growth of private social spending was, in part, facilitated by changes in public policy and increases to federal subsidies for private social welfare.

So while private social spending has grown as a proportion of GDP and total U.S. social spending, how do U.S. private-sector social welfare expenditures compare to other wealthy nations? The private-sector social system is larger in the United States than compared to any other industrialized country in the world (Adema et al. 2011). In Table 4.3, I compare private social spending as a percentage of GDP in the United States with that of eight other countries in 2007 across five categories of social policy: pensions, disability, health care, other, and total private social spending.[9] The United States appropriates more money for private social spending than any other advanced nation in the world measured as both a percentage of GDP and as a percentage of total social spending.

In the area of health care, the United States spends far more than other countries – up to 5.6 percentage of GDP. This amount is a higher percentage than any other country listed in the table and five times more than France, the second highest spending nation. In fact, the United States spends more on private health care than Canada, France, Germany,

---

[9] These categories were created by the OECD and therefore do not match my categorization of the U.S. budget.

Mexico, and Sweden combined. The United States is also near the top of the list in funding private pensions, allocating 4.3 percent of GDP toward employer-sponsored retirement plans, behind only Great Britain and Sweden. The most recent international estimate of total social expenditures puts U.S private social spending at 10.5 percent of GDP and close to 40 percent of all American social expenditures (Adema et al. 2011). Relatedly, the U.S. also ranked first internationally in the amount of government money spent on tax subsidies for private social welfare (Adema et al. 2011). The international comparison of tax expenditures, from the same OECD report, showed that in 2007 the United States spent 2 percent of GDP on tax expenditures for social programs, which was 1.5 points higher than the international average and double that of Germany, the country that spent the second most on tax subsidies (Adema et al. 2011). It is no coincidence that the United States spends the most on social tax subsidies and has the highest total of private social expenditures in the world. At the end of this chapter, I test the relationship between changes in social tax expenditures for employer-based benefits and increases in business spending on social benefits and services. I expect that an increase in social tax expenditures causes a higher level of private social spending. All total, the American private social system has grown faster than the public system over time, and is the largest in the industrialized world.

Tax Expenditures: Spending Through the Tax Code

Why is it that budget experts and policymakers treat tax breaks as a form of government spending? And how do tax expenditures relate to the private social system in the United States? I address these questions by explaining the tax expenditure concept, examining the growth of tax expenditures over time, and showing the distinct role of tax expenditures in creating and growing the private social welfare state. First, I provide a brief description of tax expenditures and contrast this alternative form of government spending with traditional budgetary expenditures. Second, I chart the growth and change of tax expenditures over the last three decades. Next, I illustrate the importance of tax expenditures for social welfare with a specific focus on the four policy areas that together make up U.S. social policy: health care, pensions, education, and welfare. Finally, I test the empirical relationship between changes in the level of social tax expenditures and changes in business spending on employee social benefits and services. My analysis shows that increases in federal tax expenditures cause a corresponding increase in private social spending.

Tax Expenditures in American Politics

The Treasury Department issued the first tax expenditure report to the United States Congress in 1968. Since the first report, not only have tax expenditures been formalized as an annual report issued by two branches of the U.S. government but also this concept has been adopted by nearly all fifty state governments and the vast majority of industrialized countries around the world (Leachman et al. 2011, Adema et al. 2011). Stanley Surrey, Assistant Secretary of the Treasury, created the tax expenditure concept in 1967 as a way to calculate how the government spends federal dollars through the tax code. Secretary Surrey argued that Congress and the White House were using tax policy not as a means to raise and collect revenue but as a "vast subsidy apparatus" to reward favored constituencies and industries, and to finance narrow policy areas (1974, p. 6). Surrey argued that there are two components of the federal tax system: the first being the structure necessary to collect income and corporate taxes, and the second, a set of special tax provisions that are deliberate departures from the accepted baseline of net income and intervene in the private economy in ways that are similar to direct government spending for public programs. This first part of the tax structure is familiar to everyone and is what citizens commonly think of when they are asked to think of federal taxes. The second part of the tax structure is also familiar to American citizens, but by a different name – tax breaks. However, the analysis here is not concerned with how citizens think of tax breaks but rather how policymakers use the tax code to distribute social benefits. Policymakers in Washington, D.C. are not confused about the nature of tax expenditures, as expressed by Senator Tom Coburn in a 2011 speech, when he remarked, "tax expenditures are not tax cuts. Tax expenditures are socialism and corporate welfare. Tax expenditures are (tax) increases on anyone who does not receive the benefit or can't hire a lobbyist or special interest group to manipulate the code in their favor" (Helderman and Kane 2011, Sonmez 2011). Secretary Surrey concerned with departures from the baseline, designed tax expenditures as a method of calculating the costs of tax breaks in dollars lost to the U.S. treasury so that special tax provisions could be reviewed side by side with traditional spending programs in order to control the budget deficit and improve policymaking. In my forthcoming analysis, I use tax expenditures in the spirit proposed by Secretary Surrey by comparing the partisan influences on traditional spending for public programs versus tax expenditures directed at private benefits.

Budget experts and economists consider tax breaks or tax expenditures to be functionally equivalent to traditional spending. Tax expenditures are best thought of as a simultaneous exchange of money – taxpayers submit a check for their full tax liability to the Treasury, and the government in return issues them a check to subsidize designated activities (e.g., home ownership, charitable contributions, employment benefits). Formally, tax expenditures are counted as revenue losses to the U.S. treasury, or the amount of money the federal government forgoes resulting from tax breaks that allow certain citizens to pay less in taxes for specified activities. Tax expenditures are provisions adopted *deliberately* by policymakers, their tax preferences, as a type of subsidy which are not unintended loopholes for income tax evasion or tax shelters. In addition, a tax expenditure program that costs the government $100 billion in lost revenue has a similar effect on the budget deficit as a new spending program for the same amount – either way the federal government is out $100 million. The effects would be similar, but not identical, because a hundred-million-dollar loss due to tax expenditures creates a different set of interaction effects than does a hundred million dollars of public spending. As one report argues, "tax expenditure analysis can help both policymakers and the public to understand the actual size of government, the uses to which government resources are put, and the tax and economic policy consequences that follow from the implicit or explicit choices made in fashioning legislation" (Joint Committee on Taxation 2011). In short, tax expenditures are a policy tool used by the federal government to spend money on specific activities or privileged constituencies through the tax code.

Tax expenditures can take the form of a deduction, exclusion, exemption, or a tax credit. The difference between exclusions, deductions, and credits relates to where each provision factors into the calculation of income and tax liability. Exclusions are tax items subtracted from gross income, which means they never enter into the "top line" calculation of a taxpayer's tax base. Normally, exclusions are not listed on a 1040 form and therefore are not counted as part of a taxpayer's reported income. For example, the income tax exclusion for employee contributions to medical and health care insurance is not reported in a taxpayer's wages or salary. A tax exemption is a reduction in taxable income for a person due to his or her status. For example, the parental personal exemption for students between 19 and 24 is available only to those parents with college-aged children who are full-time students. Deductions are items subtracted from gross income in computing taxable income. There are two forms of deductions: "above the line" and "below the line." An "above the line" deduction makes adjustments to a taxpayer's gross income (these would appear on the gross income line for a standard 1040 form). Tax deductions for higher education tuition and fees are popular forms of "above the line" provisions for social welfare. Deductions executed "below the line" occur after a taxpayer reports his or her gross income and require itemization. The popular mortgage interest deduction is an example of a "below the line" provision. Credits are allowed against the tax rates imposed by the tax code, thereby reducing an individual's tax liability. There are two types of credits: nonrefundable, which only count against a person's tax liability, and refundable. Refundable credits provide a payment to the individual even if all of her tax liability is eliminated. For example, the earned income tax credit (EITC) is a refundable credit and therefore acts as a wage subsidy for taxpayers at or near the poverty line. The EITC is based on a percentage of a worker's earnings and is usually large enough to compensate for their taxes owed and entitle the worker to a refund (Howard 1997).

Traditional spending and tax expenditures differ in ways that are salient for both politics and policy. First, the two policy instruments of traditional spending and tax expenditures travel different policy paths at the federal level. In particular, tax expenditures pass through fewer committees and face fewer legislative veto points than does spending passed through the appropriations process. Therefore, policymakers from both parties could favor tax expenditures since they are easier to pass through the legislature and once passed are more likely to become a permanent fixture of federal policy. In this way, tax expenditures are similar to mandatory spending programs such as Social Security and Medicare. Next, the two types of spending diverge ideologically in the degree to which they rely on public bureaucratic administration and, by extension, how much they assist the private market. In particular, traditional spending often uses public administration in a way that competes with the private market while tax expenditures do not rely on federal bureaucracies (outside of the light touch of the IRS) and bankroll private organizations. Finally, traditional spending and tax expenditures distribute federal income in opposing directions. Specifically, most tax expenditures are designed to regressively distribute income to wealthier households, while public spending produces a progressive redistribution effect. In conclusion, this collection of policy effects creates opposing incentive structures for Democrats and Republicans that should result in observable partisan differences in the funding of public versus private social welfare.

Tax Expenditures and the Policy Process

Some types of spending are easier to pass than others and, once passed, are more difficult to eliminate. In particular, tax expenditures face fewer veto points than appropriations spending, are not limited by committee jurisdictions, and once passed function similarly to entitlement spending (Howard 1997, Hacker 2002). In the formal budget process, direct discretionary spending must pass through both standing committees with jurisdiction over a specialized policy area as well as the Budget and Appropriations Committees that fix discretionary spending levels for each budget category. Conversely, the Senate Finance and House Ways and Means committees have exclusive jurisdiction in both approving and "appropriating" tax expenditures. Tax expenditures face less scrutiny than traditional spending, primarily because they fall on the revenue side of the budget process. Tax expenditures are created or expanded in revenue or tax reform bills (see the Appendix for a sample of tax expenditure programs passed or expanded from 1981 to 2011). On the revenue side, the tax-writing committees are simply given a revenue floor; within the revenue floor, the committees can trade off tax rate changes with tax expenditure programs, which net out of total revenue. Finally, since tax expenditures are legislated on the revenue side of the budget, increases in tax expenditures can be presented as revenue neutral in the aggregate (Kleinbard 2010a).

In addition to facing fewer legislative veto points, tax expenditures are not limited by committee jurisdiction. The tax-writing committees are not limited by substantive jurisdictions, as are most standing committees, since any issue area, such as social policy, defense, or economic development can be addressed with a tax policy solution (Kleinbard 2010b). Consequently, the tax committees have a much broader jurisdiction than do substantive committees that are subject to the appropriations process. In addition, traditional spending has to be coordinated by multiple committees and a bureaucratic agency while tax expenditures are just subject to the congressional tax committees. For example, while the Department of Education has power over direct student loans, it does not coordinate with the Office of Management and Budget (OMB) and treasury on their implementation of the Helping Outstanding

Pupils Educationally (HOPE) and Lifetime Learning tax credits for higher education.

Most importantly, tax expenditures function as a type of entitlement spending. Entitlement spending is, by definition, spending allocated to any citizen who qualifies under the law, regardless of income level. The most expensive traditional spending programs for social welfare are entitlements (e.g., Social Security and Medicare). These programs are so expensive, in part, because policymakers cannot control their costs on a year-to-year basis. Similar to these public entitlement programs, any taxpayer may claim a tax deduction, exclusion, or credit, and there is no limit on how many tax provisions an individual filer can claim or any limit on the aggregate amount of federal revenues that can be lost. Additionally, once passed, these stay in the tax code over a long period of time. According to the Joint Committee on Taxation (2008b), "of the 128 tax expenditures reported for fiscal year 1988, 100 remained in effect in fiscal year 2007. Of the approximately 270 tax expenditures either in existence in the fiscal year 1988 or adopted at any time between 1987 and 2007, 202 remained in place in 2007." Since tax expenditures are not subject to annual review, only a new piece of tax legislation can remove existing programs from the tax code. Consequently, since both mandatory direct spending and tax expenditures are not subject to annual review only around one-third of the total federal budget is reviewed by Congress in any given year. Overall, tax expenditures are both easier to pass through the legislature and, once passed, have a greater likelihood of becoming a permanent fixture of the federal social system.

Tax expenditures require less public administration than traditional spending on public programs, which is a characteristic that appeals to conservatives concerned with the size of the federal bureaucracy. First, tax expenditures are self-reported, and depend on characteristics of taxpayers or their behavior. The I.R.S. reviews eligibility only after the fact, either in an audit or through calculations on individual returns that are then compared and confirmed with third parties. Additionally, the self-reporting feature of tax returns does not carry the stigma of receiving public benefits and deters fewer people, whether they are eligible or not, from claiming tax benefits. In fact, some citizens who receive tax subsidies for social welfare might believe that they are getting back their own money or not even recognize that they are receiving government benefits (Mettler 2011). Conversely, direct spending programs base eligibility for public benefits on general criteria or the discretion of an administrator.

The delivery and administration of public benefits are usually based on uniform rules and the determination of eligibility is stringently enforced. For most public social welfare programs, beneficiaries have to file claims and sometimes appear in person before an administrator to receive a cash benefit. The administration of public welfare often results in welfare beneficiaries feeling minimalized by the process and thereby more pessimistic about government (Soss 1999).

The costs of administering direct social spending programs appear explicitly as part of the program agency's budget. On the other hand, the administrative costs of tax expenditure programs to the Internal Revenue Service (IRS) are not readily identifiable because there is no separate categorization of costs based on normal tax provisions versus tax expenditures. Economists argue that tax expenditures add complexity to the tax structure and raise the costs for the I.R.S. in their enforcement duties and taxpayer service (Surrey and McDaniel 1985). The Department of Treasury administers close to 80 tax expenditure social programs with no expertise or vested interest in any of the social welfare policies. Therefore, unlike public social welfare programs such as Social Security, which enjoy strong support from their bureaucratic administrators, tax expenditures exist in spite of the bureaucratic apathy from the IRS (Campbell 2003, Hungerford 2008). While these features may appeal to a wide swath of policymakers concerned about public backlash concerning government spending, I expect that the lack of bureaucratic oversight and administration of tax expenditure programs will be viewed more favorably by conservative Republican lawmakers, who are concerned about the reach of the federal government.

The Opposing Income Distributive Effects of Policy Instruments
The most important policy difference between traditional spending and tax expenditures is the direction in which they distribute federal money. Tax expenditures, all except refundable tax credits, have regressive effects on national income distribution – resulting in government distribution to wealthier households.[10] Since the income tax has a progressive structure, tax expenditures formulated as deductions and exclusions generally reduce the progressivity of the tax system by reducing tax rates more for

---

[10] There are only a couple of nonrefundable tax credits for social programs that help the poor; well over 90 percent of federal tax expenditure programs are exemptions, exclusions, credits or deductions that mainly benefit the rich.

TABLE 4.4. *Income Distribution for Tax Expenditures for Charitable Contributions, 2011*

Income Class	Average Benefit
Lowest Quintile	$0
Second Quintile	$5
Middle Quintile	$40
Fourth Quintile	$182
Top Quintile	$1,420
80–90th Percent	$505
90–95th Percent	$907
95–99th Percent	$1,828
Top 1 Percent	$11,474

Source: Tax Policy Center, T11-0253, Tax Expenditure Benefits; Charitable Contributions Deduction, 2011.

high-income taxpayers with higher marginal rates than for low-income taxpayers with lower marginal rates. Additionally, the use of deductions, exclusions, and exemptions excludes the poorest Americans from tax benefits for social purposes. The vast majority of social tax expenditures are upside-down subsidies that provide greater government benefits to wealthy households and very little if anything to the poorest American families (in large part due to the low level of federal income tax on the poor). One of the largest social tax expenditure programs and a typical example of the regressive distribution of federal income is the deduction for charitable contributions. Citizens who donate to religious organizations, educational institutions, or other types of nonprofits can deduct the donations from their taxable incomes if they itemize their annual tax returns. Table 4.4 shows how, on average, the wealthiest families (with the highest tax rates) receive the largest financial benefit from the tax deduction for charitable contributions with an average benefit for families in the top 1 percent of $11,474 in 2011. This table shows that the average tax benefit for the top 1 percent ($11,474) was 63 times higher than the average benefit for households in the upper middle class ($182). Table 4.4 lists nine income categories and the average financial award in each cohort for claiming the charitable deduction. There is a simple linear relationship here, since with each step up the income ladder there is a correspondingly higher benefit and this relationship is similar to most of the other social tax expenditure programs such as the various programs for private pensions (these will be discussed more in Chapter 6). It might seem strange to use the charitable contribution deduction as an example of a social program that helps the rich if we assume that most charitable giving goes toward groups that help the poor. However, the Congressional Budget Office found that the top 20 percent of income earners accrued $33 billion from this one tax break in 2013 (Joint Committee on Taxation 2012). Other studies have shown that organizations that primarily assist the poor receive only a small percentage of charitable giving in the U.S. and the majority of giving is targeted toward universities, religious institutions, and cultural organizations (Rosenberg et al. 2011). In short, social tax expenditures provide the greatest benefits to the wealthiest Americans and the least to the poorest citizens.

In contrast, both types of public social programs, means and non-means tested, redistribute more national money to working class families. Means-tested social programs such as welfare and food stamps are designed so that only households with low incomes can qualify for federal benefits and services – the redistributive effects here are obvious. Yet, even non-means tested social programs such as Social Security redistribute more money to the poor. Kelly (2009) demonstrates that 53 percent of total Social Security benefits go to those citizens in the lowest income quartile and only 23 percent goes to the top three income categories combined. In this study, I argue that political party leaders clearly understand the conflicting distributional effects of traditional social spending versus social tax expenditures and act on this when formulating their social policy strategies. I expect that Democrats will favor public policy that progressively redistributes income down the socioeconomic scale toward their constituencies while Republicans will support social policy with regressive distributive effects that benefit wealthier households.

The Growth of Federal Tax Expenditures in the United States
In 2012, the total tax expenditure budget cost the U.S. treasury over $1.2 trillion of lost revenue. In order to place this value in perspective, $1.2 trillion accounts for close to 40 percent of the national budget, or two out of every five dollars spent by the federal government. Not only are tax expenditures a significant proportion of the federal budget, but they have grown over time.[11] There has been a growth in the absolute value

---

[11] Individual tax provisions make up the bulk of all federal tax expenditures. The range of individual tax expenditures went from making up 73 percent of all tax expenditures to an upper bound of 92 percent. In my analysis, I focus exclusively on individual tax expenditures for social welfare and exclude the few from the corporate side. Therefore, my study is not of "corporate welfare" but rather how households receive compensation from private social benefits and services.

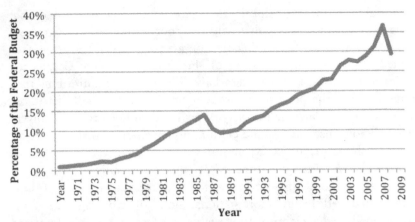

FIGURE 4.3. Federal tax expenditures as a percentage of the U.S. budget, 1970–
2009. *Source:* Policy Agendas Project and Joint Committee on Taxation data
along with author's calculation.

of tax expenditures, but this type of indirect spending has also increased
as a proportion of the total U.S. budget. Figure 4.3 displays a chart of
total federal tax expenditures as a percent of the annual U.S. budget
between 1970 and 2009. In 1970, total tax expenditures represented
just one percent of total national spending. Tax expenditures increased
about one percent per year from 1977 until 1987. The steep drop in
tax expenditures in fiscal year 1987 was a result of the Tax Reform
Act of 1986. President Ronald Reagan made a grand bargain with the
Democratically-controlled Congress that traded income and corporate
tax cuts, for the elimination of a number of tax expenditure programs for
businesses. In the twenty-year period from 1987 to 2007, tax expenditures
grew from 10 percent of the total budget to over 36 percent of total federal
spending in 2007. Democrats taking control of Congress in 2006 and the
reduction of tax receipts resulting from the Great Recession resulted in a
decrease of tax expenditures in 2008.[12] In each decade during this period
tax expenditures increased as a proportion of all U.S. spending. Tax
expenditures averaged 9 percent of total U.S. spending in the 1980s, 14.6
percent in the 1990s, and increased to 27 percent in the 2000s. All total,
federal tax expenditures have grown over the last forty years whether

---

[12] There was a one-year coding change in how federal tax expenditures were estimated in
2008 by the JCT and this might also explain some of the decline.

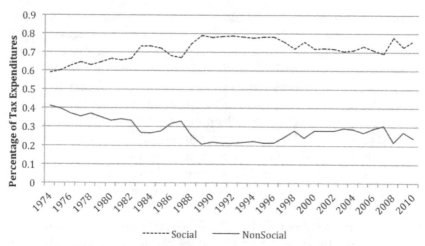

FIGURE 4.4. Social versus nonsocial tax expenditures, 1974–2010. *Source:* JCT data along with author's calculation.

measured as a proportion of the total budget or GDP – as a means for the government to finance policy goals in the United States.[13]

The Other Side of the Social Coin: Tax Expenditures

Social tax expenditures represent the majority of federal spending through the tax code and are primarily responsible for the overall growth in total federal tax expenditures. There are various categories of tax expenditures: those for economic development, energy, national defense, and those provisions for social programs. Social tax expenditures have grown in both number and value over the last forty years. First, the number of social tax expenditure programs in the tax code has tripled from 27 in 1970 to around 80 in 2008. The majority of this growth has occurred in the last 15 years during the end of the Clinton administration (after the Republicans took control of Congress) and the George W. Bush administration – a period that contained six years of unified Republican control of government. Figure 4.4 shows the growth of social tax expenditures as a proportion of all federal tax expenditures from 1972 to 2010. Social tax expenditures grew by 18 percentage points during this period from

---

[13] The growth of tax expenditures is less dramatic if measured against GDP although still trending upward. According to a recent report from the Congressional Research Service, tax expenditures as a percent of GDP was around 5.8 percent in 1974 and grew to just under 8 percent in 2009.

58 percent of total tax expenditures in 1974 to 76 percent of total tax spending by 2010. Specifically, social tax expenditures increased as a proportion of total expenditures after the Tax Reform Act (TRA) of 1986. Democrats in the legislature required that tax expenditure programs directed at businesses and energy companies be eliminated to pay for the income tax cuts proposed by the Reagan administration. The current partisan conflict is over which major tax expenditures should be reduced or capped and how the increased revenues should be used, with the Republicans arguing for tax cuts against the Democratic position of using the revenue for some tax cuts and some increased spending.

What specific programs constitute social tax expenditures in the United States? In Table 4.5, I compare the top ten tax expenditure programs from the mid-1970s to today based on the four-year estimates from the Joint Committee on Taxation. The tremendous rise in health care costs has pushed the exclusion for employment-based health care from the sixth most expensive program to the first. In the 1970s, only one out of the top five most expensive programs was related to social policy (the exclusion of employee pension contributions). Currently, three out of the five largest tax expenditure programs are for social benefits: employer health, employer pensions, and the EITC. In fact, seven out of the top ten most expensive programs are qualified as tax expenditures for social purposes. Social tax expenditures, no matter how they are measured, have become a larger and more significant part of the federal government's financial effort to provide income and economic security to citizens. In the next sections, I examine the role of federal tax expenditures in subsidizing four major social policy areas: health care, pensions, welfare, and education.

Health Care Tax Expenditures

Tax expenditure programs for employer-based health care date back to the early twentieth century. The exclusion of employer-based health and accident plans was created under the Revenue Act of 1918. The Stabilization Act of 1942 limited the amount of wage increases by businesses, yet allowed employers to create employee health insurance plans as a form of income and compensation. One year later, an IRS administrative ruling was issued declaring that contributions made by employers to third party private insurance companies for group medical and hospitalization premiums were not a form of taxable income. This ruling was later codified and expanded to more industries in the IRS code of 1954 (Bittker 1968). The 1954 ruling resulted in a shift to more group health care coverage in the United States. This ruling and the accompanying federal tax subsidies

TABLE 4.5. *A Comparison of the Ten Largest Tax Expenditures, 1975–1979 and 2010–2014*

Tax Expenditure	Total Billions (1975–1979)	Rank Order	Tax Expenditure	Total Billions (2010–2014)
Exclusion of capital gains at death	$37.6	1	Exclusion of contributions for health care	$659.4
Deduction for nonbusiness State and local taxes	$37.3	2	Deduction for mortgage interest	$484.1
Net exclusion of pension contributions	$32.4	3	Reduced rates on dividends and capital gains	$402.9
Capital gain: individual	$32.0	4	Net exclusion of defined benefits	$303.2
Deduction for mortgage interest	$25.7	5	Earned Income Tax Credit	$268.8
Exclusion of contributions for health care	$21.2	6	Deduction of State and local taxes	$237.3
Deduction for property taxes	$21.0	7	Net exclusion of defined contributions	$212.2
Exclusion of Social Security	$17.7	8	Exclusion of capital gains at death	$194.0
Exclusion of unemployment insurance	$13.6	9	Deductions for charitable contributions	$182.4
Exclusion of interest on life insurance	$9.3	10	Exclusion of Social Security	$173.0

Source: Joint Committee on Taxation, JCS-3-10 and JCS-11-75.

encouraged families to buy more coverage that resulted in a dramatic rise in the number of high-income households with group health insurance (Thomasson 2003). Over the course of this study, the addition of new tax deductions for health care purchased by the self-employed and deductions for cafeteria plans along with the pace of medical inflation has increased the total cost of tax expenditures for health care as a proportion of total social tax expenditures.

There are three broad categories of tax expenditure programs in the area of health care: employment-based health care insurance subsidies, benefits for taxpayers who have incurred major health-related expenses, and general health benefits. In the category of insurance, there are tax breaks for the exclusion of employee contributions to accident and health plans, self-employed health insurance premium deductions, and the exclusion of benefits under cafeteria plans. The majority of federal money is spent for employment-based subsidies and beneficiaries tend to be middle- and upper-income households. In the second category, there are deductions and credits to help citizens offset major medical costs. This type of tax expenditure helps the elderly, who often spend a higher proportion of their yearly income on medical expenses. The third category is a collection of deductions and credits that encourage charitable giving to health organizations, incentivize health savings accounts, assist with long-term costs, and subsidize medical research. Federal tax expenditure programs have been integral to the growth of private health care insurance in America. Tax expenditures provide government subsidies that create discounts for individual medical expenses and employment-based insurance, which increases the demand for health care insurance. Most health economists argue that in the aggregate, the private health care sector would be somewhere between 10 and 20 percent smaller without the various tax expenditure programs for health care (Phelps 2002). In 2010, the federal government spent close to $200 billion on tax expenditure programs exclusively for health care.

Tax Expenditures for Old-Age Pensions

Tax expenditures for employer-based pensions have existed since the introduction of the federal income tax. The Treasury Department ruled that pensions paid to employees were deductible to employers in 1914. The Revenue Act of 1926 exempted employer contributions to pension plans from taxation and postponed taxes on employee contributions. In 1928, a statute was enacted that allowed employers to deduct a reasonable amount necessary from their total costs to fund current pension liabilities. And after the establishment of the Social Security Act of 1935, the majority of employers integrated their plans with the new public pension program, reducing their benefits by the amount of the Social Security stipend. In addition, statutes were passed that made pension trusts irrevocable in 1938 and established nondiscriminatory eligibility rules for pension coverage, contributions, and benefits (Surrey 1974).

Tax expenditures for employment-based pension plans are formally measured as the tax revenue that the government does not currently collect on contributions and earnings amounts, offset by the taxes paid on pensions by those who are currently receiving retirement benefits. It is important to point out that tax expenditures for employer-based benefits are directed mainly at employees rather than employers. Outside of defined-benefit and defined-contribution plans, the main tax subsidies for private pension plans are directed toward employer-based IRAs and pension plans for the self-employed. There are two major types of individual retirement accounts (IRAs): the traditional IRA and the Roth IRA. The traditional IRA allows for the tax-deferred accumulation of investment earnings and is taxed at retirement. Employees can deduct annual contributions to an IRA of $5,000 per year for individuals and $10,000 per year for a family.[14] Roth IRA contributions are made from after-tax income and are not taxed upon withdrawal in retirement. The net effect of these tax provisions is the equivalent of an exemption on the retirement investment return, and if taxes in the future are lower, a loan on the principal. Self-employed taxpayers can make deductible contributions for their retirement (Keogh) plans equal to up to 25 percent of their annual income. In 2010, the federal government allocated around $260 billion toward pension programs that provided citizens with income security. During the course of this study, the various tax expenditures for IRAs and other employment-based retirement plans were increased in both generosity and eligibility.

Tax Expenditures for Welfare

Tax expenditure programs for welfare target the working poor. The earned income tax credit (EITC) is far and away the most important tax expenditure program for assisting poor families in America. The EITC has, in dollar terms, become one of the largest welfare programs offered by the federal government. The EITC increases the after-tax income of lower- and moderate-income working couples and individuals, particularly those with children. The EITC is calculated as a percentage of a taxpayer's earned income up to a maximum amount. The portion of the credit that offsets (reduces) the income tax is a reduction in tax collections, while the portion refunded to the taxpayer is treated as a federal expenditure. The EITC provides a work incentive since the more a person earns, the greater the amount of the credit.[15]

---

[14] All taxpayers without employer-provided retirement plans are eligible for IRA deductions.

[15] But within the income range over which the credit is phased out, the credit may act as a work disincentive: as the credit declines, the taxes owed increase. While the credit encourages single parents to enter the work force, the decline of the credit above the phase-out amount can discourage the spouse of a working parent from entering the workforce. This marriage penalty may also discourage marriage when one or both parties receive the earned income credit (Jones 2014).

The EITC has received strong bipartisan support through the years as both an alternative to traditional welfare and an incentive program for low-skilled labor. Policymakers have often expanded the credit since its creation in 1975. The Revenue Act of 1978 made the credit permanent, raised the maximum amount of the credit, and provided for advance payment of the credit. Both the Deficit Reduction Act of 1984 and the Tax Reform Act of 1986 raised the maximum credit available to low-income citizens. The 1986 Act also indexed the maximum earned income and phased out income amounts to inflation. The Omnibus Budget Reconciliation Act (OBRA) of 1990 increased the credit again, created an adjustment for family size, and created supplemental credits for young children and health insurance. The OBRA of 1993 increased the credit, expanded the family-size adjustment, extended the credit to individuals without children, and repealed the supplemental credits for young children and health insurance. Finally, the Economic Growth and Tax Relief Reconciliation Act (EGTRRA) of 2001 expanded the credit while also expanding the phase-out range for married couples. The U.S. Census Bureau estimates that in 2005, the EITC reduced the number of people in poverty by approximately 4.4 million or around 10.9 percent (Jones 2014).

The child tax credit, the second largest tax expenditure for welfare, was adopted in 1997 and later expanded in 2001 and made refundable in 2003. The refundable child tax credit can both reduce a low-income worker's taxable income to zero and provide a refundable credit in the form of government check, even if a taxpayer pays nothing in taxes. Since most families are eligible for the EITC and the child credit, they get back everything that was withheld from their paycheck and a refund. The Child and Dependent Care Credit, a nonrefundable tax credit, although designed to help poorer families, provides the largest benefits to households over $100,000. Since this credit is nonrefundable and since poorer families have their tax liability eliminated by the previous two refundable tax credits, this nonrefundable tax credit is used by households with higher tax responsibilities. In 2010, the federal government spent a little over $130 billion on welfare programs run through the tax code, including around $55 billion just on the EITC.

Tax Expenditures for Education
The majority of education tax expenditure programs reduce the cost of a college education. There are two major tax expenditure programs for post-secondary tuition costs: the HOPE and the Lifetime Learning credits. The Taxpayer Relief Act of 1997 introduced the HOPE and Lifetime

tax credits. The federal government spent around 50 percent more on these two education tax credits than on all Pell Grants in 2010. A Hope Scholarship Credit can be claimed for each eligible student in a family (including the taxpayer, the spouse, or their dependents) for two taxable years for qualified expenses incurred while attending an eligible postsecondary education program.[16] An eligible student is one who is enrolled on at least a half-time basis for at least one academic period during the tax year in a program leading to a degree, certificate, or credential at an institution eligible to participate in U.S. Department of Education student aid programs.[17] The per-student credit is equal to 100 percent of the first $1,100 of qualified tuition and fees and 50 percent of the next $1,100. The Lifetime Learning Credit provides a 20 percent credit per return for the first $10,000 of qualified tuition and fees that taxpayers pay for themselves, their spouses, or their dependents. The credit is available for those enrolled in one or more courses of undergraduate or graduate instruction at an eligible institution to acquire or improve job skills. There is no limit on the number of years for which the credit may be claimed. Both credits are phased out for taxpayers at higher incomes and cannot be claimed for the same student in the same tax year. In 2010, the federal government directed around $23 billion to subsidizing higher education through the tax code in the United States.

Tax expenditures represent a major financial commitment by the federal government to provide economic and income security to citizens. All total, in 2010 social tax expenditures represented close to 80 percent of all federal tax expenditures and cost the U.S. Treasury close to $600 billion in lost revenues. Each of the four social policy areas: health care, pensions, welfare, and education, cost the government hundreds of billions of dollars on a yearly basis. In some cases, such as welfare, tax expenditures are more important than the government's efforts using traditional programs. In the following section, I empirically examine the relationship between social tax expenditures and changes in private sector social spending.

Social Tax Expenditures and Changes to Employer Social Spending

How do changes in the level of federal social tax expenditures affect employer spending on social benefits and services? Policymakers add or

[16] Provided the student has not completed the first two years of undergraduate education.
[17] These include most accredited public, private, and proprietary postsecondary institutions.

expand social tax expenditures as a means to incentivize businesses to offer social goods such as health care insurance and pension plans in the private market. In the course of this chapter, I have alluded to a relationship between changes in social tax expenditures and changes in private social spending in the United States – the following is a direct test of that relationship. I hypothesize that increases in the level of federal social tax expenditures will result in a subsequent rise in the level of employer spending on social benefits and services, all else equal.

The main independent variable of interest, annual changes in social tax expenditures, is constructed using my original and unique data set of federal tax expenditures for social programs. These data capture the federal government's efforts to subsidize both the provision and purchase of private social benefits and services. The Congressional Joint Committee on Taxation estimates annual tax expenditures in terms of revenues lost to the U.S. Treasury for each special tax provision included in the U.S. tax code. A tax estimate is created by subtracting predicted revenues under the existing tax code from predicted revenue under new and expanded tax expenditure programs. In creating the variable for social tax expenditures, I subtract out the EITC and education tax expenditures since these are not used to incentivize employers in their provision of worker benefits and services. As with the previous spending measure, this variable is adjusted for inflation and per capita.

The dependent variable is a metric of private social spending. The Employee Benefits Research Institute (EBRI) organizes the data set on employment-based social spending by using information from the Department of Commerce's Bureau of Economic Analysis, and the Department of Labor's Bureau of Labor Statistics. The employer measure consists of annual business spending on private employee pension and profit sharing, group health plans, unemployment plans, defined-benefit retirement plans, defined-contribution retirement plans, and personal savings. The variable for employer social spending does include the contributions made by employers and individual employees to employment-based social insurance plans. The EBRI employer spending data along with JCT social tax expenditures data run each year from 1970 to 2009.

There are included in the model a number of control variables that account for other political and economic influences on private social expenditures. First, I control for Republican Party control of the executive and legislative branches. Republican control of the presidency is a dummy variable and Republican control of the legislature ranges from two (unified control) to one (a divided legislature) to zero (unified

Democratic control). The Republican Party has built a reputation for pursuing and passing policy that is supportive of business (Bartels 2008). Therefore, I would expect that there are conservative policies, passed under Republican administrations and not captured by the social tax expenditure variable that could positively influence more business spending on employee benefits. Next, I control for changes in unemployment since a tight labor market could result in employers being compelled to compete for employee services using fringe benefits. Additionally, I account for changes in the top income tax rate that could subtract money away from business owners that they might otherwise use for worker benefits. The results of the time series analysis of the relationship between changes in federal tax expenditures and private social spending are reported in Table 4.6.

My results indicate that increases in social tax expenditures cause businesses to grow their level of spending on employment-based social programs. The baseline model examines the relationship between changes in tax expenditures and employer social spending while controlling for Republican Party control of the federal government. An increase in social tax expenditures produces an increase in employer social spending of just over $2 million in the short run and adds $4 million more over the long term. A Granger causality test indicates that this is the proper direction of the relationship. The political party variables are signed in opposing directions and both are not statistically significant from zero. The second model, which includes the economic controls, also finds a significant correlation between increases in social tax expenditures and the level of employer social spending in the United States. The relationship is similar to the first model in that a one-unit increase in social tax expenditures corresponds to an immediate increase of $3 million in employer social expenditures and an additional $6 million in the long run. In this model, there is no statistically significant relationship between Republican control of the White House and changes to business social spending, although Republican control of the legislative branch correlates with negative changes to employer social spending. These results could be a product of Republican legislatures correlating with economic slow-downs. A short-term increase in the unemployment rate corresponds to a decrease in employment-based spending, although the coefficient is not significant. An increase in the top marginal income tax rate causes reductions to business social spending in both the short and long runs. This analysis provides evidence that income tax rates relate to business owners' abilities to increase wages and benefits for their employees.

TABLE 4.6. *The Relationship between Social Tax Expenditures and Employer Social Spending, 1970–2009*

Independent Variables	Private Social Spending (1)	Private Social Spending (2)
Short-term Effects		
Δ Social Tax Expenditures	2.22**	3.43**
	(1.12)	(1.13)
Δ Republican President	139.0	111.2
	(151.2)	(147.1)
Δ Republican Congress	73.12	68.16
	(89.93)	(82.47)
Δ Top Tax Rate		−22.25**
		(11.17)
Δ Unemployment		−30.22
		(59.55)
Long-Term Effects		
Social Tax Expenditures$_{t-1}$	4.26**	6.62***
	(1.12)	(1.78)
Republican President$_{t-1}$	57.78	−49.43
	(111)	(117)
Republican Congress$_{t-1}$	−90.31	−176.7**
	(72.39)	(73.90)
Top Tax Rate$_{t-1}$		−12.38**
		(4.82)
Unemployment$_{t-1}$		21.35
		(47.26)
Error Correction Rate		
Private Spending$_{t-1}$	−.376**	−.700***
	(.126)	(.179)
Constant	1314**	3004***
	(433.2)	(705.9)
Adjusted R^2	.189	.330

N = 38 for all columns. ***p<.001,**p<.05, *p<.10
OLS coefficients with two-tailed tests; Standard errors in parentheses.

The precipitous rise in private social spending in the United States has been fueled, in part, by increases in social tax expenditures by the federal government. My analysis provides evidence that while private social spending is determined by industrial-level decisions and macroeconomic forces, it is also influenced by policymakers use of tax subsidies. This dual rise of tax expenditures and private social spending has shifted both public and private resources to wealthier citizens for the purpose of greater economic security. This regressive distribution is a unique trait of the U.S. social welfare state – no other country in the world allocates so much government money to assisting wealthier citizens gain access to social insurance. In the following chapter, I put together the pieces of the last two chapters to examine the politics of the divided social welfare state in America.

Conclusion

This chapter discussed two important and understudied aspects of the divided social system in the United States – the private social state and the federal tax expenditures that subsidize it. There are a number of salient points to reiterate going forward in analyzing the politics of the divided social system. First, the American private social system is the largest in the world and has been growing over time. This growth is not just a product of business decisions and macroeconomic factors. The growth in private social programs has been assisted by the expansion of government tax subsidies aimed at employer-provided benefits, as demonstrated in the analysis at the end of this chapter. Next, a significant number of American citizens are enrolled in both employer-sponsored health care insurance and pension programs and these workers are likely to be wealthier, white, and working as professionals in large companies. Although these populations are not directly enrolled in government assistance programs, they receive a significant amount of government aid in the form of tax expenditures. Therefore, just who exactly is a beneficiary of federal government welfare spending is more expansive and complex of a category than just the elderly, the disabled, and the poor.

In the next chapter, I continue my analysis of the divided social welfare state by examining the relationship between Republican Party power and changes in tax expenditures for private benefits. First, I discuss the Republican Party's efforts to use tax subsidies to privatize social welfare programs over the last four decades. I then review the main theoretical argument on the relationship between political parties and changes to the divided social welfare state. I argue that both major political parties use social policy to further their electoral and ideological goals. In particular, Republicans use tax expenditures for private social benefits to distribute federal money and services to their constituencies while promoting conservative policy goals. The political parties design social policy to accomplish these goals in both the short and the long run. Political parties do not face the simple choice of whether to raise or lower total social spending but rather the more complex task of selecting the proper ratio between direct social spending for public benefits and social tax expenditures for private programs. This theory is tested using an error correction model in two ways. First, I examine the dynamic relationship between Republican Party control of the federal government and changes in social tax expenditures. Second, I test for both the short- and the long-term relationship between changes in political party control and the modality of social expenditures in the United States. The results provide empirical evidence for my theory of political parties and the divided social system.

Appendix to Chapter 4

Federal Social Tax Expenditures, 2012

TAX EXPENDITURE ESTIMATES BY BUDGET FUNCTION

EDUCATION, TRAINING, EMPLOYMENT, AND SOCIAL SERVICES
Education and Training
Deduction for interest on student loans
Deduction for higher education expenses
Exclusion of earnings of Coverdell education savings accounts
Exclusion of scholarship and fellowship income
Exclusion of income attributable to the discharge of certain student loan debt
     and NHSC educational loan repayments
Exclusion of employer-provided education assistance benefits
Exclusion of employer-provided tuition reduction benefits
Parental personal exemption for students age 19 to 23
Exclusion of interest on state and local government qualified private activity
     bonds for student loans
Exclusion of interest on state and local government qualified private activity
     bonds for private nonprofit and qualified public educational facilities
Credit for holders of qualified zone academy bonds
Deduction for charitable contributions to educational institutions
Deduction for teacher classroom expenses
Exclusion of tax on earnings of qualified tuition programs:
Prepaid tuition programs
Savings account programs
Qualified school construction bonds

Employment
Exclusion of employee meals and lodging (other than military)
Exclusion of benefits provided under cafeteria plans
Exclusion of housing allowances for ministers
Exclusion of miscellaneous fringe benefits
Exclusion of employee awards

Exclusion of income earned by voluntary employees' beneficiary associations

Special tax provisions for employee stock ownership plans (ESOPs)

Deferral of taxation on spread on acquisition of stock under incentive stock option plans

Deferral of taxation on spread on employee stock purchase plans

Disallowance of deduction for excess parachute payments (applicable if payments to a disqualified individual are contingent on a change of control of a corporation and are equal to or greater than three times the individual's annualized includible compensation)

Limit on deductible compensation

Work opportunity tax credit

Social Services

Credit for children under age 17

Credit for child and dependent care and exclusion of employer-provided child care

Credit for employer-provided dependent care

Exclusion of certain foster care payments

Adoption credit and employee adoption benefits exclusion

Deduction for charitable contributions, other than for education and health

Credit for disabled access expenditures

HEALTH

Exclusion of employer contributions for health care, health insurance premiums, and long-term care insurance premiums

Exclusion of medical care and TRICARE medical insurance for military dependents, retirees, and retiree dependents not enrolled in Medicare

Exclusion of health insurance benefits for military retirees and retiree dependents enrolled in Medicare

Deduction for health insurance premiums and long-term care insurance premiums by the self-employed

Deduction for medical expenses and long-term care expenses

Exclusion of workers' compensation benefits (medical benefits)

Health savings accounts

Exclusion of interest on State and local government qualified private activity bonds for private nonprofit hospital facilities

Deduction for charitable contributions to health organizations

Credit for purchase of health insurance by certain displaced persons

Credit for orphan drug research

Premium subsidy for COBRA continuation coverage

Tax credit for small business purchasing employer insurance

Credits and subsidies for participation in exchanges

INCOME SECURITY

Exclusion of workers' compensation benefits (disability and survivors payments)

Exclusion of damages on account of personal physical injuries or physical sickness

(continued)

Exclusion of special benefits for disabled coal miners
Exclusion of cash public assistance benefits
Net exclusion of pension contributions and earnings:
Plans covering partners and sole proprietors (sometimes referred to as "Keogh
   plans")
Defined benefit plans
Defined contribution plans
Individual retirement arrangements:
Traditional IRAs
Roth IRAs
Credit for certain individuals for elective deferrals and IRA contributions
Exclusion of other employee benefits:
Premiums on group term life insurance (excludes payroll taxes)
Premiums on accident and disability insurance
Additional standard deduction for the blind and the elderly
Deduction for casualty and theft losses
Earned income credit
Phase out of the personal exemption and disallowance of the personal
   exemption and the standard deduction against the alternative minimum tax
Exclusion of survivor annuities paid to families of public safety officers killed in
   the line of duty
Exclusion of disaster mitigation payments

VETERANS' BENEFITS AND SERVICES
Exclusion of veterans' disability compensation
Exclusion of veterans' pensions
Exclusion of veterans' readjustment benefits
Exclusion of interest on State and local government qualified private activity
   bonds for veterans' housing

Source: Joint Committee on Taxation, JSC-1-13.

Employer-Based Health Care Plans, 2010

Enrolled Beneficiaries of Employer-Based Health Care Plans, 2010

Characteristic	Percent
Race	
White	70.6%
Black	67.9%
Latino	65.7%
Income as % of Poverty	
138 percent or less	50.5%
401 or higher	73.2%
Education	
Less than high school	53.3%
High school or some college	64.8%
College degree	74.5%
Sex	
Male	73.9%
Female	65.3%
Occupation	
Professional	76.8%
Service	55.0%

Source: U.S. Census 2011.

5

A Republican Welfare State?

The last chapter documented the growth of social tax expenditures over the last four decades and demonstrated how an increase in tax expenditures produces a corresponding rise in private sector social spending. I now turn to formally examining the political factors that cause changes to the level of social tax expenditures for private social welfare and test for the possibility of a Republican welfare state. I argue that the Republicans' electoral and policy incentives coalesce in motivating party members to ratchet up social tax expenditures for private welfare as a way to distribute benefits to important constituencies and fundamentally alter the ideological direction of federal policy. In addition, I theorize and expect that the Republican Party will pay for growing subsidies for private social benefits through reductions in traditional public social spending both as a practical means to control overall spending and as a political means to penalize the Democratic Party and its supporters (the reverse is also true, that Democrats will raise public spending at the expense of tax subsidies for the same reasons).

I operationalize and test these theoretical arguments by using a unique data set of federal social tax expenditures from the nonpartisan Congressional Joint Committee on Taxation (JCT). I use a dynamic model (the same model used in Chapter 3 to test party control and public spending) that accounts for partisan effects on both short-run and long-run changes in social tax expenditures, and a ratio of social tax expenditures to total social spending. If my theoretical arguments are correct, then Republican control of the federal government will result in both increased social tax expenditures for private welfare and a greater ratio of social tax expenditures to overall social spending. A rise in the social expenditure ratio represents an increase of government funding for the wealthy paid for by cutting public social spending that mainly targets the poor.

This chapter is organized into the following sections. First, I examine recent works on Republican efforts to privatize public social programs, with particular emphasis on the use of tax expenditures. Second, I explain the model for the partisan theory of the divided social welfare state as it applies to testing the private side of the social system. This section includes an introduction of the testable hypotheses stemming from the theoretical argument. Third, I discuss the variables used to test the relationship between Republican Party power and changes to the different forms of social spending and briefly reexamine the time series model. Next, I present an analysis of Republican Party control and changes in the level of social tax expenditures. I find that, as expected, Republicans do expand social tax expenditures for private welfare when in office both as a stand-alone spending category and as a ratio of total social spending. In order to account for changes in political ideology over time, I rerun the analysis substituting measurements of political party leader ideology for party control and find that more conservative Republican presidents and Senate majority leaders correspond to increases in the social expenditure ratio. Finally, I test the alternative explanations of divided government and polarization alongside party control to determine if partisanship is truly responsible for changes in social tax expenditures. The results indicate that Republican power produces growth in social tax expenditures for private welfare, even when controlling for divided government and polarization. The major implication of these results is that as Republicans replace Democrats in office federal social spending shifts away from programs that assist the poor and toward subsidizing both businesses and wealthier citizens in the provision and consumption of private social welfare.

The Republican Party, Tax Expenditures, and the Privatization of Social Welfare

Subsidies, and particularly tax expenditures, are important components of the Republican Party's legislative strategy to privatize the public social welfare state. In the subsequent section, I examine some of the recent studies of the Republican Party's privatization efforts at the federal level. The political logic of using tax subsidies for private welfare benefits is as follows. Republican Party elites (including members of Congress, big donors, and conservative lobbyists) argue that popular social programs passed by the Democratic Party (i.e., Social Security, Medicare) are a primary reason for why voters support Democratic candidates for office. Using this logic, there are a significant number of voters who receive (or plan to receive) public social benefits and, therefore, vote for Democratic candidates to both protect and expand these government programs. In addition, the Republicans' main legislative priority of cutting taxes is restricted as long as large social programs remain popular with the public. Republican Party leaders, beginning with conservative think tanks, argued to their members that if they were able to successfully dismantle public social programs then electoral support for the Democratic Party would erode over time (Teles 2007). Starting in the 1970s, Republican legislators, especially the influential Jack Kemp, began to subscribe to the "Two-Santa Theory." Here is the theory as described by its author, Jude Wanniski: "The Democrats, the party of income redistribution, are best suited for the role of Spending Santa Claus. The Republicans, traditionally the party of income growth, should be the Santa Claus of Tax Reduction. It has been the failure of the GOP to stick to this traditional role that has caused much of the nation's economic misery. Only the shrewdness of the Democrats, who have kindly agreed to play both Santa Clauses during critical periods, has saved the nation from even greater misery" (Wanniski 1976). Wanniski's argument is that Republicans' concern with balanced budgets and controlling inflation resulted in Republican tax increases during times of inflation and spending cuts during recessions. These policy changes were not popular with voters and consequently hurt the Republican Party at the ballot box. The Republican Party had to counter the Democrats' spending with spending of their own – spending through the tax code.

Tax expenditures not only help the Republican Party play Santa Claus to the voters but are also part of another popular conservative theory, commonly referred to as "starve the beast." The proponents of this theory argue that Republicans should cut taxes and increase tax expenditures so as to reduce federal revenues for public social programs now and into the future – so that government can be small enough to "drown it in a bathtub." In addition, some Republican leaders argue that the best strategy to replace traditional public social programs is to create and promote comparable private alternatives. If social spending is diverted from popular programs to government subsidies for private alternatives, then citizens could be untethered from associating the Democratic Party with the social safety net (Smith, 2000, 2007). For example, one study argues that the Republican Party designed an attack on Social Security that required two steps: first, a weakening of public confidence in the future guarantee of retirement benefits from the federal government, and second, increasing citizens' reliance on and familiarity with private alternatives (Teles 2007). This study highlighted the importance of tax expenditure programs for private pension plans in efforts to privatize Social Security. Steven Teles argues "instead of describing an abstract idea, widespread use of IRAs would allow conservatives to point to something a wide range of individuals were already using and encourage them to compare their returns from Social Security and their IRA" (p. 170). A recent example of this strategy was President George W. Bush's attempt to legislate private alternatives to Social Security at the beginning of his second term in 2005 as part of an overall privatization strategy called the "ownership society."

When President George W. Bush was reelected in 2004, he promised to spend his new political capital on social policies through ushering in the ownership society, which would introduce new federal subsidy programs to encourage Americans to save on their own for education, health care, unemployment, and retirement. The ownership society was an overarching governing philosophy that called for public programs to be replaced by more federal support for savings accounts, which would foster greater personal responsibility among citizens. Former Bush advisor Jay Lefkowitz described the ownership philosophy this way: "government's job has to become to help people become self-reliant" (Swindell et al. 2004). President Bush during his reelection campaign proposed a number of new tax expenditure programs such as health savings accounts, college tuition savings, unemployment savings accounts, and private retirement plans. Democrats opposed reducing the direct role of government in providing economic security to people and described the proposed tax expenditure programs as follows: "their major effect is to provide tax breaks for saving that high-income households would have done anyway" (Swindell et al. 2004). The Republican Party had just implemented a successful change to the Medicare program in 2003 that created federal subsidies for private prescription drug plans. Republican leaders wanted to build on this momentum to transform the other large, popular public social program Social Security into a federal subsidy program for private investments.

The foundation of this ambitious plan was rolled out right after President Bush took his second oath of office and centered on transferring a portion of Social Security into newly created "personal investment" accounts. The personal investment account proposal involved two new tax expenditure programs: one program would collapse the three existing tax expenditure programs for IRAs into one new IRA program

but without tax restrictions on withdrawals, and the second proposed combining the various tax expenditure programs for employment-
provided retirement plans (401ks) into one tax expenditure program
for employment-based retirement and increasing the contribution limits.
These plans would be phased in gradually by allowing younger workers to divert 2 to 4 percent of their payroll taxes (which are currently
dedicated to Social Security) into these new accounts or having workers make contributions to the new programs that would be matched by
the federal government. The opposition to the proposed tax expenditure
programs came mostly from the Democratic Party. Democrats wanted to
protect their signature policy achievement, Social Security, and called the
proposals risky since trillions of dollars would be moved from the guarantee of Social Security into private accounts that were dependent on the
performance of the stock market and by extension placed more risk on
individual retirees. The financial industry, although nervous at first about
collapsing the numerous existing tax subsidies into just two programs
for private retirement investments, was assuaged by the promise to divert
Social Security money into new investments. The financial industry has
long promoted the idea of diverting the billions that go into Social Security into private retirement products – in a sense it is the political Holy
Grail for investment firms.

President Bush was so committed to the idea of replacing part of Social
Security with new tax expenditure programs he went on a national campaign, called "60 stops in 60 days," to sell the idea to the public. Peter
Wehner, White House director of strategic initiatives, argued in an email
to Republicans that "the Social Security battle is one we can win – and
in doing so, we can help transform the political and philosophical land-
scape of the country" (Warshaw 2009). Republican leaders viewed the
tax expenditures for private investments not only as good policy but also
as a political necessity to sever the link between popular social programs
and support for the Democratic Party. The implied message from the
party is that the more citizens who are invested in the private market, the
better the political environment would be for Republicans in future elections. Bush's national campaign for private accounts, while succeeding
in convincing Americans that there were big problems with the solvency
of Social Security, did not persuade the mass public that private investment accounts were the best solution. A Pew poll taken during Bush's
national campaign showed that people with the most knowledge of the
plan were also the least supportive of it and the reasons given most often
for their opposition were that the plan would cut Social Security benefits

and expose people to new risks. Andrew Kohut, president of the Pew Center, discussed the public opinion problem with President Bush's proposals this way: "people have multiple values: they believe in the free market and an ownership society, but they also believe in a social safety net, and in the role of government providing it" (Nather and Bettelheim 2004).

In Congress, there was a split over the plan between the few moderate Republicans left and the increasing number of conservative Republicans motivated to make history by privatizing Social Security, the cornerstone of the New Deal. One moderate Republican, Sherwood Boehlert, said that he did not "want to engage in a crap shoot with retiree benefits" so close to the midterm election (Nather and Bettelheim 2004). A real hurdle in the Republican efforts to transform Social Security came from the estimated transition costs of diverting federal money from public programs into new tax expenditure programs or vouchers. The estimated transition cost of the Bush private investment proposal was over $1 trillion and provided obstacles to persuading some Republicans concerned about the national debt. Bush was in a partisan bind on the pension reform since the component that drew the most support from conservatives in Congress, diverting Social Security funds into a new tax expenditure program, alienated the most Democrats. As the 2006 midterm elections approached, vulnerable Republicans in Congress became nervous over Bush's reform efforts, especially after the AARP lobby started a visible and well-funded campaign against the plan. Ultimately, there was never a vote on the plans in Congress given the unpopularity of the proposals with the American public, the unified Democratic opposition, the opposition of AARP, and the potential for some Republican house members to lose their seats if they had to debate and vote on the proposals so close to an election.

While this attempt at major social policy reform was not successful, the Bush administration was successful in getting other social tax expenditures passed and paved the way for future Republican efforts at privatization. The passage of Medicare Part D by a unified Republican government demonstrated how the privatization movement could be used to create wholly new private programs under the guise of a popular public program. Morgan and Campbell (2011) described this process as "delegated governance": when the government uses indirect policy tools (such as tax expenditures) and private institutions to provide social welfare or other public goods. Medicare Part D is a federal program that provides subsidies to seniors to offset private insurance premiums and costs for prescription drugs. The passage of Medicare Part D was made possible by including a new tax expenditure program that the more conservative members of the Republican Party supported. The tax expenditure sweetener for conservatives was a long-sought-after Republican program for health savings accounts that allowed taxpayers with high deductibles for health insurance to save and withdraw tax-free money to pay for personal medical expenses. The new feature of the health savings accounts (HSAs), which differed from most other social tax expenditure programs, was that both contributions and withdrawals to the program were tax free. It was the HSA tax expenditure program that brought conservative Republicans aboard the President's plan for Medicare reform.

Morgan and Campbell (2011) argue that three factors usually bring about delegated governance in the area of social policy: conflicted public opinion about social spending, special interests with investments in the provision of private social benefits, and the difficulty of passing changes to public programs through a legislative body with multiple veto points. Morgan and Campbell (2011) document in *The Delegated Welfare State* how Newt Gingrich, as the Republican Speaker of the House in 1995, designed a legislative strategy that would push private-sector health care reforms as an indirect attack on the popular Medicare program (pp. 84–85). They further argue that the Republicans in Congress proposed Medicare Part D as a political strategy to alleviate public pressure for social spending, initiate a market-based reform that benefited private drug companies, and take away a potential issue from the Democratic Party (Morgan and Campbell 2011, pp. 107–109). Paul Ryan's 2012 House Budget proposal, more recently, included a plan to change Medicare into a program that offers federal government grants to the elderly so they can purchase private health care insurance. In short, the Republican Party has proposed a parade of policy alternatives to Social Security and Medicare that have the common denominator of using federal money to support and subsidize the private provision and administration of social welfare benefits and services. So whether a Republican lawmaker is playing Santa Claus, starving the beast, or promoting an ownership society, it all results in a legislative strategy of increasing social tax expenditures.

A Model of Political Parties and the Divided Social System

I argue – in the partisan theory of the divided social system – that both political parties confront public demand for federal social welfare spending and respond in ways that distribute government benefits to their constituencies and shift the ideological direction of public policy. In Chapter 3, I examined the theory and found that the election of a

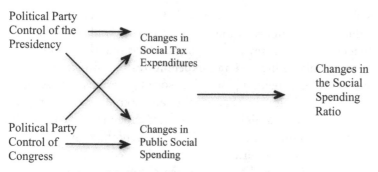

FIGURE 5.1. A model of the politics of the divided social state.

Democratic president results in an immediate increase in public social spending. These results align with the argument that Democrats, when in power, will increase federal social spending that supports the public administration of social welfare and progressively redistributes federal resources to their electorally important constituencies. In this chapter, I turn to examining the relationship between Republican Party power and changes in both the level of tax expenditures for private social welfare and the proportion of tax expenditures to overall federal social spending.

Figure 5.1 shows how the partisan theory of the divided social system will be operationalized and tested in this chapter. I represent political party power in government through measurements of political party control of both the executive and legislative branches. There is evidence from past studies that party control of both branches can influence changes in government spending. Next, I expect that not only will political party control result in changes to direct spending and tax expenditures as individual categories of spending but will also produce predictable changes in the ratio of tax expenditures and discretionary spending plus tax expenditures (referred to here as total social spending). A change in the ratio reflects a political party's desire to pay for increases in social benefits targeted to its constituency with cuts in spending going to the opposing party's supporters.

My theoretical argument represented in the model in Figure 5.1 generates two hypotheses about the relationship between Republican Party power and the divided social system. First, I hypothesize that Republican Party control of the federal government results in higher annual levels of tax expenditures for social programs. Tax expenditures for private social benefits can be considered a form of conservative social policy given that it is a subsidy executed through the tax code, it regressively distributes federal money up the income ladder, and it is designed to encourage the private administration of social services and consumption of social benefits. However, my primary argument is that the Republican Party desires not only to increase tax expenditures but also to decrease or hold constant federal spending for public social programs. The second hypothesis tests the relationship between greater Republican control of the federal government and higher ratios of tax expenditures to overall social spending. The subsequent tests of these two hypotheses will demonstrate that there are clear empirical differences between the Democratic and Republican parties over how to finance social welfare and which socioeconomic groups should receive government assistance. In the next sections, I discuss the variables and time-series model that are used to empirically evaluate the partisan theory of the divided social welfare state.

The Relationship between Political Parties and Social Tax Expenditures

I test the partisan theory of the divided social system using new measurements of federal social spending in a dynamic model. First, I have created a new set of variables that measure the federal government's annual efforts to subsidize private social benefits and services through the tax code. The first dependent variable of interest, the annual level of social tax expenditures, is constructed using an original data set of federal tax expenditures for social programs. The Congressional JCT estimates annual tax expenditures in terms of revenues lost to the U.S. Treasury for each special tax provision included in the U.S. tax code. Each tax estimate is a function of subtracting predicted revenues under the current law from predicted revenue under new and expanded tax provisions. A tax provision has traditionally been listed as a tax expenditure if it deviates from the normal income tax structure and it results in more than a de minimis revenue loss ($50 million). The normal tax structure for individuals, according to the JCT, includes the following: a personal exemption and one for each dependent, the standard deduction, deductions for certain business expenses, and the current tax schedule. While there are some disagreements among economists over what constitutes a tax expenditure, most tax breaks for social purposes are safely classified as exceptions to the normal income tax law.[1] According to the JCT and

---

[1] Please see the Appendix to this chapter for a more detailed discussion of this issue.

the Tax Policy Center (TPC), these estimates have been excellent predictions of actual changes in government tax receipts as calculated by IRS returns or modeled estimates (Joint Committee on Taxation 2008, Burman et al. 2008a).

The JCT methodology reflects certain assumptions about taxpayer behavior, and bases its estimations on federal government projections of revenue baselines and gross income.[2] A tax expenditure is estimated separately, under the assumption that all other tax expenditures remain constant by measuring the revenue loss under the existing law with revenue that would be raised if the tax expenditure program did not exist, assuming constant taxpayer behavior and no changes to the normal tax structure. As an example, revisions of tax expenditure estimates reflect changes to tax law and changes that alter the baseline or normal income tax structure (e.g., tax rate schedule, standard deduction). Tax expenditures are reported and organized using budgetary categories identical to those used by the Office of Management and Budget (OMB) for the appropriations budget. In order to remain consistent between analyzing the public and private social systems, I match the budget categories previously used to measure public social spending to my newly constructed variables for social tax expenditures. There are six budget categories that qualify as federal social expenditures: education, training, employment and social services; health; Medicare; income security; Social Security and railroad retirement, and veterans' benefits and services.[3] I matched the budget categories from the OMB and the JCT to construct both the individual measure of social tax expenditures and the ratio of tax expenditures to all federal social spending. All of the social expenditure variables are adjusted for annual changes to inflation and per capita to account for any increase in spending that is attributable to overall price levels and population growth.[4]

I constructed the following dependent variables for social spending using tax expenditures data from the JCT. The first is a measurement of

---

[2] I do not measure "corporate welfare" but rather the tax benefits accrued mainly to citizens through filing their annual individual income tax returns. There are many more details on the measurement issues surrounding tax expenditures available in the Appendix to this chapter.

[3] Since some social policy scholars consider housing to be a component of federal social welfare policy, I run an analysis that includes housing as a part of overall social spending and have placed the results in the Appendix to this chapter.

[4] I used the inflation adjustment values from the Policy Agendas Project to adjust the values for tax expenditures so as to match public social spending with social tax expenditures.

federal tax expenditures for private welfare, which excludes the two programs that supplement public programs (Social Security and Medicare).[5] The second dependent variable is a measurement of social tax expenditures for private welfare that have regressive distributive effects and therefore subtracts out the earned income tax credit (EITC).[6] I expect that increases in Republican Party power at the federal level will result in large and positive changes to the annual level of social tax expenditures for both variables, with a stronger relationship between Republican control and changes to regressive social tax expenditures.

In the second set of models, I introduce a new variable, the social expenditure ratio, which represents the political and policy trade off between federal spending for public social programs and tax subsidies for private welfare benefits. The social expenditure ratio variable measures annual social tax expenditures for private welfare as a proportion of aggregate social spending, which sums yearly discretionary spending plus yearly tax expenditures.[7] Again, there are two measurements of federal social spending: one variable with the EITC, and a second metric without the EITC so as to capture the differences in spending and distribution effects. A higher proportion of social tax expenditures to aggregate social spending signifies years in which tax expenditures grew at a faster pace than direct social spending. All total, I expect that greater levels of Republican Party control of the federal government will produce increased social tax expenditures and a higher social expenditure ratio.

[5] I subtracted out these two programs because they can be considered a form of augmented public spending (since they just make public social spending tax free) and changes to the annual estimates will be driven by the percent of the population over the age of 65. The estimates are consistent across the time series except for 2008. There was a one-year change in how the JCT estimated tax expenditures (e.g., changes to some of the underlying assumptions) and that may result in the 2008 estimates differing from other estimates.

[6] There was no tax expenditure report produced by the JCT for 1973 – therefore the data for this year are interpolated using the data from 1972 and 1974. The JCT has reported estimates of tax expenditures in every year from 1967 to 2012 except for 1973. An ECM with more than one piece of missing data would typically use stochastic imputation techniques and run them several times, combining (essentially averaging) the results to capture the added uncertainty in the imputation (otherwise the imputed data is improperly being treated as observed data and the uncertainty is underestimated). However, one missing observation treated through linear interpolation is appropriate in a time-series context.

[7] I use discretionary social spending for the simple reason that it can be raised or lowered by the political party in power as opposed to using total public social spending, which has increasingly been dominated by mandatory spending and therefore changes mainly due to growth in the elderly population.

Measurement of Political Party and Economic Influences on Social Expenditures

The main independent variables of interest measure Republican Party control of the federal government. I use Republican Party control, over the more common Democratic Party control, since the expectation is for a positive correlation between Republican Party power and increased social tax expenditures. The independent variables separate out control of the executive and legislative branches. Republican control of the executive branch is represented by a dummy variable that is coded one for a Republican president and zero for a Democratic president. Republican Party control of the legislature is represented by a variable that ranges from unified Republican control (2) to divided legislative control (1) to unified Democratic control (0). I expect greater Republican Party strength in the legislature to correspond to higher levels of tax expenditures for private social benefits.

Moreover, I expect that changes to political party control will result in changes to social tax expenditures even when accounting for economic factors. The first economic control variable is the annual change in gross domestic product (GDP). An increase in GDP, which signals a strengthening economy, should influence social spending through the tax code. A rise in the national production level indicates more business spending (including on employee benefits), correlates with a tighter job market, and relates to increased charitable giving. Next, I include the inflation level in the model, since increases in inflation may push some taxpayers into higher marginal income tax brackets (prior to the Tax Reform Act [TRA] of 1986) and therefore increase the amount of new or existing tax expenditure programs claimed by taxpayers as a way to lower their overall tax burden.[8] In addition to economic controls, I include a variable for changes in marginal income tax rates. Marginal tax rates directly relate to the value of tax expenditure programs so any increase in federal income tax rates will result in more taxpayers claiming tax relief and an overall increase in the value of federal tax expenditures for social programs. Altogether, these variables will help determine if changes in political party power in government affect social spending once economic and policy factors are taken into consideration.

I use an error correction model (ECM) since the relationship between Republican Party control and social tax expenditures (and the social

---

[8] The Tax Reform Act of 1986 addressed the problem of bracket creep by formalizing an adjustment for inflation.

expenditure ratio) will have both short-term and long-term effects (for more on this model, please see the full explanation in Chapter 3). When there is a change in Republican Party control there is an immediate impact on spending that will be represented in tax bills (and in discretionary spending) for that following year, but since many increases in tax expenditure programs are lagged and since these programs act as a form of entitlement spending, the full effects will not be felt all at once. The expectation is that Republican Party control will lead to higher levels of social tax expenditures and a larger social expenditure ratio in both the short and the long runs. For Republican control of the federal government, I provide the long-run multiplier (LRM) that represents the total expected change in the social expenditure ratio for each unit change in Republican influence in both branches. In addition, the two data sets act as an integrated time series. First, social tax expenditures are determined by changes to the tax code, which are non-mean reverting. Next, the social expenditure ratio is composed of two spending data sets, both of which are non-mean reverting. The numerator is the annual level of social tax expenditures. The denominator is the summation of annual discretionary spending in the budget process that is determined by the previous year's estimates and therefore is a strictly cumulative process, plus social tax expenditures.[9] In the next section, I turn to formally analyzing the relationship between Republican Party control of the federal government and social tax expenditures for private welfare.

Political Party Control and Social Spending in the United States, 1970–2012

Since the relationship between Republican Party control and social tax expenditures is at the core of my analysis, I begin with some descriptive statistics on political party control of the White House and changes to the average level of social tax expenditures. In Figure 5.2, I examine the change in social tax expenditures by presidential administration from 1970 through 2012. After President Carter, who presided over a period of hyperinflation, the next largest increases in social tax subsidies were under presidents Reagan, Nixon, Ford, and George

---

[9] Also, I ran multiple Augmented Dickey–Fuller (ADF) tests with a constant, a time trend, and one lag for all four measures: annual social tax expenditures, annual regressive social tax expenditures, and the two social expenditure ratios. All of the dependent variables reported values higher than −3.50 so the null hypothesis of a unit root cannot be rejected.

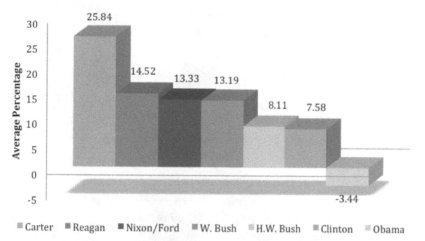

FIGURE 5.2. Percentage change in social tax expenditures by president, 1970–2012. *Source:* JCT data along with author's calculation.

W. Bush.[10] The largest yearly increases under Republican presidents, not surprisingly, occurred in years where Republicans controlled one or both chambers of Congress. For example, the five largest one-year increases in social tax expenditures over the last thirty years were in 1983 (48.8%), 1981 (36.1%), 2008 (22.9%), 2004 (21.4%), and 2003 (18.4%). The Republican Party had unified control of government in 2003 and 2004, and controlled the White House and the Senate in 1981 and 1983. In contrast, the only decrease in annual social tax expenditures across presidential administrations occurred during President Obama's first term. Surprisingly, President Clinton – considered to be a moderate Democrat with a proclivity for social spending through the tax code – presided over a modest increase of around 7 percent.

[10] In 1980, President Carter campaigned on a platform of severely cutting tax expenditure programs as a means to make the tax structure more progressive. He failed at stemming the increase of social tax expenditures and there are three reasons for the large increase that occurred during the Carter administration. First, the rise of inflation during the Carter administration accelerated the use of existing tax expenditures as families were pushed into higher tax brackets. Second, President Carter faced a fiscally conservative Congress who fought for more tax expenditures and, in particular, conservative Democrats in power positions on the tax-writing committees such as Wilbur Mills and Al Ullman. Finally, there was a rising conservative public mood during this period that was animated by antitax sentiment represented by the passage of Proposition 13 in California. The cumulative result was that social tax expenditures rose despite the preferences of President Carter for progressive tax reform.

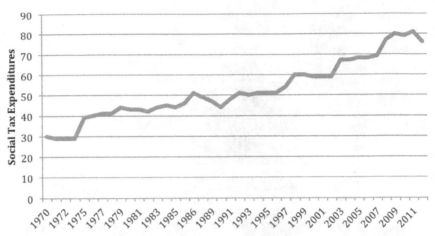

FIGURE 5.3. Change in the number of social tax expenditure programs, 1970–2012. *Source:* Author's calculation using JCT data.

Over the last forty years, Republican presidents have produced – on average – a 12 percent annual increase in social tax expenditures (compared to 9 percent for Democratic leaders) and Republican-controlled Senates have produced a 14 percent increase in annual social tax expenditures (compared to 9 percent for their Democratic counterparts). Only the House of Representatives experienced a reverse partisan relationship with Democratic control resulting in more social tax subsidies. While these partisan patterns of spending are suggestive of a relationship between Republican Party control and increases in social tax expenditures they do not account for changes over time or control for other economic and societal explanations for changes in federal tax expenditures.

While the previous figure shows that Republican administrations result in the faster growth of social tax expenditures, it does not speak to whether this is due to the addition of new programs or the expansion of existing ones. In Figure 5.3, I chart the growth of social tax expenditure programs over time. The largest increases in the number of programs occurred under Republican executives – President Ford and President George W. Bush. Overall, the number of programs grew exponentially from just 29 in 1970 to 81 in 2011, a 179-percent increase. I have included in the Appendix to this chapter a table that shows the expansion and addition of major tax expenditure programs through the years. Many of the large and older social tax expenditure programs expanded their eligibility, expanded their contribution limits, had caps removed, or were indexed to inflation during years of Republican Party control of the federal government. President George W. Bush alone presided over the passage of 14 significant tax bills during his tenure in office.[11]

Here, I examine the relationship between political party control of government and tax expenditures for private social programs across two models. The first model examines the relationship between Republican control of the federal government and changes to social tax expenditures for private social welfare programs. The second model reports the results from testing the relationship between Republican power and changes in the annual level of social tax expenditures for private social welfare excluding the most progressively redistributive program. I claim that one reason Republicans support social tax expenditures is that this type of spending distributes federal dollars up the income ladder toward wealthier voters, who tend to vote Republican. If this claim is correct, then the results should strengthen when excluding the progressively structured earned income tax credit (EITC).

The results from the two models in Table 5.1 confirm the hypotheses that increased Republican Party control of the federal government produces higher levels of tax expenditures for social programs even when controlling for economic and policy factors. The Republican welfare state is run through the tax code and directed at private social programs and their wealthier beneficiaries. Specifically, a Republican executive in the White House results in significant expansions of federal tax subsidies for private social welfare. First, a switch from a Democratic to Republican president causes an immediate increase in the level of social tax expenditures of over $100 million. This amount of change represented one fifth of the average yearly value of social tax expenditures during this entire period. In the long run, the impact of a Republican president is even

---

[11] It is also possible that yearly changes to the largest programs are driving the overall changes and not the addition and expansion of newer programs. I separated out three of the largest programs from all the other social tax expenditures for each year from 1970 to 2012. The three programs I separated out are the EITC, the employment-based health care exclusion, and the employment-based private pension exclusion. These three programs totaled to over $200 billion in 2012. First, I examined the average change of the big three programs versus all other social tax expenditures during the study. The big three grew at an average of 8 percent a year over forty-two years while the other programs grew at an average of over 9 percent annually. Second, I examined the average percentage change in the big three versus all other social tax expenditures in years following a Republican increase in power. Again, the category of newer social tax expenditures grew at a faster pace, on average, than changes to just the top three programs.

TABLE 5.1. *Republican Party Power and Changes in Social Tax Expenditures for Private Welfare, 1970–2012*

	Social Tax Expenditures	Social Tax Expenditures (−EITC)
Short-Term (Immediate) Effects		
Δ Republican President	102.6**	83.88*
	(52.96)	(50.52)
Δ Republican Congress	7.59	−1.44
	(29.7)	(27.69)
Δ GDP	.040	.060
	(.050)	(.049)
Δ Inflation	19.56**	16.27**
	(9.13)	(8.59)
Δ Top Tax Rates	2.07	1.57
	(3.31)	(3.11)
Long-Term Effects		
Republican President$_{t-1}$	121.8**	115.3**
	(38.39)	(36.42)
Republican Congress$_{t-1}$	−15.62	−16.19
	(25.47)	(23.39)
GDP$_{t-1}$	.099***	.115***
	(.026)	(.026)
Inflation$_{t-1}$	−.781	−1.85
	(8.63)	(8.09)
Top Tax Rates$_{t-1}$	4.59**	4.47**
	(1.91)	(1.76)
Error Correction Rate		
Tax Expenditures$_{t-1}$	−.604***	−.823***
	(.165)	(.193)
Constant	−500.1	−493.2
	(160.1)	(146.9)
Long Run Multiplier		
Republican President	201.6**	140.4**
	(69.23)	(44.99)
Republican Congress	−25.85	−19.66
	(39.57)	(26.89)
Adj. R²	.379	.424

Note: N = 42. Entries are OLS estimates with standard errors in parentheses.
One-Tailed Significance Levels: ***p ≤ .01, **p ≤ .05, *p ≤ .10.

larger (over $120 million). These results are a function of designing tax expenditure benefits to rise with expected inflation and the entitlement nature of some tax expenditure programs that grow gradually over time. An increase in Republican control of the legislature, although positive in the short run, is negatively signed in the long term and both coefficients are not statistically significant from zero. The second test of Republican control and changes to regressively structured social tax expenditures again produce positively signed and statistically significant coefficients. The election of a Republican to the White House results in an immediate growth of more regressive social tax expenditures and additional long-term effects. As predicted, the election of a Republican president actually produces larger changes to the measure of regressive social tax expenditures (since a change of $84 million is larger than one fifth of the total value of social tax expenditures once the EITC is subtracted out). In addition, a changeover to a Republican executive results in an overall $200 million annual change in social tax expenditures as represented by the long-term multiplier effect and an additional $140 million long-run effect. In total, Republican presidents favor higher social spending for private welfare and especially for private welfare with upwardly distributive effects.

The economic and political controls all impact changes in social tax expenditures in the expected direction, although some take effect in the short run and others more over time. In the short term, as inflation increases – and pushes taxpayers into higher brackets – there is a corresponding increase in social tax expenditures. In the long term, a rise in economic production results in higher levels of social tax expenditures. This result could be due to a number of factors, such as increased charitable giving, more employment-based benefits, or individuals buying more health and retirement products. Next, an increase in the marginal tax rates for the richest citizens also produces an increase in social tax expenditures. As income taxes grow higher, social tax expenditures become more valuable, especially to wealthier households. These control variables perform similarly across both models. The results here show that a Republican in the White House produces substantial increases in social tax expenditures, regardless of how they are measured.[12] The following

[12] Since this model has 42 observations, I ran a baseline model with just two variables for Republican control of the White House and Congress. The main results are the same as Table 5.1 with a switch to a Republican president resulting in a statistically significant increase in social tax expenditures of over $100 million (see the Appendix).

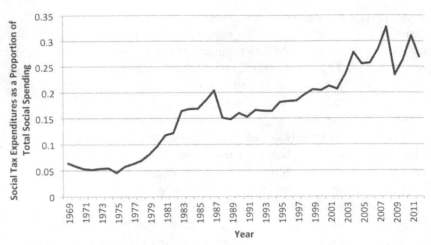

FIGURE 5.4. Changes to the annual ratio of social tax expenditures to federal social spending, 1970–2012. *Source:* Author's calculation using JCT and PAP data.

analysis examines if the Republican Party pays for increases to tax subsidies for private welfare with cuts to public social spending for more vulnerable populations.

Republican Party Control and Changes to the Social Expenditure Ratio

Up to this point, I have shown that Democratic control of the federal government results in increased social spending for public programs and that Republican power results in higher levels of social tax expenditures for private welfare. Yet I argue in the partisan theory of the divided social system that a political party in power not only increases its preferred form of social spending but pays for it with cuts or slowdowns in the opposing party's desired form of social spending. This political trade off in preferred social spending types can be represented by the social expenditure ratio.

Figure 5.4 shows the change in the ratio of social tax expenditures to total federal social spending across the period of study. As the social tax expenditure ratio grows, so, too, does the proportion of federal social spending conducted through the tax code. In 1970, tax expenditures were just 5 percent of the government's efforts to provide social services and benefits. By 2011, social tax expenditures had risen as a proportion of total social spending to over 30 percent – a six-fold increase over forty years. More importantly, the social expenditure ratio has not grown linearly over time. The ebbs and flows in the trend line are a function of the political and policy decisions made by parties in power. For example, there was a sharp rise in the ratio starting in the mid-1970s and continuing through the late 1980s when social tax expenditures topped out at 20 percent of federal social spending. The Tax Reform Act of 1986 dropped the level of tax expenditures, but then tax expenditures consistently increased again over the next decade. The sharpest rise in social tax expenditures took place during the early George W. Bush administration, reaching a global high of 32 percent of all social expenditures in 2008. However, this ratio is driven not only by changes in social tax expenditures but also by social spending for public programs. President Reagan presided over an average decrease in discretionary social spending of −1.36 percent during his eight-year presidency. In comparison, President Obama – due mainly to the stimulus – increased discretionary social spending by 12.8 percent during his first term. The following analysis evaluates the political, economic, and policy factors that determine changes to the trade off between social tax expenditures for private welfare and federal social spending for public programs.

Table 5.2 examines the relationship between Republican Party control of the federal government and ratio of social tax expenditures to aggregate federal social spending. The expectation is that as Republicans gain power there will be corresponding increases in the level of social tax expenditures while the growth of discretionary social spending for public programs is cut back or held constant. I import the political variables of interest from the previous analysis using a dummy variable for Republican control of the White House and an ordinal measure of Republican control of Congress. Additionally, I carry over the control variables that exercised the most influence in determining changes in social tax expenditures (the inflation rate and marginal tax rates) and discretionary social spending (households below the poverty line). The expectation for the following tests is that as Republicans gain more institutional control at the federal level, they will increase social tax expenditures for private welfare at the expense of public social spending, resulting in a higher social expenditure ratio in both the short and the long run.

The election of a Republican president in the short term and the increased power of legislative Republicans in the long term results in a higher ratio of social tax expenditures to overall federal social spending. The first model shows that a switch to a Republican President moves the ratio around six points toward more tax expenditures at the expense of

TABLE 5.2. *Republican Party Power and Changes in the Social Expenditure Ratio, 1970–2012*

	Social Expenditure Ratio	Social Expenditure Ratio (-EITC)
Short-Term (Immediate) Effects		
Δ Republican President	.059**	.064**
	(.025)	(.024)
Δ Republican Congress	.019	.017
	(.015)	(.015)
Δ Inflation	.005	.006
	(.005)	(.005)
Δ Top Tax Rates	−.004	−.001
	(.008)	(.001)
Δ Poor Families	.042**	.041**
	(.020)	(.020)
Long-Term Effects		
Republican President$_{t-1}$	−.003	−.002
	(.018)	(.017)
Republican Congress$_{t-1}$	.040**	.043**
	(.014)	(.014)
Inflation$_{t-1}$	−.008*	−.009*
	(.005)	(.005)
Top Tax Rate$_{t-1}$	−.001*	−.002*
	(.001)	(.001)
Poor Families$_{t-1}$	.029**	.031***
	(.009)	(.009)
Error Correction Rate		
Tax Expenditures$_{t-1}$	−.413***	−.467***
	(.127)	(.130)
Constant	.015	.037
	(.158)	(.159)
Long-Run Multiplier		
Republican President	−.007	−.007
	(.043)	(.042)
Republican Congress	.098**	.098**
	(.031)	(.030)
Adj. R^2	.309	.356

Note: N = 42. Entries are OLS estimates with standard errors in parentheses.
One-Tailed Significance Levels: ***p ≤ .01, **p ≤ .05, *p ≤ .10.

stagnant or less public social spending. This impact, similar to the previous model of just social tax expenditures, occurs soon after the president takes office. Recent Republican presidents have enjoyed both high levels of public approval and legislative environments favorable to making these types of social spending trade offs in their first few years. The impact of a Republican executive grows larger in the second model when the social expenditure ratio reflects just regressively redistributive tax expenditure programs. A Republican Congress increases the social expenditure ratio in the long run. The long-run multiplier indicates that increased Republican power in the legislature results in a ten-point shift toward tax expenditures in the ratio. Again, the relationship between Republican power and changes in the ratio are stronger in the second model, which isolates more regressive social tax expenditure programs. There were actual increases in the size of the long-term multiplier coefficient in 1983, 1986, 2003, and 2004 all years of majority Republican control of the federal government. These results point to significant social expenditure trade offs being made during the first term of President Reagan and during the period of unified Republican control under President George W. Bush. Altogether, Republican power at the federal level produces a social policy trade off with increased subsidies for private social welfare coming at the cost of stationary or reduced public social spending.[13]

The economic and societal control variables had minimal and somewhat surprising effects on changes in the ratio. Most surprisingly, an increase in the number of poor families corresponds with an increased social expenditure ratio. In Chapter 3, the empirical results indicated that changes in families below the poverty line negatively correlated with public spending. Recent research (Bartels 2008, Gilens 2012) has shown that policymakers tend to systemically ignore the public preferences of the poor. An increase in inflation produces negative changes in the ratio in the long term. The negative relationship between inflation and spending could be due to decreased overall government spending after periods of high price levels.[14]

---

[13] These results are similar when political party control is tested against a ratio of social tax expenditures that includes housing as a category of social policy as reported in the Appendix to this chapter.

[14] Since the following two models only have 42 observations, I ran a baseline model with just the primary political variables of interest. The main results are similar to those in Table 5.2 with a switch to a Republican president resulting in a statistically significant increase in social expenditure ratio.

In conclusion, the Republican Party uses federal money to finance an American social welfare state. However, this unique welfare state is one that is subsidized through the tax code, is administered by private entities – mainly businesses through employment-based social programs – and benefits more economically secure citizens. Not only is there evidence of Republican control resulting in higher levels of tax subsidies for private welfare but these increases in tax expenditures come at the expense of discretionary public programs that serve the poor, veterans, and schoolchildren. However, the aforementioned set of analysis treats political party control the same over the years so that Republican control of the White House in the 1970s is operationalized the same as Republican control in the 2000s. Republican party leaders have become more conservative over time and Democratic leaders more liberal. I would, therefore, expect a larger shift in the social expenditure ratio between a liberal Democrat and conservative Republican than between moderates from different parties. In the next section, I examine how changes in the political ideology of political party leaders in government determine changes to the social expenditure ratio.

Political Party Leader Ideology and Changes to Federal Social Spending

How do changes in the ideology of political party leaders determine changes in federal social spending in the United States? The Republican and Democratic parties of 1970 are not the same two political parties of 2012. In the previous analysis, for example, Republican Party control of the White House is measured the same in 1974 with Gerald Ford coded as 1 as it is in 2008 with George W. Bush also coded as 1. We know from experience and DW-NOMINATE measurements of ideology that President Bush was a more conservative executive than President Ford even though both were Republican presidents. The ideological distance has not only grown between presidents from the same party but at the legislative level as well – within and between congressional party leaders. In the recent 112th Congress (2011–2013) the most conservative Democratic member was more liberal than the most liberal Republican; in essence there was no ideological overlap between members of the two political parties. In comparison, the 92nd Congress (1971–1973) had significant ideological overlap between the two parties with conservative members of the Democratic Party and liberals in the Republican ranks (McCarty, Poole, and Rosenthal 2000).

The increased ideological homogeneity within both the Democratic and Republican parties has made it easier for party leaders to organize and coordinate their members around ideologically distinct social policy strategies. As ideological uniformity has increased, each political party can work more as a unitary actor in the policy process resulting in "conditional party government" (Aldrich and Rohde 2000). Aldrich and Rohde argue conditional party government results in strong majority parties when the members of a party are ideologically homogenous. Once members' policy preferences homogenize, the legislators within each party have greater incentive to provide party leadership with the power and resources to force ideological discipline on the party members in government. Most importantly, the major source of intraparty homogeneity is that members' electoral constituencies have become more uniform in their policy demands and preferences (Aldrich and Rohde 2000). These changes have allowed party leaders to convince members that party-sponsored bills can be used to distribute benefits to broad groups of partisan voters. This partisan change is a stark shift from the bipartisan omnibus bills used in the 1960s and 1970s to distribute benefits to members' individual districts. The increased ideological homogeneity of a political party has meant that party leaders are expected to put forth any bill that enjoys the support of a majority of the party's members. Political party leaders in the majority have not only gained power through increased member homogeneity but also through institutional changes in government. Various studies demonstrate that since procedural changes started in the 1970s, majority party leaders have exerted more influence on committee assignments, committee transfers, aggregate expenditure levels, and roll-call voting (Kiewiet and McCubbins 1991, Cox and McCubbins 1993, Rohde 1991). Therefore, political party leaders are selected by the membership to reflect the dominant ideology of the party's majority and, once selected, have the tools to map the majority's ideological position onto legislation. These trends mean that as party power switches from Democrats to Republicans, the ideological direction of social policy swings from the center-left to the right or far right. Therefore, I expect that as political party leaders become more ideologically extreme over time, changes in party power will result in larger changes in the modality and magnitude of federal social spending.

In the following model, I replace the variables of political party control of the two branches with the first dimension DW-NOMINATE scores of the President, Speaker of the House, and the Senate Majority

Leader.[15] The DW-NOMINATE scale is calculated from all nonunanimous roll call votes cast across all Congresses with each vote recorded on a liberal–conservative dimension ranging from −1.0 (most liberal) to 1.0 (most conservative) (McCarty et al. 1997). I expect that as Republican Party leaders become more conservative (scores moving closer to one) there will be a corresponding increase in the ratio of social tax expenditures for private benefits to aggregate federal social spending. I import the two dependent variables from the previous model. These variables also allow separate analysis of the relationship between control of the House of Representatives versus the Senate and changes in social spending. The first model measures changes in the social expenditure ratio using tax expenditures for private programs. The second model employs a ratio that uses changes in regressive social tax expenditures (minus EITC).

Table 5.3 shows that, as expected, more conservative Republican leaders in the White House and Senate resulted in a higher proportion of social tax expenditures to total federal spending. In the first model, as the president becomes more conservative there is a corresponding increase in the short-run level of social tax expenditures for private welfare (and a positive but insignificant relationship in the long term). In addition, a more conservative Senate majority leader produces larger changes to tax subsidies for private social benefits of around six percentage points in the short term and an additional seven to eight percentage points in the long term. Interestingly, there is a negative relationship (although statistically not significant from zero) between the ideology of the House Speaker and changes to social tax expenditures in the long term. This result is probably due to the fact that Republicans controlled the House for eight years during the Clinton and Obama presidencies. It also might help explain why Republican control of Congress in previous models was at times negatively signed and not statistically significant from zero – Republican control has divergent effects in the House versus the Senate. In the second model, more conservative Republican Presidents resulted in a higher social expenditure ratio in the short term while more conservative Republican Senate Majority leaders produced higher ratios in both the short and the long term. The relationship, as expected, between conservative Republican control and the social expenditure ratio grew stronger in the second model, where three out of the four party leader coefficients were higher than the previous model. A Republican Senate

---

[15] The terms of office compiled from official House and Senate websites and Eric Lomazoff at the Russell Sage Foundation prepared the data.

TABLE 5.3. *Political Party Leader Ideology and Changes in Federal Social Spending, 1970–2012*

	Social Expenditure Ratio	Social Expenditure Ratio (-EITC)
Short-Term (Immediate) Effects		
Δ President	.053**	.057**
	(.019)	(.019)
Δ House Speaker	−.011	−.011
	(.035)	(.015)
Δ Senate Majority Leader	.060**	.057**
	(.033)	(.032)
Δ Inflation	.004	.004
	(.005)	(.005)
Δ Top Tax Rates	−.001	−.001
	(.001)	(.001)
Δ Poor Families	.034**	.043**
	(.020)	(.020)
Long-Term Effects		
President$_{t-1}$	.003	.001
	(.014)	(.014)
House Speaker$_{t-1}$	.004	.003
	(.031)	(.030)
Senate Majority Leader$_{t-1}$	.078**	.086**
	(.030)	(.029)
Inflation$_{t-1}$	−.011**	−.012**
	(.005)	(.005)
Top Tax Rate$_{t-1}$	−.001	−.002**
	(.001)	(.001)
Poor Families$_{t-1}$	.024**	.025**
	(.011)	(.011)
Error Correction Rate		
Social Spending$_{t-1}$	−.401***	−.462***
	(.129)	(.131)
Long-Run Multiplier		
President	.009	.002
	(.037)	(.031)
House Speaker	.011	.006
	(.076)	(.065)
Senate Majority Leader	.195*	.186**
	(.079)	(.066)
Constant	.106	.148
	(.174)	(.175)
Adj. R²	.307	.364

Note: N = 42 for all models. Entries are OLS estimates with standard errors in parentheses. One-tailed Significance Levels: * p ≤. 10; **p ≤ .05; ***p ≤ .01.

Majority leader produces a significant long-run multiplier effect in both models of close to 20 points. The totality of these results speaks to the additive effects of legislative control to presidential power in shaping social policy. All total, more conservative Republican leadership at the federal level produces a higher proportion of social tax expenditures to federal social spending.

There are a number of implications that stem from this analysis. First, it is not just Republican Party control of the federal government that is driving increases in social tax expenditures. The Republican Party's move to the right has produced large shifts in tax subsidies for private social welfare as a proportion of total social spending. These results call into question claims that tax expenditures are the preferred policy tool of moderates as a way to split the difference between Democrats' desire for more spending and Republicans' preferences for a lower tax rate. The Republican movement to privatize social welfare corresponds with the increase in the number of conservative Republicans in legislative leadership positions. In addition, since Republicans have become more conservative over time these results indicate larger changes later in the time series than were experienced in earlier periods of Republican control of the federal government. Another implication of these results is that Republican control of the Senate is more important to the expansion of social tax expenditure than is partisan control of the House of Representatives. These results could be driven more by Republican control of the Senate during part of President Reagan's tenure and the first six years of the George W. Bush administration. There could also be something structural about the Senate, and, more specifically, the Senate Finance committee's role in tax legislation, which is producing these results. The Senate Finance committee has historically shown more initiative in creating and expanding tax expenditures while the House Ways and Means, burdened by a larger jurisdiction and more political actors, often acquiesces to the Senate's proposed changes to the tax code.

Up to this point, I have theorized and demonstrated that political party control of the federal government causes changes to the modality and magnitude of social spending. In order to fully investigate the influence of political parties on social spending, I extend the analysis from measures of political party control to include party polarization and divided government. Party polarization and divided government are proven to result in changes to public policy independent of and in some cases in addition to political party control (McCarty et al. 2000, Alt and Lowry 1994). If it is these trends that are causing yearly increases in social tax expenditures and not partisanship than the previously reported relationship between political party control of the federal government and changes in social welfare expenditures must be amended.

Testing Alternative Explanations for Changes to Federal Social Spending

While the previous analysis found that political party control of the federal government determines both the modality and degree of social spending, there are other possible explanations for changes in social expenditures. For one, it is possible that social tax expenditures are not just the preferred spending mechanism of the Republican Party but rather a compromise policy position in an era of increased polarization and divided government. Tax expenditures may represent a compromise policy position that attracts Democratic support as a form of government financing for popular social goals and appeals to Republicans as a way to reduce citizens' tax burden. For example, if the president's party does not control Congress, resulting in divided government, then it makes passing sizeable changes to traditional public social spending more difficult for Democrats and large-scale tax cuts harder to achieve for Republicans. Therefore, it could be the case that the two political parties negotiate an increase to social tax expenditures as a politically acceptable, although not preferred, policy outcome. If I find that either divided government or party polarization is responsible for changes to the social expenditure ratio (and not Republican control of the federal government) then the idea that political party control determines social spending changes must be modified. The following sections review the extant literature on polarization, divided government, and social spending.

There has been a dramatic rise in the ideological polarization between the two major political parties since the 1970s, whether it is measured by interest group scores (Groseclose et al. 1999) or roll call votes (Poole and Rosenthal 1997, McCarty et al. 1997). Political polarization is the increased intraparty preference homogenization as evidenced by the ideological position of each party's members moving closer together in space and time (Poole and Rosenthal 1984, McCarty et al. 1997). In plain language, Democrats have become more liberal and Republicans much more conservative over time. As the two major political parties pull apart ideologically, they are also becoming more uniform internally as measured by the decreased variance of each party's voting coalition in the legislature. Since 1990, more than half of congressional votes have featured a majority of one party opposing a majority of the other (McCarty et al. 2006). The major implication of party polarization for policymaking is that it makes bipartisan legislation more difficult to pass. McCarty, Poole, and Rosenthal (2006) in their study of party polarization and income inequality reveal that party polarization in Congress is associated with diminished social spending. If polarization has caused less public social spending then it may incentivize Democrats to compromise with Republicans to increase the use of social tax expenditures. And although both political parties have polarized, they have not polarized equally. While the Democratic Party has moved to the center-left, Republicans have become much more conservative (Hetherington 2001, Mann and Ornstein 2012, McCarty et al. 2006). The unequal polarization of the two parties may favor the use of tax expenditures as a compromise position, as that position has moved from the ideological center to a center-right position.

Political party polarization also has consequences for the creation of new social tax expenditure programs. Howard (1997) finds that, historically, more moderate members of Congress sponsored important new tax expenditures. So besides making compromise across the legislative aisle more difficult, party polarization also signals a decrease in the amount of moderate legislators. The replacement of moderate legislators with more ideologically extreme members has repercussions for changes to social policy. If moderate members of both political parties have been responsible for doing the heavy lifting of creating and shepherding new social tax expenditures through the legislature then the decrease in moderate members may reduce the use of a potentially moderate policy tool – social tax expenditures. In addition, as more ideologically extreme members dominate the internal party negotiations it has become more difficult for a majority party leader to design social policy that attracts members of the minority party without alienating the most ideologically extreme members of his or her own coalition. Jones (2001) argues that party polarization results in legislative gridlock. He concludes that by including party polarization and party seat division in a model along with divided government, the divided government effects on legislative gridlock go away while polarization and seat division are highly correlated with gridlock. If polarization makes legislative compromise more difficult between the two parties then social tax expenditures are less likely to increase.

In the following model, I place political party polarization alongside political party control of the federal government in testing the political causes to changes in social spending. I represent political polarization using the Congressional difference of party means measure. This measure is created by scaling the DW-NOMINATE scores that allow the House and Senate to be compared across time and space, with higher values signaling more party polarization (Poole 1998). I use the overall Congressional measure of party polarization instead of using the separate measure for the House and Senate since the two chamber measurements correlate so highly with the overall measure. There are two possible outcomes with party polarization included as an independent variable. If tax expenditures are a moderate compromise position, then polarization should make compromise less likely and reduce the level of tax expenditures. A second possibility is that as the Republican Party has moved to the far right the compromise policy position between the two parties has moved from the center to center right, which would cause more tax expenditures to be passed by the legislature.

Divided Government and Social Spending

How does divided government influence federal social spending? Divided government was a common occurrence during the period of this study. The elections, between 1952 and 2012, generated unified governments at the national level just over 30 percent of the time. This era stands in stark contrast to the period between 1900 and 1950, when unified governments were elected 84 percent of the time. The traditional divided government hypothesis argues that proposed legislation is less likely to become policy when the president's party does not hold a majority of seats in both chambers of Congress. An additional institutional obstacle to passing legislation, over the last forty years, is the growing supermajoritarian requirement of the U.S. Senate that requires control of sixty seats by the majority party in order to thwart the threat of a filibuster from the minority party. The logic of the traditional divided government theory is simply that a political party is more likely to solve the collective action problem of legislative coordination through intraparty negotiations rather than interparty negotiations that require having to work and compromise across political party lines. If a political party is forced to negotiate across party lines, during periods of divided government, it lowers the probability of success. Therefore, periods of divided government are more likely to stifle the majority party's ability to increase their preferred form of policy. The implication for the relationship between parties and social spending is that if a social tax expenditure program is a compromise position between Democrats and Republicans then, all else equal, these subsidies should rise during periods of divided government. In the matter of government spending, Jones, Baumgartner, and True (1998) find no statistical difference between unified Democratic control and divided government in changes to the budget authority. Kiewiet and McCubbins (1991) found that Democratic control of Congress and the Presidency results in greater domestic social spending. Those authors also report that when there is a split Congress, social welfare spending grows slower than under Democratic control but faster than when there is unified Republican control of government.

Over the last thirty years, the increase in divided government has corresponded closely to periods of social welfare drift and devolution. Policy drift occurs when social and economic changes alter the effects of policies without significant changes to the actual policy. Hacker (2004) argues that social risks have changed drastically for most workers, without much change to the federal law that governs public and private social insurance. Additionally, devolution is the shifting of public responsibilities, such as financing, management, and/or regulation, from the national government to the subnational level. The movement of social programs from the federal level to a joint federal-state partnership has lowered the overall generosity of these programs (Goetz 1995, Rao 1998). Although these types of changes have reduced the scope of some welfare programs, the continued popularity of Social Security and Medicare inhibited the Republican Party from making deep and lasting cuts. Paul Pierson (1996, p. 17) defines social welfare retrenchment as "policy changes that either cut social expenditures, restructure welfare state programs to conform more closely to the residual welfare state model, or alter the political environment in ways that enhance the probability of such outcomes in the future." Pierson's evaluation of retrenchment in the U.S. and U.K. demonstrates that partisan barriers both inhibit social program expansion and create obstacles for legislators who want to completely dismantle the existing social welfare state. As Paul Pierson writes in his assessment of social policy in America, "economic, political, and social pressures have fostered an image of welfare states under siege. Yet if one turns from abstract discussions of social transformation to an examination of actual policy, it becomes difficult to sustain the proposition that these strains have generated fundamental shifts" (Pierson 1996, p. 173). Pierson's conclusions would align with those of scholars who argue that divided

TABLE 5.4. *Political Party Control and Average Changes to Federal Social Spending, 1970–2012*

	Discretionary Social Spending	Total Public Social Spending	Tax Expenditures for Private Welfare
Unified Democratic Control	13.4%	8.5%	12.6%
Democratic Majority	15.2%	9.1%	7.9%
Republican Majority	−1.7%	5.7%	14.1%
Unified Republican Control	8.2%	6.1%	13.1%

Source: Author's calculations using PAP and JCT data.

government restrains majority political parties from enacting policy that matches their members' preferences.

How does divided government affect changes to social tax expenditures, direct discretionary social spending, and a ratio of the two? I have argued that the most important factor in predicting changes in both the modality and the level of social spending is political party control of the federal government. Specifically, as Republicans gain more federal control there is evidence for a higher level of social tax expenditures, less public social spending, and a higher social expenditure ratio. If social tax expenditures represent a compromise position between Republicans' preferences for lower marginal tax rates and Democrats' preferences for higher public social spending, then in years of a divided government social tax expenditures should increase and the coefficients for Republican Party power should be smaller or not statistically significant from zero. The next section examines descriptive statistics that compare unified party control of government with divided control.

The differences between divided and unified government are first examined by observing the average spending changes from 1970 to 2012 by both government condition (divided and unified) and social spending type (discretionary, public, and social tax expenditure). The four rows are ordered from unified Democratic control to unified Republican control with divided government in between. The divided government rows are organized by which political party controlled at least two of the following three units: the White House, the House of Representatives, and the Senate. In Table 5.4, the first column shows that divided government with Democratic control of two out of the three units produces the largest, on average, increases in discretionary social spending.

Unified Democratic control also produces a sizeable yearly change to discretionary public spending. Not surprisingly, unified Republican Party control resulted in low growth and in the case of Republican-leaning divided government reduced discretionary social spending. The second column measures changes in total public social spending (mandatory plus discretionary). Here there are not visibly large differences between unified and divided government, although Democratic Party power did result in higher average changes as compared to Republican control of government. The next column measures changes in social tax expenditures for private welfare. There is no recognizable difference between Republican unified and divided control of government in annual changes in social tax expenditures, though on the Democratic side, unified control did result in higher averages. This table does provide supportive evidence for the idea that Democrats favor discretionary social spending and Republicans prefer social tax expenditures. However, these measures provide descriptive information about the impact of divided government on spending so I now turn to the full model.

In the following tables, I rerun the previous models of partisanship and changes in social spending with variables for divided government and party polarization. The models in Table 5.5 are again ECMs that report both a short-run and a long-run effect on the relationship between the independent and dependent variables. The first model in the table examines the relationship between Republican Party control and changes in the social expenditure ratio controlling for divided government, and the second model examines the relationship between Republican Party control and changes in the social expenditure ratio controlling for political party polarization. I represent divided government as a binary variable with one representing years of divided government and zero representing years of unified political party control. In the second model, I characterize political party polarization using a single DW-NOMINATE measure of party polarization in the U.S. Congress, with higher values representing more polarization.[16] I expect the relationship between political party control of the federal government and changes in social spending to hold even when explicitly accounting for the presence of divided government and political party polarization.

Republican Party control of the government determines changes in the social expenditure ratio even when controlling for periods of divided

---

[16] House and Senate party polarization correlate at over a 0.90 level; the same results occur when using just House polarization.

TABLE 5.5. *Divided Government, Polarization, and Changes in Social Spending, 1970–2012*

	Social Expenditure Ratio (1)	Social Expenditure Ratio (2)
Short-Term (Immediate) Effects		
Δ Republican President	.042	.073**
	(.034)	(.024)
Δ Republican Congress	.017	.016
	(.015)	(.015)
Δ Divided Government	.019	
	(.028)	
Δ Party Polarization		−.221
		(.413)
Δ Inflation	.002	.008*
	(.005)	(.005)
Δ Top Tax Rates	−.001	−.001
	(.001)	(.001)
Δ GDP	−.001	
	(.016)	
Δ Poor Families	.046**	.028
	(.022)	(.021)
Long-Term Effects		
Republican President$_{t-1}$	.003	.013
	(.019)	(.020)
Republican Congress$_{t-1}$	.043**	.042**
	(.014)	(.013)
Divided Government$_{t-1}$	−.027	
	(.022)	
Party Polarization$_{t-1}$		.237*
		(.155)
Inflation$_{t-1}$	−.012**	−.005
	(.006)	(.005)
Top Tax Rate$_{t-1}$	−.002	−.002*
	(.001)	(.001)
GDP$_{t-1}$	−.010	
	(.027)	
Poor Families$_{t-1}$	.026**	.037***
	(.009)	(.009)
Error Correction Rate		
Social Spending$_{t-1}$	−.475***	−.550***
	(.135)	(.148)
Constant	.123	−.146
	(.174)	(.193)
Adj. R^2	.300	.372

Note: N = 42 for all models. Entries are OLS estimates with standard errors in parentheses. One-tailed Significance Levels: * p ≤ .10; **p ≤ .05; ***p ≤ .01.

government and party polarization. In the first model, Republican control of the legislature produces increases in social tax expenditures in the long run. The inclusion of a variable for divided government seems to alter the statistical significance of a Republican presidency in the short run. This finding suggests that a president having party control in the legislature is important for passing a significant change in social tax spending. The coefficient for divided government is positively signed in the short run and negatively signed in the long run but not statistically significant from zero in either case. This model provides evidence against the idea that tax expenditures serve as a compromise policy position between the two parties during periods of divided government. So while there are cases such as that of President Clinton and Congressional Republicans working together to create new education tax credits in 1997, this is the exception rather than the rule of changes to social tax expenditures.

In the second model, Republican control of government again correlates with higher social tax expenditures. In addition, political party polarization causes increased social tax expenditures in the long run. As with the previous social expenditure ratio models, a Republican president produced an immediate increase in social spending and increased Republican power in Congress altered the social expenditures ratio in the long term. The control variables of economic growth, inflation, tax rate changes, and poverty responded similarly to the previous models of partisanship and social spending. These results taken together with the analysis of political party leader ideology provide conclusive evidence that polarization is driving changes to federal social policy. Party polarization results in higher social tax expenditures in two ways. First, more conservative presidents and Senate majority leaders (and presumably Senate Finance committee chairmen) are prioritizing the creation and expansion of social tax expenditure programs. Second, increased party polarization, with the Republican Party moving to the far right of the ideological spectrum, has changed the median chamber position during periods of Republican power. The asymmetric polarization of the Republican Party in the legislature means that even Republican presidents may be pulled to the right, having to either offer up more tax expenditures or deeper cuts in discretionary spending in order to pass a bill through Congress. These results here identify some of the specific mechanisms alluded to by McCarty, Poole, and Rosenthal (2006) in their analysis showing a relationship between polarization and higher levels of income inequality. Specifically, political party polarization has increased the magnitude of social tax expenditures as a proportion of total federal social spending. Overall, the results from the two models confirm that Republican Party control and political polarization drive higher levels of social spending through the tax code.

Conclusion

The analysis in this chapter provides evidence for the partisan theory of the divided social state. In particular, I show that political party control of government determines which type of social spending is utilized and, by extension, who administers social services and who receives social benefits. Republican Party control of the federal government produces decreases in direct discretionary social spending, increases in social tax expenditures for private benefits, and higher ratios of tax expenditures to total social spending. Therefore, a shift in political power to the Republican Party at the federal level moves resources and financial support from public programs that serve more disadvantaged populations to private benefits and services, which primarily benefit wealthier households. These results give empirical support to Lowi's theory of interest-group liberalism. Lowi (1969) argued that the American style of pluralist government was liberal in that it offered a positive view of the power and ability of government to shape societal outcomes. Therefore, the overall level of government activity and spending does not dramatically change with changes in political party power but rather the real change is the perception of the public good and this is determined by the majority party's special interest coalition. Specifically, the public good of economic security oscillates back and forth between Democratic support for working-class constituencies and Republicans' use of federal subsidies for private welfare benefits.

There are a number of important implications that can be drawn from the analysis in this chapter. First, the changes documented here mean that for many Americans, federal support for their social insurance is not stable and fluctuates with party power in Washington, D.C. Interestingly, while the political rhetoric from both parties is mainly about helping the middle class, the main financial beneficiaries of federal social programs are either the working poor or the rich. Next, the empirical analysis here provides evidence that the Republican Party has embraced the "Two-Santa Theory" and distributes government goods and services through the tax code as a way to counter the Democrats' spending Santa. Republican presidents increase the level of social tax expenditures in the short run and Republican legislatures in the long run, signaling a real commitment by the party to practice distributive politics. Finally, the Republican Party has been successful in not only building a private social system through increases in tax expenditures but reducing the scope of public programs by cutting or slowing discretionary spending. The Republican increase in social tax expenditures along with cuts in marginal income tax rates have increased the nation's debt level. In short, the relationship between Republican power and increases in the social expenditure ratio provide tangible support for the "starve the beast" strategy being more than a theory.

The primary test in this chapter was between Republican Party strength and changes in federal subsidies for private social welfare as represented by social tax expenditures, yet this is only one part of the partisan theory of the divided social state. I have argued that political parties distribute both financial support for social programs and monetary benefits through altering the direction of national redistribution. In the next chapter, I examine the relationship between the modality of federal social spending and changes in the level of income inequality in America. In a previous chapter, I alluded to the fact that direct spending and tax expenditures are known to distribute federal money in opposing directions. Direct spending for public programs is collected from various taxes and allocated more to working-class populations. In contrast, even though the wealthy pay a large share of federal taxes, this same group enjoys an even larger share of the total benefits from social tax expenditure programs, producing a regressive distribution of income (and for some programs regressive redistribution). It's possible that changes in social spending determine citizens' economic security not only through the financing of social insurance but also through changes in the government's role in influencing the national income distribution.

Appendix to Chapter 5

Summary Statistics of the Major Variables

Variable	Mean	Standard Deviation	Minimum	Maximum
Tax Expenditures	635.4	606.2	23.6	2044.5
Tax Expenditures (-EITC)	593.4	540.3	23.6	1870.4
Social Expenditure Ratio	.528	.197	.117	.776
Social Expenditure Ratio (-EITC)	.521	.192	.117	.760

Baseline Model of Republican Power and Changes to the Social Tax Expenditures, 1970–2012

Variables	Social Tax Expenditure	Social Tax Expenditure (-EITC)
Republican President	114.5*	117.3**
	(47.47)	(45.44)
Republican Legislature	.199	− 6.88
	(38.1)	(30.27)
Constant	43.11	38.16
	(22.52)	(16.88)
Adjusted R^2	0.070	0.085

N = 42, ARIMA specifications with standard errors in parentheses.
Two-Tailed Significance Levels: *p ≤ .05.

Baseline Models of Republican Power and Changes to the Social Expenditure Ratio, 1970–2012

Variables	Social Expenditure Ratio	Social Expenditure Ratio (-EITC)
Republican President	.054*	.058*
	(.024)	(.027)
Republican Legislature	.016	.015
	(.014)	(.015)
Constant	.011	.010
	(.008)	(.008)
Adjusted R^2	0.097	0.099
PARTY LEADER IDEOLOGY		
President	.045*	.048*
	(.018)	(.019)
House Speaker	−.004	−.003
	(.033)	(.034)
Majority Leader	.044	.040
	(.033)	(.034)
Constant	.011	.010
	(.008)	(.008)
Adjusted R^2	0.094	0.092

N = 42, ARIMA specifications with standard errors in parentheses.
Two-Tailed Significance Levels: *p ≤ .05.

Republican Power and Changes to the Social Spending (with Housing), 1970–2012

	Social Expenditures	Social Expenditure Ratio
Short-Term (Immediate) Effects		
Δ Republican President	79.21*	.055**
	(47.04)	(.025)
Δ Republican Congress	6.81	.017
	(25.72)	(.014)
Δ Inflation	13.71*	.004
	(8.03)	(.004)
Δ Top Tax Rates	1.76	−.002*
	(2.93)	(.001)
Δ Poor Families		.055**
		(.018)
Long-Term Effects		
Republican President$_{t-1}$	98.71**	−.023*
	(33.06)	(.016)
Republican Congress$_{t-1}$	−3.74	.058***
	(21.81)	(.014)
Inflation$_{t-1}$	−2.47	−.013*
	(7.61)	(.004)
Top Tax Rate$_{t-1}$	3.10**	−.003*
	(1.62)	(.001)
Poor Families$_{t-1}$		.040***
		(.008)
Error Correction Rate		
Tax Expenditures$_{t-1}$	−.649***	−.640***
	(.186)	(.123)
Constant	−367.4*	.146
	(134.3)	(.148)
Adj. R^2	.351	.484

Note: N = 42. Entries are OLS estimates with standard errors in parentheses.
One-Tailed Significance Levels: ***p ≤ .01, **p ≤ .05, *p ≤ .10.

Changes to Social Tax Expenditures, 1981–2010

Provision	Reagan
	Economic Recovery Tax Act of 1981
Deductions	New deduction for two-earner married couples; permit unlimited marital deduction for estate and gift tax
IRAs/Pension	Extended eligibility for IRAs to include active workers in employer pension plans; increased Keogh annual contribution limit to $15,000
Tax Credits	Increased estate tax credit to exempt all estates of $600,000 or less
Capital Gains	Reduced maximum capital gains rate to 20%
	Deficit Reduction Act of 1984
Tax Credits	Increased EITC
Capital Gains	Reduced long-term capital gains period from 1 year to 6 months
	Tax Reform Act of 1986
Deductions	Increased standard deduction to $5,000 for couples and personal exemption to $2,000 and phased in deduction for self-employed health insurance
Exclusions	Repealed exclusion of unemployment benefits
IRAs/Pension	Limited IRA eligibility and pension contributions
Tax Credits	Increased EITC; extended research and experimentation credit; created new low-income housing tax credit; repealed the investment tax credit
	Omnibus Budget Reconciliation Act of 1987
Deductions	Limited mortgage interest deduction to debt less than $1 million
	H.W. Bush
	Omnibus Budget Reconciliation Act of 1990
Deductions	Created a 25% health insurance deduction for the self-employed
Exclusions	Created exclusions for employer-provided legal and educational assistance
Tax Credits	Adjusted EITC benefit levels and phase-in and phase-out rate for family size; created low-income credit for premium costs of health insurance; extended tax credits for research, business energy, targeted jobs, fuels credit, created small business credit for accommodations for disabled persons
Capital Gains	Capped capital gains rate at 28%

(continued)

Provision	
	Clinton
	Omnibus Budget Reconciliation Act of 1993
Deductions	Reduced business meals and entertainment deduction
IRAs/Pension	Expanded taxable portion of Social Security benefits from 50% to 85% when modified AGI goes above $44,000 (joint) or $34,000 (single)
Tax Credits	Extended EITC to single workers earning $9,000 or less
	Taxpayer Relief Act of 1997
IRAs/Pension	Extended AGI phase outs for deductible IRAs; allowed tax-free withdrawals from first time home purchases; created new Roth and Education IRAs
Tax Credits	Introduced a $500 per child tax credit; introducing Hope and Lifetime Learning nonrefundable education credits; increased the unified estate tax credit from $600,000 to $1 million
	W. Bush
	Economic Growth and Tax Relief Reconciliation Act of 2001
Deductions	Increased the standard deduction for joint filers; limited tax deduction for higher education expenses
Exclusions	Permanently extended exclusion of employer provided education assistance; excluded any fringe benefit for qualified retirement planning service
IRAs/Pension	Annual dollar contribution limit raised to $3,000 for 2002–04, $4,000 for 2005–07, and $5,000 for 2008 and thereafter; annual contributions for 401ks increased to $15,000 over four years; increased from $500 to $2,000 annual limitation on Education IRAs
Tax Credits	Child care credit increased to $1,000; permanent extension of adoption credit; established employer-provided child care credit; increased phase out of the EITC for joint filers by $1,000 for 2002–04, $2,000 for 2005–07, $3,000 for 2007
	Job Creation and Worker Assistance Act of 2002
Tax Credits	Extended work opportunity credit; welfare to work credit; allowance of nonrefundable personal credits
	Jobs and Growth Tax Relief Reconciliation Act of 2003
Deductions	Accelerated increase in the standard deduction for joint filers from EGTRRA to begin in 2003 rather than 2009
Tax Credits	Accelerated EGTRRA increase in the child tax credit to $1,000 to 2003 instead of 2005
Capital Gains	reduced rates for adjusted capital gains and dividends

Provision	
	Working Families Tax Relief Act of 2004
Deductions	Extended standard deduction for couples
Tax Credits	Extended child tax credits to 2009; increased refundability of child credit to 15%; extended credit for research, work opportunity, welfare to work credit
	Tax Increase Prevention and Reconciliation Act of 2005
Exemptions	Extended certain exemptions for income of controlled foreign corporations; accelerated adjustment of foreign earned income
IRAs/Pension	Allowed taxpayers to convert traditional IRA into Roth IRA; eliminated the income limit on Roth IRA conversions ($100,000) in 2010
Tax Credits	Allowed companies to carry foreign tax credits forward 10 years
Capital Gains	Extended the reduced rates for adjusted capital gains and dividends through 2010
	Katrina Emergency Relief Act of 2005
Deductions	Suspended limits to donations for Katrina relief efforts; expanded deduction for donated food and books; created additional exemption for housing Katrina victims
Exclusions	Excluded discharges of debt for victims
IRAs/Pension	Exempted early penalty withdrawals from retirement plans for victims; allowed rollover contributions for home purchase
Tax Credits	Extended work opportunity credit to Katrina employees; created employee retention credit; allowed displace people to use 2004 income for EITC
	Gulf Opportunity Zone Act of 2005
Deductions	Extended charitable contributions for Rita and Wilson efforts; extended suspension of limitation on causality and theft loss deductions
IRAs/Pension	Extended special retirement fund rules for victims
Tax Credits	Extended various credits for victims including employee retention, low-income housing, New Markets, and Hope and Lifetime
	Pension Protection Act of 2006
Exclusions	Permanent tax-free withdrawals for qualified tuition accounts
IRAs/Pension	Permanent increase in annual contribution limit for IRAs and 401ks
Tax Credits	Extended coordination of Hope and Lifetime Learning credits

(*continued*)

Provision	
	Tax Relief and Health Care Act of 2006
Deductions	Extended deductions for state and local taxes, school related expenses, qualified tuition expenses, computer technology, and energy efficient buildings
IRAs/Pension	Allow one time transfer from IRA to Health Savings Account
Tax Credits	Extended new market credit, research credit, work opportunity credit, welfare to work credit, included combat pay in earned income for EITC, credit for new energy
	Mortgage Forgiveness Debt Relief Act of 2007
Exclusions	Excluded debt forgiveness on primary home from taxable income
	Housing Assistance Tax Act of 2008
Deductions	Allowed non-itemizing homeowners to deduct up to $500 ($1,000 for joint filers) of property taxes paid during 2008
Tax Credits	Allowed a refundable credit for first-time homebuyers; increased and simplified low income housing credit
	Emergency Economic Stabilization Act of 2008
Deductions	Extended through 2009 the property tax deduction for nonitemizers, the deduction for state and local sales taxes, the deduction for qualified tuition expenses, and the deduction for expenses of school teachers
Exclusions	Extended the exclusion of debt forgiven on principle residence from taxable income through 2009
Tax Credits	Lowered the threshold for the refundable portion of child care tax credit to $85,000; extended research and new markets tax credits
	Obama
	American Recovery and Reinvestment Act of 2009
Deductions	Allowed a deduction for sales tax on new cars in 2009
Exclusions	Exempts up to $2,400 of unemployment compensation
Tax Credits	Created Making Work Pay and American Opportunity tax credits; increased the EITC; lowered the threshold for the child tax credit; converted homebuyer credit to refundable credit; expanded the Work Opportunity and New Markets credits
	Patient Protection and Affordable Care Act of 2010
Deductions	Deduction floor on unreimbursed medical expenses raised to 10% of AGI; deductibility of remuneration for services; deduction for Medicare Part D limited; organizations not meeting 85 ratio standard are ineligible for certain deductions

Provision	
Exclusions	Indian tribe benefits are excluded from income; state expansions of health care in underserved areas is eligible for income exclusion
IRAs/Pension	Additional tax on withdrawals from Health Savings Accounts and Medical Security Accounts not used for medical expenses
Tax Credits	Adoption Credit and Adoption Assistance Credit extended and made refundable

Source: Author's amended table from the Tax Policy Center's "Major legislation by act, 1981–2013"

Methodological Issues Concerning Tax Expenditures

In order to determine the baseline income tax structure (from which tax expenditures are exemptions) there needs to be agreement on what qualifies as taxable income. The normal tax baseline in based on the Schanz-Haig-Simons (S-H-S) definition of income. The S-H-S concept defines net income as an increase in net economic wealth between two points of time plus consumption during that period. The S-H-S method does not specify which accounting techniques should be used in formulating consumption so the treasury uses standard business accounting techniques in establishing the baseline. Essentially, by declaring a provision a tax expenditure the treasury is stating that the provision is not a function of the normal tax structure. The S-H-S concept does not include some items that might be considered part of the income baseline, such as capital gains. The U.S. Department of Treasury also constructs tax expenditure estimates using two baselines: the normal structure (like the JCT) and the reference income tax structure. Nearly all of the federal social tax expenditure programs would be counted as tax expenditures regardless of how expansive the basic tax baseline is defined. It is relevant to note that there are disputes among both tax lawyers and economists about some of the assumptions used in measuring tax expenditures (see Burman 2003). As a practical matter the tax expenditure concept and methodology has been part of the formal budget process for close to 40 years and is a widely accepted metric of the government's effort to provide subsidies through the tax system. Some economists claim that caution should be used in the summation of individual tax provisions since there is a possible interaction effect. The revenue estimate for a tax expenditure is based on the assumption that it alone is repealed and that all other provisions remain constant. There are two potential issues when summing individual tax expenditure programs: interaction effects and the intersection of tax expenditures with the alternative minimum tax (AMT). As the JCT analysis states, in general, elimination of several itemized deductions would increase revenue by less than the sum of revenue gains measured by eliminating each item separately because more taxpayers would use the standard deduction (Joint Committee on Taxation 2009). Conversely, elimination of multiple items that are exclusions from the adjusted gross income would increase revenue by more than the sum of individual gains because taxpayers would be pushed into a higher tax bracket (Joint Committee on Taxation 2009). I use the latest reported estimates from the JCT in aggregating yearly social tax expenditures. For example, the JCT booklet released in 2010 estimates tax expenditures from 2010 to 2014 – I use this booklet's estimates and not earlier ones in recording 2010 tax expenditures. In this study, I aggregate all tax expenditures for social purposes for each year from 1970 to 2012. According to a recent study by Burman et al. (2008a), summarization of tax expenditure estimates has proven to produce similar aggregate estimates as models that take into account the interaction effects of all tax expenditures under the alternative minimum tax structure. Burman et al. (2008a) find "that adding separate tax expenditures to compute total costs produces significant errors for some subgroups of provisions, but in the aggregate (and for many subcategories) comes close to the correct sum." They also find that exclusions, and credits underestimate the totals while deductions overestimate. Since I'm aggregating across multiple social welfare categories that represent between 60 and 80 percent of total federal tax expenditures (depending on the year), there is a small likelihood that the aggregate tax expenditures are greatly over- or underestimating the true value. And although the AMT is thought to reduce the value and desirability of itemized deductions in the aggregate, Burman et al. (2008a) find that the AMT does not influence the value of aggregating all individual itemized deductions. The standard deduction is not allowed under the AMT so more taxpayers will itemize. The phase-out of itemized deductions for high-income taxpayers does apply to the AMT. The AMT and the passive activity loss rules are not viewed by the JCT as an aspect of the normal tax law. They are considered as provisions that diminish the magnitude of each tax expenditure. For example, the AMT reduces the value of the charitable contributions by not allowing the deductions to be claimed in the calculation of AMT liability. The passive loss rules defer otherwise allowable deductions until the taxpayer has passive income or cashes in their assets.

The possible interaction effects in totaling estimated direct outlays do not preclude analysts from summing total direct spending. A repeal of one of the public welfare programs may not reduce total outlays by the amount associated with the program. This could occur if benefits under the repealed welfare program must be counted in determining an individual's eligibility under another welfare program. In essence, repeal of one public program could make more people eligible for other programs, and total government outlays would increase for the program continued. No one asserts that budget outlays cannot be added to produce a total outlay figure even though the interaction effect described here exists. Nor should this interaction effect prevent tax expenditure items from being totaled (see Surrey 1974).

There are timing issues when it comes to some pension tax expenditure programs. Tax expenditures are measured as the revenue lost to the U.S. Treasury from an individual provision in a given year. Traditional and Roth IRAs both exempt the return on savings from taxes, but traditional IRAs allow the taxpayer to defer payment of tax on contributions until money is withdrawn from the account, while Roth IRAs tax contributions and exempt withdrawals. So, an expansion of the traditional IRA would show a much bigger revenue loss in a given year but over the long run an expansion of the Roth could cost the government just as much. Some tax breaks, such as private pensions, pay out over many years. Traditional IRAs allow a deduction for contributions and earnings with qualifying withdrawals fully taxable. The use of time-series analysis allows me to capture a portion of these lagged effect changes to social tax expenditure policy.

6

The Modality of Social Spending and Income Inequality in America

The previous chapter demonstrated that increased Republican Party control of the federal government results in higher levels of social tax expenditures at the expense of public spending for social programs. A major implication of these results is that changes to political party control determine whether the government increases financial aid for public versus private social assistance and by extension which populations receive more federal support for their social benefits and services. Yet these first-order effects are not the only major consequences of changes in the modality of federal social spending. I argue that social policy not only bestows tangible benefits to certain groups (such as a retirement account or health insurance) but also takes money from one socioeconomic group and gives it to another, creating redistribution effects. The increased use of public social spending produces progressive income redistribution effects that help the working class, and, conversely, a growth in tax expenditures regressively distributes federal money to wealthier families. Therefore, changes in the modality of social spending not only produce first-order effects for the provision of social benefits but also create second-order effects that determine the government's role in redistributing national income and by extension the level of income inequality.

So how do changes in social spending impact the level of income inequality in America? In this chapter, I explore the evidence for the divergent income distribution effects of public social spending versus social tax expenditures, and test in a dynamic model the impact of changes to the social expenditure ratio on the level of income inequality. I expect that when the federal government shifts tens of billions of dollars between the two sides of the divided social state from one year to the next, there will be a noticeable impact on changes to the ratio of national income share between the wealthiest and poorest Americans in both the short and the long runs. First, I examine the differences between Democrats and Republicans on the issues of income inequality and income redistribution. Second, I review the research and findings on the rise of income inequality in the United States over the last forty years. Third, I examine the recent literature on the role of political factors in contributing to increases in the level of income inequality. Next, I revisit the model of political parties, social spending, and income inequality and connect my theoretical argument to recent studies that establish opposing income redistribution effects for public social spending and tax expenditures. Finally, I analyze the relationship between federal social tax expenditures and variations in the level of income inequality over time. My results show that as social tax expenditures become a larger proportion of federal social spending there is a corresponding increase in the ratio of income share controlled by the wealthiest households.

Income Inequality in America

An analysis of the partisan differences over rising income inequality is necessary to understand why Democrats and Republicans select different social spending mechanisms with divergent distribution effects. On September 17th, 2011, an estimated group of 1,000 citizens gathered together at Zuccotti Park in New York City (in what later became known as the Occupy Wall Street movement) to protest against rising income inequality and its effect on American politics. Occupy Wall Street (OWS) protesters called attention to the disproportionate power of large corporations in the political process, and, in particular, the excessive influence of the financial sector on shaping federal policy. The Occupy Wall Street movement adopted the slogan "We are the 99%," which highlighted the changes in the national income share between the top 1 percent of income earners and the rest of the country. Soon after the initial protest, the national media started to cover the NYC protests and similar protests around the country and around the world. The spread of OWS protests and the intense media coverage that followed moved income inequality to the front and center of the national political agenda, and consequently, revealed the stark differences between the Democratic and Republican parties on the role of government in assuaging the growing income gap in the United States.

In the months after the OWS protests, Republican leaders scrambled to offer a response to the public's growing concern about income inequality in ways that meshed with their members' ideology. Republican House Speaker John Boehner even went so far as to say that he "understood people's frustrations (with rising inequality)" and House Majority Leader Eric Cantor scheduled a major speech on income inequality at the University of Pennsylvania (it was eventually canceled due to the threat of OWS protests). The long-held Republican policy positions of lower taxes, private-sector solutions, and support for business did not lend themselves easily to offering solutions to rising income inequality. While some Republican members tried to shoehorn inequality into their existing legislative strategy, other party members rejected the issue outright. Republican Steve LaTourette, representative from Ohio, when asked about income inequality, replied that "it's redistribution of wealth – which is socialist, which is communist and all of that – but I do think that when you pit millionaires and billionaires against everyone else, that's a nice populist message, and we've got to get our hands on it" (Cogan and Sherman 2011). The 2011 Republican House budget reflected the party's ideological position (and reluctance to directly address income inequality) by proposing lowering both corporate and marginal income tax rates while cutting public social spending and converting Medicare into a federal subsidy program for private health care insurance. President Obama during this time period sought to link his economic policies (and by extension the Democratic Party) with the related goals of reducing inequality, and restoring upward mobility for the working class. In a major 2011 economic speech, President Obama argued,

for the top one hundredth of 1 percent, the average income is now $27 million per year. The typical CEO who used to earn about 30 times more than his or her worker now earns 110 times more. And yet, over the last decade the incomes of most Americans have actually fallen by about 6 percent. Now, this kind of inequality – a level that we haven't seen since the Great Depression – hurts us all.... Inequality also distorts our democracy. It gives an outsized voice to the few who can afford high-priced lobbyists and unlimited campaign contributions, and it runs the risk of selling out our democracy to the highest bidder. Obama 12/6/11.

So while no political party is supportive of rising income inequality, the Democratic Party's platform lends itself more easily to rallying its base around federal policy solutions such as raising taxes on the rich and providing more income redistribution to the poor. In the year leading up to the 2012 election, President Obama highlighted his administration's effort to raise taxes on the very rich as a means to pay for more benefits for the middle class and poor. President Obama's stump speeches emphasized how his administration curbed the worst practices of Wall Street, passed a health care bill that raised taxes on the rich to pay for health care insurance for the poor, doubled the number of Pell Grants (college assistance for needy students), and passed a law that required equal pay for equal work for women. President Obama often combined these policies under the framework of addressing the problem of income inequality, even going so far as to claim the growing income gap was "the defining issue of our time" in his 2012 State of the Union (SOTU).

In the year running up to the 2012 election, Democratic Party leaders, in particular President Obama and Senate Democrats, used the increased attention surrounding the issue of income inequality to continually bring up "wedge" issues that forced Republicans to vote for either increased taxes on the very rich or increased spending for the poor (the two most direct policy mechanisms for addressing the income gap). Democrats in Congress proposed a number of bills that would raise taxes on millionaires and allow the Bush tax cuts to expire on the wealthiest households (those making more than $250,000 a year). One piece of legislation designed to draw a contrast between the two parties' positions on inequality was the Democratic proposal for creating a "Buffett rule" for effective marginal tax rates (effective rates are what taxpayers actually pay the government once all their tax expenditures are netted out). The "Buffett rule" would create a minimum 30 percent tax rate for citizens making over a million dollars a year (this is named after famed billionaire Warren Buffet who argued that he should not pay a lower effective lower tax rate than his secretary). As reported in *Politico*, Democratic Senator Charles Schumer argued that pushing the "Buffett rule" was a sound political strategy since "it is an emerging contrast with Republicans. We think the wealthy should share even more of the sacrifice" (Weisman 2012, Wong 2012). While the Democratically controlled Senate passed a bill with a "Buffett rule" that would have raised taxes on the richest households, generating an additional $47 billion in federal revenue, the Republican House voted down the "Buffett" measure and passed its own bill, which included a 20 percent decrease in taxes on small businesses. Some Democrats on the campaign trail discussed the partisan differences in addressing income inequality by highlighting the vote on the "Buffett rule" along with other unpopular Republican votes on allowing payroll taxes to rise, voting against raising the minimum wage, and cuts to the food stamp program. This collection of votes was purposely put on the agenda by Democrats to put Republican legislators on the defensive concerning the issue of inequality in the run up to the 2012 Presidential election.

In the 2012 election, Governor Romney's personal background along with his selection of Representative Paul Ryan as his vice presidential candidate reinforced the public's perception of the Republican Party as the party of the rich. Governor Mitt Romney, the Republican candidate for president, reported a net worth of $250 million and made his fortune through the private equity industry. The media attention surrounding Romney's untactful portrayal of who benefits from federal policy at a fundraiser (i.e., 47% of people pay no income taxes and are dependent on government programs) was coupled with stories about the low tax rate Governor Romney paid in 2011 (around 14%). Governor Romney's background story made any attempts by the Republican Party to convincingly propose programs that would help the middle and working classes more difficult. On the campaign trail when asked about the political relevance of income inequality, Governor Romney declared that this topic was about the politics of "envy" and "class warfare" and that it should only be discussed in "quiet rooms." Next, the vice presidential nominee Representative Paul Ryan was the chief architect of the Republican budget proposal that would reduce marginal tax rates for wealthier individuals and corporations, and pay for it by drastically reducing federal social spending on Medicaid, college assistance, and food stamps. Democrats called Ryan's budget the "reverse Robin Hood" plan. Other Republicans sought to blame the federal government for inequality and offered up private market solutions to the growing income gap. Republican Congressman Bill Flores, for example, when asked about income inequality, responded, "absolutely, there's huge income inequality, and it started right here in Washington. The way we fix that is getting the government out of the way of the private sector so we can put these people to work" (Cogan and Sherman 2011). All total, the perception of the two political parties is that federal money will be filtered down to the working class under Democrats and transferred up to the rich by Republicans (Bartels 2008).

As Democratic and Republican policymakers have revealed divergent public positions on the importance of income inequality as a political issue, partisans in the electorate have followed suit. In particular, a number of studies have shown that Democratic voters consider income inequality to be an important issue and react more negatively to policy that distributes federal money to wealthier citizens (Bartels 2008, Faricy and Ellis 2014, Page and Jacobs 2009). According to a report from *Politico*, a poll taken during the height of the Occupy Wall Street movement revealed that more than three times as many Democrats as compared to Republicans considered income inequality to be an important political issue facing the nation (Mak 2011). A more recent study shows that while similar numbers of Democrats and Republicans recognize that income inequality has grown over the last decade (68% and 61% respectively), there is a partisan division on whether or not the government should actively work to reduce the income gap. The study finds that 90 percent of Democrats say the government should do some or a lot to reduce inequality compared to only 45 percent of Republicans who wanted government action on the issue (Pew Research Center 2014). When pressed in the survey about possible policy actions that could be used to address income inequality, it is not surprising that Democrats and Republicans disagree on the best course of action. Democrats were twice as likely as Republicans to favor raising taxes on the wealthy to pay for programs for the poor and Republicans were three times more likely to favor lowering taxes on the wealthy and corporations (Pew Research Center 2014). In short, while partisan voters do not differ on recognizing growing income inequality, they differ on the importance of inequality as a political issue and their preferred policy prescriptions for addressing income inequality.

Trends in U.S. Income Inequality

Even though the rise of income inequality in America is – by now – well documented, it is worthwhile to revisit the basic facts. There are many ways to measure income inequality yet by any measure available, the gap between the rich and poor has widened over the last four decades (Piketty 2014, Piketty and Saez 2003, 2006, Neckerman and Torche 2007). Inequality has increased whether measured in pre-tax or post-tax dollars, whether or not capital gains are included, and whether measured in terms of income or wealth. During the period of this study, the Gini coefficient in the U.S. rose from 0.394 in 1970 to 0.469 in 2010.[1] Since 1970, income inequality in the United States has risen each consecutive year except for the recession periods of 1990–1991, 2001, and 2007. The following sections present evidence and analysis of growing income

---

[1] The Gini coefficient, the most common measurement of income inequality, reports a single value that ranges between 0 and 1, with higher values indicating greater income inequality. Although the U.S. Census changed its calculation of the Gini in 1993, since that time – a period with a consistent measure – the rise has been over five percent.

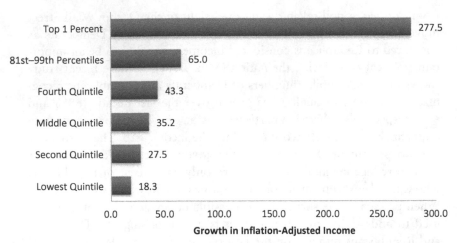

FIGURE 6.1. Percentage change in after-tax income across quintiles, 1979–2007. *Source:* Author's compilation using CBO income data.

inequality in America, including a focus on the unique role of gains made by the top 1 percent of income earners and a comparison of income inequality across countries.

Income inequality has been driven largely by the dual trends of extraordinary income gains by the wealthiest households and decreasing income shares for middle- and working-class American families. The U.S. Census rank orders all households by income from highest to lowest, and then divides the households into five cohorts or quintiles (from highest to lowest income). If total income for the population were evenly divided, then each quintile (from the bottom 20% of income earners to the top 20% of income earners) would account for 20 percent of the total income. Therefore, the degree to which each income cohort is above or below a 20 percent share of the total serves as a measure of income inequality. Figure 6.1 displays the share of household income held by each income quintile – in twenty-year snapshots – from 1969 to 2009.

As Figure 6.1 shows, national income has become more unevenly distributed over time, with the greatest shares going to the wealthiest Americans. The after-tax income gains grow not only with each step up the income ladder but, within the top quintile, triple-digit gains are reserved for those at the very top of the income distribution scale. In 1969 the bottom 80 percent of households earned 57 percent of the nation's income while the top 20 percent controlled 43 percent of national income. By 2009, the wealthiest families saw their share of national

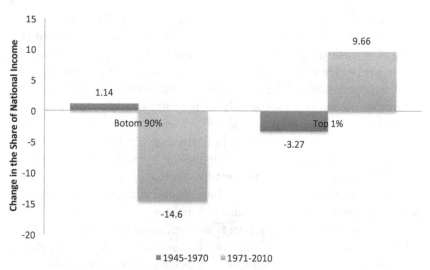

FIGURE 6.2. Changes in national income share between the bottom 90 percent and the top 1 percent. *Source:* Author's calculation from data from Alvaredo et al., *The World Top Incomes Database.*

income rise by seven points to 50.3 percent while the bottom 80 percent lost seven points of their average income shares. The families in the top quintile of income have not controlled this much of America's wealth since 1928 (U.S. Census 2010). And while households in the top quintile have experienced large income gains, their gains pale in comparison to those in the top 1 percent.

The Top One Percent

The rise of income inequality is not just attributable to changes in the top income quintile; the top 1 percent's income gains has driven the growth of U.S. income inequality. Figure 6.2 shows the change in the share of national income between the bottom 90 percent of income earners and the top one percent in two periods: 1945–1970 and 1971–2010.

In 1945, the bottom 90 percent started out with just over two-thirds of the nation's income and that share grew to just under 70 percent by 1970. Conversely, the top one percent lost share of the national income going from 11.2 to 7.8 percent in the same twenty-five-year period. The postwar period was known for widely distributed income gains among the population, and this period also coincided with President Johnson's Great Society programs. However, the majority of the country (the bottom 90 percent) lost out during the last forty years, going from controlling around

70 percent of the national income to around 53 percent. The top 1 percent went through a boom period, more than doubling their portion of the national income from just under 8 percent to a 17.4 percent share. In fact, in the decade before income inequality started to rise, from 1960 to 1970, over 60 percent of the national income gains went to households in the bottom 90 percentile while only 11 percent accrued to the wealthiest 1 percent. This rate of income growth was reversed during the Bush presidency from 2002 to 2007, where the top 1 percent received over 60 percent of the total income gain while the bottom 90th percentile of households took in under 13 percent (Stone et al. 2012).

A number of economic studies have found that the largest income gains have been within the exclusive territory of the top one percent. For example, according to a report from the Congressional Budget Office (CBO),[2] between 1979 and 2005 the bottom half of the top 1 percent experienced an income increase of 105 percent. The next highest four-tenths of the top 1 percent witnessed its real income rise 161 percent. Next, the top one-tenth of one percent had its inflation-adjusted income rise an astounding 294 percent. Finally, the top one one-hundredth of one percent, approximately 11,000 families, had a real income increase of 384 percent. Thomas Piketty and Emmanuel Saez (2003, 2006) demonstrate in a series of articles, using income data from IRS returns, that income gains by the top wage earners (within the top one percent) decreased in the period after World War II but rose sharply starting in the mid to late 1960s. Piketty and Saez examine changes in the income share for those households at 99th, 99.5th, 99.9th, and 99.99th percentile levels. They show that families in the 99.99th percentile saw their share of national income increase *five-fold* over a forty-year period (0.55 to 3.34) compared to the 99th percentile, who more than *doubled* their share of national income from 8.02 to 18.29. Not only have the wealthiest households enjoyed larger income gains than the rest of America; the richest American families have experienced the largest income gains in the Western world.

An International Comparison of Income Inequality

The current level and rapid escalation of income inequality in the U.S. stands out among the wealthy, industrialized nations in the world (Brandolini and Smeeding 2006, Leigh 2007, Pontusson and Kenworthy 2005). According to the most recent data from the OECD, the United

---

[2] 2007, Historical Effective Tax Rates 1979 to 2005.

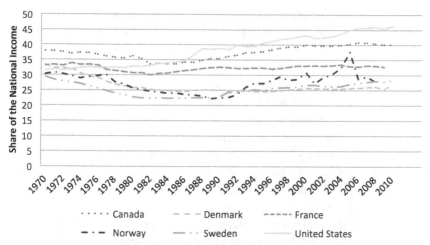

FIGURE 6.3. An international comparison of the top 10 percent of income earners, 1970–2010. *Source:* Alvaredo et al., *The World Top Incomes Database.*

States has the highest level of income inequality in the post-industrial world. In fact, U.S. inequality level is seven percentage points higher than the European average (Luxembourg Income Study 2013). In another measure of international income inequality from 2010 – the ratio of income of households in the 90th percentile compared to the average income of those families in the 10th percentile – the United States reports a ratio that is more than double any other wealthy nation (Luxembourg Income Study 2013). In research on international income inequality, the United States reports a greater level of income inequality compared to every Western European country in both the pre- and post-tax estimates.[3] In a study from Pontusson and Kenworthy (2005), ten of eleven industrialized countries experienced increased income inequality during the 1980s and 1990s, and nine of these countries responded with more assertive distributive social policies at the end of the period. The United States was not one of these nations.[4]

Figure 6.3 compares the change in the share of national income of the top 10 percent of income earners across six countries. The six countries

---

[3] The Luxembourg Income Study (LIS) began in 1983 and is a cross-national study that reports on a number of demographic characteristics, including family and personal income.

[4] In addition, they show that although the median income level in the United States is higher than that of most other countries, far more American citizens are poor relative to the median income.

represented in the figure are the United States, France, Canada, Sweden, Denmark, and Norway. The American wealthy started this period in the middle of the pack but experienced larger income gains over the forty-year period compared to their European counterparts. In 1970, the top 10 percent in the United States accrued around 31 percent of the nation's income, which was lower than the income share of the wealthiest families in Canada, Denmark, and France. Over time the wealthiest households in the United States experienced larger and larger gains and by 2010 this group controlled over 46 percent of the nation's income. In comparison, the top 10 percent of income earners lost national income share in Denmark and France during this same period. And although many countries have experienced increases in income inequality, nations with more traditional social welfare states that progressively redistribute money have much lower levels of comparative income inequality (Saez and Veall 2005).

The Politics of Income Inequality

What has caused the recent rise in income inequality? Economic and sociological research have unearthed numerous causes that range from increased globalization to changes in technology to changes in the family structure to disparities across workers' education and skill level, and including the diminished power of labor unions (Cashell 2009, Gustafsson and Johansson 1999, Levy and Murnane 2001, Alderson and Nielsen 2002, Golden and Wallerstein 2011). Recently, political scientists have turned their collective attention to examining the relationship between politics and income inequality. In 2004, the American Political Science Association's (APSA) Task Force on Inequality and American Democracy released a report that chronicled how political behavior, political institutions, and public policy affect income inequality and how, in turn, the rise of income inequality has influenced the quality of democracy. More recent scholarship has provided evidence that political party control of government, mass public opinion, and changes to public policy have contributed to growing income inequality in the United States (Bartels 2008, McCarty et al. 2006, Kelly 2009, Hacker and Pierson 2010, Gilens 2012). The following sections describe how political parties use changes to public policy as a means to distribute income and, in turn, influence the level of national income inequality.

Republicans and Democrats have produced divergent patterns of income growth over the last fifty years. Specifically, Democratic presidential administrations correlate with greater income gains for the working class and Republican presidential administrations produce greater income growth for the wealthy (Hibbs 1987, Bartels 2008, Kelly 2009). Early work from Douglas Hibbs (1987), which examined income trends from 1948 to 1978, found that income inequality decreased on average by 25 percent during periods of Democratic control of the White House and remained relatively unchanged under 17 years of Republican executive power. These same partisan patterns of income distribution are evident in more recent studies on the politics of income inequality. Bartels (2008) examines change in the income ratio between those households in the 80th percentile of distribution (the wealthiest 20 percent of families) and those in the 20th percentile (the poorest 20 percent of families) from 1948 to 2005. Income inequality went up under six Republican presidents and down under four out of five Democratic leaders. This same study argues that applying consistent income growth patterns experienced under Democratic presidents every year from 1948 to 2005 would almost have negated the real rise in economic inequality over five decades. Conversely, Bartels (2008) shows that the application of Republican income growth patterns during the last fifty years would have resulted in 80 percent more growth in U.S. income inequality. In addition, Kelly (2009) examines roughly the same time period (1947–2000) and tests the relationship between partisan control and two forms of income inequality: pre-tax income (income prior to taxes and spending) and post-tax income (pre-tax income plus income from government redistribution). He finds that Democratic presidents reduce overall income inequality through changes to pre-tax income distribution and – to a lesser extent- explicit redistribution through public policy.[5] Altogether, the literature shows that working class families experience a rise in their income levels during Democratic administrations and wealthier families fare better under Republican presidents.

How do Democrats and Republicans use public policy to produce divergent patterns of income distribution? The majority of evidence, to date, finds that political party control of the federal government has the largest impact on income distribution through influences to the overall economy. In particular, the two major political parties advance opposing fiscal policies that result in different consequences for the macroeconomy

---

[5] This trend is a consistent finding across the aforementioned studies of income inequality in that political factors are more determinative in moving pre-tax income inequality as opposed to post-tax income inequality.

and, by extension, income inequality. Historically, Democrats in office have pursued higher taxes on the wealthy and full employment policies that have resulted in patterns of income redistribution that accrue more resources to the working class. For example, from 1948 to 2001, the average unemployment rate was 30 percent lower and economic growth 40 percent higher under Democratic presidents than Republican presidents (Bartels 2008). During this period, as GDP grew and unemployment went down, the working and middle classes experienced more of the nation's income growth. Another study found similar evidence in that Democratic administrations reduced the ratio of pre-tax income inequality (the pre-tax income shares going to the top 20 percent versus the bottom 40 percent of the income distribution), while Republican presidencies corresponded with years of increased pre-tax income inequality (Kelly 2009). Therefore, Democratic administration fiscal policies that bring about higher levels of GDP growth and lower levels of unemployment account for most of the recent decreases in pre-tax income inequality and the majority of change in the total level of income inequality (both pre- and post-tax and transfer). However, these studies operationalize policy mainly through changes in public spending and therefore do not account for the myriad of changes in tax policy that may have impacted changes in the national income distribution.

Republican administrations have enacted fiscal policies that focus on lowering inflation and decreasing taxes, especially for wealthier individuals, and the cumulative effects of these policies are to distribute money up the income ladder (Hibbs 1987, Bartels 2008, Kelly 2009). Hibbs (1987) argued that Republicans accepted lower economic production and growth as a means to fight potential expansions of inflation. He theorized the Republican economic strategy reflected, in part, their electoral goals since wealthier families obtain a significant portion of their wealth from capital and assets and these forms of wealth are eroded by high levels of inflation. In support of this idea, Bartels (2008) found that inflation rates grew at a slightly slower pace under Republican presidents (as opposed to Democratic presidents) from 1948 to 2005. While political parties have been found to predominantly influence income distribution indirectly through fiscal policy, they also can more directly affect changes in income inequality through social policy. In the next section, I examine the income distributive effects of public social spending (favored by Democrats) and social tax expenditures (preferred by Republicans).

How Public Spending and Tax Expenditures Affect Income Inequality

The relationship between social policy and income inequality can only be fully understood by accounting for both public social programs and private welfare. Studies of changes in public social programs and income inequality only explain how changes in federal spending impact families at the lower end of the income distribution. And while studies of how government activity determines the income of poor families are important, there are areas of social policy that influence the income of wealthier families too. The particular rise of American income inequality has been driven by the large income gains going to the top 1 percent, and, therefore, the following analysis of social tax policy, is well suited to measure the impact of politics and policy on changes in inequality. Federal subsidies and tax expenditures are known to distribute more money, on average, to wealthier families than they do to middle- and working-class groups. While a number of studies have shown that Republican Patry power produces increases in income inequality, the particular policy mechanisms through which this occurs remain enigmatic. The federal government spends hundreds of billions on social tax subsidies every year resulting in wealthier families receiving tens of thousands and sometimes even hundreds of thousands in government funds. If there is going to be a systematic relationship between public policy and changes to income inequality, it is most likely to be found through an examination of the tax code.

Earlier, I theorized that political parties use the distributive effects of policy to target benefits to their constituencies and move the ideological direction of public policy. The partisan use of a public policy's distributive effects has been made possible due to an increasingly divided mass electorate along the lines of partisanship and income class (McCarty et al. 2006). While a citizen's party identification has not always been related to class, over the period of this study more working-class citizens have become Democratic Party supporters while wealthier voters have aligned with the Republican Party. The major implication of this bifurcation is that political parties can deliver federal money to their constituencies by changing the direction of national income redistribution. These redistributive effects are especially important in that the socioeconomic groups that Democrats and Republicans want to target, the rich and the poor, are often not very popular with the public (Gilens 1999, McCall 2013). Therefore, a political party can create programs for popular social goals such as home ownership and target money to the very wealthy through second-order distributive effects without worrying about public backlash given the information asymmetry between policymakers and the public.

In the following sections, I examine the literature on the distributive effects of public social spending and social tax expenditures. I establish that federal spending for public social programs, both means and non-means tested, progressively redistributes federal income. In contrast, tax expenditures, in general and those explicitly designed for private social programs, distribute income from all taxpayers toward wealthier households. I argue that political parties know and take into account the divergent distributive effects of public spending versus social tax expenditures when deciding changes to social policy and that these divergent distributive effects are observable when evaluating fluctuations in the distribution of national income.

The Progressive Distributional Effects of Direct Social Spending

The main objective of public social programs is to provide citizens with social insurance, services, or benefits. A secondary effect of government social spending is the redistribution of federal income down the income ladder to poorer families. Public social programs collect revenue from federal taxes (payroll and income) and then redistribute a disproportionate amount of financial benefits to middle- and working-class families. For example, Kelly (2009) finds that the combined income effect for all federal social programs reduced income inequality by around 14 percent. Additional studies have found similar results; Hungerford (2009) found that the combination of government social programs and the progressive income tax structure reduces the Gini coefficient by around 16 percent. Therefore, as spending on public social programs goes up, the level of national income inequality goes down (Bartels 2008, Kelly 2009, Cashell 2009).[6] The majority of public social programs that are means tested, such as Medicaid, welfare, and food stamps, are directly designed to provide financial assistance to the poor. Means-tested social programs take the level of family income into account when determining the eligibility and sometimes the generosity of a program's benefits. The program means test is used to deny benefits to families that have sufficient income to provide themselves economic security. These programs have relatively

---

[6] These studies measure the impact of direct social spending by comparing the distribution of pre-tax or market income, which excludes income and benefits from government sources, with the national distribution of post-tax and transfer income that is market income minus taxes and plus government income.

TABLE 6.1. *A Comparison of Medicaid Recipients and Employment Beneficiaries, 2010*

Medicaid			
By Employment	Full Time	Part Time	Non Worker
	11%	29%	41%
By Income (FPL)	Low	Middle	High
	43%	18%	2%
By Gender	Female	Male	
	18%	16%	
By Race	White	Black	Hispanic
	12%	29%	27%
Employer-Based			
By Employment	Full Time	Part Time	Non Workers
	68%	27%	15%
By Income (FPL)	Low	Middle	High
	14%	48%	86%
By Gender	Female	Male	
	57%	56%	
By Race	White	Black	Hispanic
	65%	42%	37%

Source: Author's compilation using data from the Kaiser Family Foundation.

small annual budgets (outside of Medicaid) and rather obvious progressive redistributive income effects.

There is a socioeconomic division between who receives means-tested federal health insurance and those employees who enroll in the employment-based health system. Table 6.1 compares the recipients of Medicaid to those of employment-based health care insurance across employment status, income level (as measured by a household's position above the federal poverty line), gender, and race. Each category represents the rate of coverage in percentage terms. Medicaid is a joint federal–state health insurance program that is means tested for families and individuals with low-income who cannot afford other sources of health care insurance. As is to be expected, Medicaid covers more disadvantaged groups and those households that are better off enroll at higher rates in the employment-sponsored health care structure. Households in which no one works and that are closest to the federal poverty line (under 100 percent) have rates of Medicaid use over 40 percent. In comparison, full-time workers who earn income well above the poverty line (400 percent or higher) are enrolled at the highest rates in the employment-based system. While there are not substantive gender differences, racial minorities benefit more from Medicaid than do whites, while the opposite is true in the private health care system (although more racial minorities enroll in private plans at higher rates than Medicaid).

All total, more vulnerable populations rely on and are served by Medicaid while wealthier workers who are in privileged positions in the labor market reap the benefits of the tax expenditures that subsidize employer-provided health care and pensions. Yet even large, non-means-tested social programs targeted toward the elderly such as Social Security and Medicare have a higher benefit-to-cost ratio for poorer families than for wealthier households.

Social Security, Medicare, and Income Redistribution
The progressive distribution of Social Security and Medicare benefits is a function of both design and demographics. The progressive redistributive effects of Social Security and Medicare are substantial, given that these two programs alone cost the federal government $1.4 trillion in 2012 (Office of Management and Budget 2012). Social Security replaces a larger proportion of lifetime earnings for low-income workers than for high-income workers. In addition, if the disability portion of Social Security is included in calculating redistributive benefits then the working class accrues even more of the financial rewards from the program. In particular, Social Security redistributes national income from upper middle- and high-income employees to low-wage retirees.[7] A common method used to determine the redistributive winners and losers of Social Security is to measure the "money's worth ratio" or taxes paid versus benefits received by different groups. According to the Government Accountability Office the replacement of benefits-to-taxes paid is the highest for low-income workers at 49 percent, is second highest for average-income workers at 37 percent, and is lowest at only 24 percent for the highest income earners (Government Accountability Office 2005). Another study found that not only do working-class households make out better than wealthier families from Social Security but that women do better than men, and minorities tend to do better than whites (Bucks et al. 2009). One recent analysis (Liebman 2002) demonstrates that lower-income households, women, and those with less than a high school education benefit the most

---

[7] There is some evidence that the progressiveness of Social Security is mitigated by families in which one spouse is a high earner and the other a low earner, and wealthier people living longer (Bosworth et al. 1999).

from Social Security. In Liebman's study, those families closest to the poverty line (less than 50 percent) received back roughly $90 of benefits for every dollar paid through taxes. Conversely, the wealthiest families (with incomes higher than 300 percent over the poverty line) only received back twenty-six cents for every dollar contributed through payroll taxes. Since racial and ethnic minorities are more likely to be poor and work in lower-wage jobs there is also a racial disparity in Social Security benefits. Next, women received roughly double the benefits-to-taxes compared to men. Similarly, those without a high school diploma accrue nearly three times the lifetime Social Security benefits than those with a higher education. In total, Social Security redistributes financial benefits down the income ladder and toward constituencies that are electorally important for the Democratic Party.

Medicare, a universal program of health insurance for the elderly, provides more financial assistance to low-income families as opposed to higher-income families (McClellan and Skinner 1999, 2006, Bhattacharya and Lakdawalla 2006, Lee et al. 1999). As an example, one study examined the ratio of benefits to taxes for Medicare over a lifetime for three simulated couples: average earner/low earner, average earner/average earner, and high earner/average earner. The couple with one average earner and one low earner received back more benefits from Medicare than the two wealthier couples, with the greatest benefit gap being between the low-earning and high-earning couples (Steuerle and Carasso 2003). Kelly (2009) found that 37 percent of total Medicare benefits go to the lowest income quintile while only 6 percent accrue to those in the top income quintile. In addition, the benefit of Medicare for working-class households goes up substantially once the insurance value – in addition to the financial value – of the program is accounted for in the benefit-cost ratio (McClellan and Skinner 1999, 2006). The insurance value relates to the fact that poor, elderly households could not afford health insurance on the private market absent the Medicare program.[8]

Kelly (2009) found that Social Security alone reduces income inequality by 6.9 percent and Medicare, by itself, reduces income inequality by 3.6 percent. These two programs are largely responsible for the low

---

[8] The income redistribution effect for Medicare is smaller than that of Social Security in large part due to how Medicare is financed through the tax system. Medicare Part A (hospital) is financed by a payroll tax and Medicare Part B (physician care) is financed through general federal revenues. In addition, Part B relies on a uniform monthly premium paid by enrollees, which takes more disposable income from lower-income retirees.

level of poverty among the elderly in America. For example, according to a report from the Social Security Administration (SSA), without the cash payments from Social Security, more than half of the elderly population would have fallen into poverty in 2007. Overall, Social Security, Medicare, Medicaid, and other means tested programs have substantial progressive redistributive effects on national income. These redistributive effects are well known among policymakers and therefore provide an explanation for why Democrats have been stalwart supporters of Social Security and Medicare while Republicans have continually attempted to transfer these programs to the private market.

The Regressive Income Distributional Effects of Tax Expenditures

In the United States, wealthier citizens accrue the vast majority of federal income benefits from tax expenditure programs (Burman et al. 2008b, Hungerford 2009, Toder et al. 2011). Tax expenditures alter the horizontal and vertical equity of the basic tax system by allowing exemptions, deductions, and credits for specialized groups or activities. In particular, tax expenditures designed to subsidize employee fringe benefits provide more government money to wealthier workers. There are three main reasons for the upside-down income redistribution effects of tax expenditures: the progressive federal income tax structure, the relationship between employment benefits and social tax expenditures, and the role of itemization in claiming social tax expenditures.

The progressive structure of the federal income tax system results in tax expenditures becoming more valuable as the marginal rate rises. For example, if a worker in the 35 percent bracket is allowed to exclude $10,000 from her income, she receives a tax benefit of $3,500. If another worker in the 10 percent bracket is allowed to exclude the same $10,000 from her income, her tax break is only $1,000. In comparison, if instead of a tax expenditure each worker received a direct government payment of $10,000 and the receipt was taxable, the lower-income worker benefits more with $9,000 available to her after tax, whereas the other worker is left with just $6,500. Therefore, as a taxpayer's income rises, so too does the value of using social tax expenditure programs to reduce their total tax liability. The JCT (2011) estimates that families earning over $100,000 a year accrued 64 percent of the total benefits from the mortgage deduction, 81 percent of the benefits for the state and local tax deductions, and 80 percent of the redistributed income for tax deductions aimed at private pensions. So even with the top 20 percent of income earners paying 70 percent of federal taxes, there are tax expenditure programs that redistribute back a higher percentage of benefits than these families pay into the federal coffers (Toder et al. 2002).

Second, and as discussed in previous chapters, wealthier workers in larger corporations disproportionately benefit from social tax expenditures for employment-based benefits. First, professional workers, who earn high incomes and often work in corporations, are highly likely to both be offered and enroll in employment-based health care insurance and pension plans. Conversely, lower-income workers are often in jobs that do not offer employment-based health care insurance and pension plans. Workers who enroll in employment-based plans have their social insurance contributions excluded from their yearly taxable income through various tax expenditure programs.[9] Second, recent changes to private social programs allow wealthier workers with higher disposable income to invest more of their earnings in employer-based retirement and insurance plans offered by third parties. The more that wealthier employees contribute to employment-based social plans, the more income they are able to exclude and deduct from their annual tax returns. This disparity occurs not only because of their higher salaries, but also because of the integration of many private retirement plans with Social Security.[10] These integration rules allow a smaller fraction of income to be allocated to pension benefits for lower-wage employees. Not only do wealthier workers benefit more from the various tax expenditures for employee pensions, once retired, wealthier Americans rely more on employer based pension payments for their income. Analysis of the March 2008 Current Population Survey shows that pension income constituted less than 7 percent of total family income for elderly individuals in the poorest two income quintiles (the poorest 40 percent of elderly individuals). Pension income, however, accounted for about 20 percent of total family income for those in the richest two income quintiles. Together, wealthier workers' higher enrollment in employment-based plans and their ability to make greater contributions to these plans, with the accompanying higher tax expenditure benefits, result in a federal tax expenditure system that provides the greatest benefits to wealthier workers.

Finally, wealthier families that own large homes and claim the mortgage interest deduction are much more likely to itemize their tax returns

---

[9] There are some programs for the self-employed and after the passage of the Affordable Care Act (ACA) all workers have to be covered or pay a penalty into the system.

[10] Under a plan that is integrated with Social Security, employer-derived Social Security benefits or contributions are taken into account to determine whether the plan discriminates in favor of employees who are officers, shareholders, or management.

than the average American household. Taxpayers who itemize their returns claim more tax expenditure programs than those families who take the standard deduction. In 1998, 124 million tax returns were filed with the U.S. government. Close to 70 percent of those returns (86 million people) claimed the standard deduction, which is considered part of the normal tax structure. Therefore, only 3 out of 10 taxpayers (38 million) could claim sufficiently high enough tax subsidy values on their returns to exceed the standard deduction (Internal Revenue Service 2003).[11] According to data from the IRS, taxpayers in higher income brackets are much more likely to itemize their deductions than those citizens in lower brackets. In 2005, 93.3 percent of taxpayers making a yearly income of $200,000 and above itemized their returns. In the same year, 89.5 percent of taxpayers making $100,000–$199,999 itemized their taxes, as compared to 76.2 percent of taxpayers in the income bracket of $75,000–$99,999. In the lowest income group – those making under $50,000 – only 17.9 percent of citizens itemized their federal income tax returns. Additionally, the use of deductions, exclusions, and exemptions excludes non-taxpayers, the poorest Americans, from tax benefits for social purposes. In the following sections, I explore in more detail how tax expenditure programs for employment-based health care insurance and pensions regressively distribute national income to wealthier individuals.

The Regressive Distributive Effects of Tax Expenditures for Retirement Income and Health Care

While Medicare and Medicaid direct more assistance to the working class, the largest federal tax expenditure program in the United States provides the majority of its benefits to the wealthiest households. The most expensive tax expenditure program is for the exclusion of contributions to employment-based medical insurance and services. In 2012, the tax expenditure programs for private health care insurance cost the U.S. Treasury around $150 billion. These tax expenditure programs accrue more income to wealthier households for many of the same reasons as tax expenditures for private retirement plans. Gruber (2010) finds that the design of employment-based health care tax expenditure programs accrues more benefits to those with higher incomes, and that employees with higher incomes spend more on their

---

[11] Taxpayers list their itemized deduction on the U.S. Individual Income Tax return form 1040 Schedule A.

TABLE 6.2. *Distributional Effects for Employer-Based Health Care Tax Expenditure, 2015*

Income Quintile	Share of Total Tax Benefits
Lowest	0.3
Second	8.6
Middle	17.1
Fourth	22.6
Top	51.4
Top 1 Percent	3.8

Source: Tax Policy Center's Table T13–0264, Tax Benefit of Employer-Sponsored Health Insurance Premiums.

health insurance, which results in a regressive distribution of federal income from tax expenditure programs. Table 6.2 presents the distribution of tax benefits for the primary tax expenditure program for health care – employer-based health care insurance premiums. The majority of these tax benefits accrue to the families in the top income quintile, although the income benefits here are more evenly distributed in comparison to the tax subsidies for private pensions. The top income quintile's share of tax money is more than double that of the middle class, and higher than the lowest three income quintiles combined. The top 1 percent receives about $5,000 on average from just this one social tax expenditure program for health care. The implication of the discussion here is simply that as tax expenditures increase at the expense of public spending then national income moves from the middle and working classes to the rich. In the next section, I empirically test to determine if changes in the proportion of social tax expenditures to total social spending result in widening the income gap between the rich and the poor in the United States.

The Relationship between Social Spending and Income Inequality

I have argued, throughout the book, that political parties make changes to social policy as a means to distribute both social welfare *and financial benefits* to their constituencies and to alter the ideological direction of policy. In the previous chapter, I demonstrated that political party control of government determines which side of the divided social system, public or private, receives more federal money. In particular, I found that

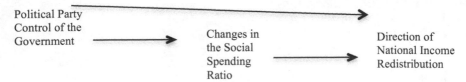

FIGURE 6.4. A model of political parties, policy, and income inequality.

increased Republican power caused a higher ratio of social tax expenditures to aggregate social spending in both the immediate and the long term. Social policy not only helps citizens receive tangible benefits such as health insurance and old-age pensions; it also takes money from one socioeconomic group and redistributes it to another. Therefore, I argue that the two political parties are keenly aware of the redistributive effects of social policy and consider these effects when crafting social policy.

If changes to the modality of social spending alter the government's role in the distribution of federal income then changes to the social expenditure ratio should be observable in corresponding changes to the level of income inequality. A partial model showing the relationship among political parties, social spending, and income distribution is shown in Figure 6.4 (the full model can be found in Chapter 1). I argue that political parties contribute to the level of income inequality, in part, through changes to the modality of federal social spending. Therefore, as political party control in government changes so too will the proportion of tax expenditures to total social spending and by extension the level of income inequality. For both electoral and ideological reasons, Republicans favor public policy outcomes that regressively distribute federal income up to wealthier households. In particular, I expect that increased Republican Party control results in more social tax expenditures and lower levels of discretionary public spending – together resulting in higher levels of income inequality.[12]

A change in the modality of federal social spending affects the level of income inequality in both the short and the long term. First, and as argued in the previous chapter, political parties design social policy with the intent of spending some federal money now to assist their

---

[12] In contrast, as Democrats gain political power there will be a shift of federal revenue to social programs that target more economically vulnerable populations. This increase in public social spending is partially offset, by reductions in social tax expenditures (through sunsets, reducing the scope and generosity of current programs, or eliminating programs).

members in reelection and also to create institutional changes that allocate spending over time in ways that reflect the party's ideology. Next, the
social expenditure ratio includes some new spending, expanded spending, or contracted spending, all of which have an immediate impact on
the after-tax income share of wealthy versus poorer families. Next, most
changes to tax expenditures for private benefits will have income effects
that extend out over multiple periods of time (a new or expanded tax
deduction claimed in year one, for example, can also be claimed in years
two, three, etc.). Therefore, I again use an error correction model (ECM)
since the relationship between the modality of federal social spending and
income inequality will have both short-run and long-run effects.[13]

I measure income inequality using the T10B10 ratio, which is the
top 90th percentile's (wealthiest 10%'s) share of the national income as
opposed to those families in the bottom 10th percentile. My period of
analysis is from 1970 to 2010 since this period overlaps with the two
variables of interest. The dependent variable – the T10B10 measure –
runs from 1967 to 2010 and the social spending data is between 1970
and 2012. This measurement comes from the U.S. Census Bureau and
is a comparison of the mean income level for households in the 90th
percentile (top 10%) with the mean income level for households in the
10th percentile (bottom 10%).[14] In 1970, the average household in the
wealthiest 10 percent of income earners had an annual income a little
over nine times that of the poorest 10 percent. By 2010, the T10B10 ratio
had grown so that the wealthiest families accrued an average income
over eleven times larger than the average household income in the 10th
percentile. The T10B10 measure correlates with the Gini coefficient at a
0.95 level but is a better measurement of income inequality, for this study,
since it focuses on incomes at the very top and bottom of the distribution.
As was discussed previously, social tax expenditures and discretionary
social spending are often targeted at the rich and the poor.

I am primarily concerned with the influence of social policy on changes
in income inequality so the main variable of interest is the social expenditure ratio that measures the annual amount of social tax expenditures
as a proportion of total social spending (tax expenditures plus discretionary social spending). This variable best captures the policy tradeoff

---

[13] There is a more complete explanation of this model choice in Chapter 3.
[14] U.S. Census uses pre-tax money income that includes wages, salaries, dividends, rent,
child support, alimony, pensions, Social Security, and welfare but does not include
SNAP, Medicare, Medicaid, or employer-based health insurance.

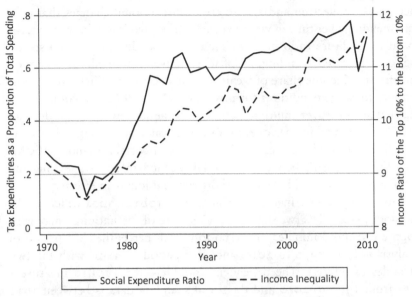

FIGURE 6.5. The social expenditure ratio and income inequality, 1970–2010.

between increased tax expenditures and stagnant or decreased levels of discretionary social spending. As the ratio of tax expenditures to all social spending goes up, so, too, should the government distribution of federal revenues to those households in the top 10 percent versus those in the bottom 10 percent. For each independent variable, there are two estimates of the population parameters: one is an estimate for the immediate change in income inequality resulting from the annual change in the social expenditure ratio and the other estimator along with the error correction rate is used to determine the long-term effect of the various independent variables on changes in the ratio of income going to the top 10 percent versus the bottom 10 percent.

I present a graphical representation, in Figure 6.5, of the relationship over time between the social expenditure ratio and changes in income inequality. The changes to the social expenditure ratio are measured on the left Y-axis, the change in income inequality is measured on the right Y-axis, and time is represented on the X-axis. First, income inequality has grown steadily over the years. The T10B10 ratio starts the series in 1970 at over a nine-fold difference and then steadily increases over the decades to finish the series with the wealthiest households having twelve times the income of the bottom ten percent. Similarly, tax expenditures start at around 30 percent of total social spending – decrease to below

20 percent during the mid 1970s – and then increase at a faster pace than discretionary spending to finish the study at over 70 percent of total social expenditures. The two trend lines move together remarkably well, correlating at over a 0.9 level. While these two variables correlate highly, the absence of other control variables in a full model can only offer the suggestion of a statistically significant relationship over time.

I include a number of economic and political control variables in the full model, which represent relevant ideas about potential causes in changes to the level of income inequality. First, I include a dummy variable for Republican control of the White House. I use this measure since Republican control of the executive branch has been shown to influence income inequality in multiple studies (Bartels 2008, Kelly 2009). In addition, the inclusion of a Republican presidency captures potential regressive redistributive policies not included in public social spending or social tax expenditures. In fact, two of the most regressive tax expenditure programs, the mortgage interest deduction and the deduction for capital gains, are not included in my data set of social tax expenditures. The inclusion of this variable also accounts for the fact that Republican control of the federal government results in a higher social expenditure ratio.

The control variables are divided between the models, with factors that influence the income share of low-wage families in the first model and variables that determine higher income growth for wealthier families in the second model. In model one, I include popular economic and sociological explanations for recent changes to the bottom end of the national income distribution, such as changes in the national immigration rate and changes to the industrial sector of the economy. As the national immigration rate rises, wages for low-income jobs should experience downward pressure from the increased competition among low-skilled workers. In addition, as immigrants flow into the service sector and drive down prices, it allows wealthier citizens to keep more disposable income since they pay less for the same high-end goods and services. Next, the industrial sector in the twentieth century has been responsible for creating good paying jobs for citizens with lower levels of formal education and manufacturing skills. Therefore, any decrease in the proportion of manufacturing jobs in the overall economy might cause an increase in income inequality as low-skilled workers get laid off, fight for fewer jobs, have to enter retraining activities, or take other jobs in different sectors of the economy. Altogether, I expect that in the first model an increase to the social expenditure ratio will result in higher income inequality even when controlling for party control of government, immigration, and changes in the manufacturing sector.

In the second model, I control for trends that exacerbate the incomes of the wealthiest Americans, thereby increasing income inequality. First, I include a variable that controls for changes in the top marginal income tax rate for the wealthiest families. The wealthiest Americans benefited recently from large cuts to their marginal income tax rates that should increase their share of the total national income. During the course of this study, the top marginal rate for the wealthiest households went from 70 percent down to 35 percent. After a cut to the highest marginal tax rate, wealthier families benefit in the following year and each subsequent year. Second, I incorporate a variable that represents the financial sector as a proportion of all domestic economic activity. The deregulation of the financial industry along with increased globalization has increased the profit ceiling for financial institutions and by extension their share of GDP. As the financial sector has grown, more money has been concentrated at the very top of the income distribution. In total, I expect that an increase in the federal social expenditure ratio will cause higher levels of income inequality, all else being equal.

The Social Expenditure Ratio and Changes in U.S. Income Inequality

A change in the modality of social spending causes an increase in the level of income inequality in the United States. Specifically, as the proportion of tax expenditures to total social spending grows, so, too, does the level of income inequality. The first model in Table 6.3 shows that an increase to the social expenditure ratio has both an immediate and a long-term effect on increasing income inequality (a little over 1.01). The two control measures, immigration and the manufacturing sector, are not statistically significant from zero in the short run (although manufacturing is signed in the right direction with income inequality). In addition, Republican control of the presidency is also negatively signed and not statistically significant. In the long-run portion of the model, all of the variables are signed in the right direction and again the social expenditure ratio correlates with an increase in income inequality (although the impact on income inequality is smaller and noisier than the short run relationship). A Republican executive is positively signed with increases in income inequality, but not significant. A decrease in the size of the manufacturing sector significantly relates to higher levels of income inequality. As manufacturing has declined, low-skilled laborers

TABLE 6.3. *The Social Expenditure Ratio and Changes in Income Inequality, 1970–2010*

Independent Variable	T10B10 (1)	T10B10 (2)
Short-Term Effects		
Δ Social Expenditure Ratio	1.03**	1.16**
	(.516)	(.507)
Δ Republican President	−.066	−.126*
	(.083)	(.085)
Δ Manufacturing	−7.97	
	(7.70)	
Δ Immigration	−.128	
	(.135)	
Δ Financial Sector		20.11*
		(11.89)
Δ Income Tax Rate		−.006
		(.007)
Long-Term Effects		
Social Expenditure Ratio$_{t-1}$	.462*	.481
	(.351)	(.484)
Republican President$_{t-1}$	.038	.052
	(.061)	(.064)
Manufacturing$_{t-1}$	−7.53***	
	(2.23)	
Immigration$_{t-1}$	.069	
	(.123)	
Financial Sector$_{t-1}$		23.51***
		(6.54)
Income Tax Rate$_{t-1}$		−.001
		(.004)
Long-Run Multiplier		
Social Expenditure Ratio	1.01**	1.02
	(.494)	(.883)
Error Correction Rate		
Income Inequality (T10B10)$_{t-1}$	−.489***	−.467***
	(.123)	(.128)
Constant	5.87***	3.02**
	(1.50)	(1.05)
Adj. R^2	.325	.295

Note: N = 40, Entries are OLS estimates with standard errors in parentheses. One-Tailed Significance Levels: *p ≤ .10, **p ≤ .05, ***p ≤ .001.

have had to accept pay cuts in the industry or even have been struc-
turally shifted out to the service industry. An increase in the immigration
rate, in the long term, is positively associated with more income inequality
although not statistically significant from zero. Altogether, the movement
of federal social policy from discretionary spending on public programs
to tax expenditures for private social benefits has an observable impact
on changes in the level of income inequality even when controlling for
political party power, immigration rates, and changes in the role of manufacturing in the economy.

Model two in Table 6.3 shows that an increase to the social expenditure
ratio results in higher levels of income inequality – in the short term –
even when controlling for political party control of government, and
factors known to increase the income share of the rich. An increase in
the social expenditure ratio produces a larger gap between the income
share of the wealthiest and poorest households than in the first model.
The long-run multiplier for social spending is signed in the right direction
but not statistically significant from zero.[15] Finally, an increase in the
social expenditure ratio produces long term growth in the income gap
between the wealthiest and poorest families in both models (although the
long-run multiplier is only significant in the first model). The results of the
two models provide evidence, unsurprisingly, that when tax expenditures
increase at a faster pace than discretionary social spending the income
share of the top 10 percent grows larger and the national income share
of the poorest 10 percent of households goes down. Since a household's
income level relates to its economic security, as the social expenditure
ratio increases both government financial assistance for social insurance
and federal money are distributed upward, so that wealthier families
experience a twofold gain in income security.[16]

The economic and policy controls are both signed in the right direction.
Yet only the growth of the financial sector measure is statistically significant and this variable reports the largest coefficients in both models. The

---

[15] I ran a model with all the control variables and the social expenditure ratio. The social
expenditure ratio is positively signed and significant in both the short and the long
runs although all the control variables report too much variance to rise to the level of
significance.

[16] In the appendix, I report two models with the Gini coefficient as the dependent variable.
In the baseline model, the social expenditure ratio correlates with a positive increase in
the Gini coefficient in both the short and the long run. In the second model with more
controls, the social expenditure ratio positively correlates with a higher Gini coefficient
in the long run.

financial sector doubled during this time period from representing just over 4 percent of GDP to accounting for over 9 percent of GDP by 2010. The profits for Wall Street firms and the large bonuses enjoyed by their highly paid workers are, by now, legend, so it comes as no surprise that the growth of the financial sector is so highly correlated with the recent rise in economic inequality. The top marginal income tax rate is related to income inequality in the direction we would expect (when the top rate goes down, income inequality goes up), yet there's too much variance in the reported coefficient for the relationship to be statistically significant. A switch from a Democratic to Republican president results in an immediate decrease in the T10B10 ratio, however, in the long run the relationship is positive yet not statistically significant from zero. This surprising short-term relationship is probably due to two reasons. First, Republican presidents George H. W. Bush and George W. Bush presided over two recessions during their terms in office. These recessions in the early 1990s, 2001, and 2007 when the income share of the top 10 percent took a bigger hit relative to other income cohorts.[17] Next, it is possible that many of the party control effects are being soaked up by the inclusion of the social expenditure ratio and the regressive distribution effects it represents.

Conclusion

In conclusion, increases in social tax expenditures at the expense of direct spending redistribute national income from the working class to wealthier households in both the near and the long term. This relationship is true even when accounting for partisan control of government, income tax rates, and economic theories of income inequality. In putting together the empirical analysis from the last two chapters, I have shown that greater Republican control of the federal government produces a higher level of social tax expenditures and less discretionary social spending and that these social policy changes, as represented by the social expenditure ratio, correlate with rising levels of income inequality. One of the important political implications of these results is that political parties can target their socioeconomic constituencies through choosing public policies with clear distributive effects. Previous studies have shown that

---

[17] Since this model has forty observations, I ran a baseline model with just two variables: the social expenditure ratio and Republican control of the White House. The main results are the same as those in Table 6.3, with an increase in the social expenditure ratio correlating with an increase in the level of income inequality.

increased spending for public social programs reduces income inequality (Bartels 2008, Kelly 2009); however, the inclusion of social tax expenditures highlights a mechanism whereby the federal government distributes income toward wealthier households all in the name of economic security. The irony for many social tax expenditure programs, such as the ones for private retirement accounts, is that citizens who enjoy the most economic security also receive the largest federal subsidies. In an era of tight budgets, large deficits, and constant demands to cut Social Security, the U.S. government spends hundreds of billions of dollars every year to subsidize the retirement security of the least vulnerable citizens. While the wealthy have experienced steady and significant gains in their income, middle-class incomes have been stagnant for fifteen years, and middle-class families have lost the ability to save and create wealth through the values of their homes and due to increases in household debt. It would be unjustifiable in normal economic times for the federal government to annually allocate hundreds of billions of federal funds to the wealthiest citizens but this level of regressive distribution during a period of extreme income inequality defies logic.

Next, while the analysis here shows that an increase in social tax expenditures influences the rise of income inequality, it is hard to imagine that the rise of tax expenditures has not contributed to the growing gap in wealth inequality as well. Piketty (2014) has argued that when the rate of return on capital income grows faster than the rate of return from economic growth there will be a corresponding concentration of wealth. Tax expenditures along with rate structures privilege capital income over wage income in the United States. The analysis here does not contain the tax expenditure for capital gains, the home mortgage interest deductions, and estates – all subsidies that help wealthy families pass down huge amounts of wealth to their children. The large numbers of tax expenditures that subsidize capital income have encouraged businesses, financial institutions, and wealthier individuals to transfer as much income as possible over to capital, assets, and investments. And while income inequality has grown tremendously in the United States, wealth inequality has grown faster and is higher than income inequality. The high level of wealth inequality (that can be passed from generation to generation) is the largest threat to reduced social mobility in America now and moving forward. It would be important for future studies to examine the politics of tax expenditures in contributing to the rise of wealth inequality in America.

Finally, my analysis of social tax expenditures and changes in the level of income inequality provides a tangible policy mechanism for what other scholars have categorized as market effects or market conditioning. The best analyses of the political effects on income inequality, to date, show that majority parties' main effect on changes in the national income distribution is found in pre-tax and transfer income patterns (Bartels 2008, Kelly 2009). One of the main puzzles of these works is why political party control of the federal government has more influence on pre-tax and transfer income inequality than it does on post-tax and transfer inequality (which takes into account public social spending). The answer has been that a political party's general fiscal policy determines certain macroeconomic outcomes and that these patterns of unemployment and economic growth are then translated into income distribution patterns that either benefit the working class under Democratic presidents or the wealthy under Republican presidents. I would argue that the direct role of public policy on patterns of income distribution has been vastly understated because changes to tax policy, which disproportionately impact the rich, have not been formally theorized, operationalized, and tested. There is more work needed so that we may fully evaluate the impact over time of changes in federal and state-level tax policies on the rise of income inequality in America.

Appendix to Chapter 6

Baseline Model of the Social Expenditure Ratio and Changes in Income Inequality, 1970–2010

Variables	Income Inequality	Income Inequality
Social Expenditure Ratio	1.14*	
	(.512)	
Social Expenditure Ratio (-EITC)		1.06*
		(.527)
Republican President	−.080	−.079
	(.087)	(.088)
Constant	.046	.048
	(.029)	(.029)
Adjusted R²	0.062	0.050

N = 40, ARIMA specifications with standard errors in parentheses.
Two-Tailed Significance Levels: *p ≤ .05.

Republican Power and Changes in Income Inequality, 1970–2010

	Gini Coefficient	Gini Coefficient
Short-Term (Immediate) Effects		
Δ Social Expenditure Ratio$_t$	.016*	.010
	(.012)	(.013)
Δ Republican President$_t$	−.005*	−.005*
	(.002)	(.002)
Δ Manufacturing$_t$		−.035
		(.220)
Δ Finance$_t$		.283
		(.350)
Long-Term Effects		
Social Expenditure Ratio$_{t-1}$	.017**	.018**
	(.008)	(.008)
Republican President$_{t-1}$	−.001	−.003*
	(.001)	(.001)
Manufacturing$_{t-1}$		−.035
		(.100)
Finance$_{t-1}$		.681**
		(.358)
Error Correction Rate		
Gini Coefficient$_{t-1}$	−.130**	−.424***
	(.059)	(.141)
Constant	.050*	.165**
	(.022)	(.075)
Adj. R^2	.102	.161

Note: N = 40. Entries are OLS estimates with standard errors in parentheses.
One-Tailed Significance Levels: ***p ≤ .01, **p ≤ .05, *p ≤ .10.

7

The Implications of the Divided American Welfare State

In an era of stagnant economic mobility, wage volatility, and rising income inequality – the ability of America's social system to provide citizens economic security has never been more important. A traditional welfare state is a system in which the disproportionate amount of government benefits are directed to the country's most vulnerable populations as a means to produce more equitable distributions of wealth and income security. The United States has not created a traditional welfare state. In every major area of U.S. social policy, there are examples of programs designed to help the very poor and programs that accrue the most financial support to the rich (with the middle class being partially served by both public and private programs). For example, take the policy area of retirement security. The federal government kept 22 million elderly Americans above the poverty line in 2012 through the replacement rate structure of the Social Security program and then turned around and handed out over $200 billion worth of subsidies for private pension plans to the country's wealthiest families. In health care, the federal government spent over $200 billion on Medicaid to assist the poor but also subsidized employment-based health care insurance for wealthier workers to the tune of over $120 billion. And in the area of education, while students and families making under $20,000 a year receive the majority of benefits from federal Pell grants for higher education, at the other end of the income spectrum households that make between $100,000 and $200,000 accrue around 50 percent of the total benefits from the college tuition and fee tax deductions (Congressional Budget Office 2012; Joint Committee on Taxation 2012). The United States has an expensive and complicated social welfare state that offers a patchwork of programs for the poor, a number of public and private programs that benefit the middle class, and a collection of tax subsidies that disproportionately provide benefits and money to the rich. I have shown here that partisan politics determines how social insurance is provided, who benefits, and, consequently, the direction of income inequality in America.

In the following sections, I examine the political and policy implications of the partisan politics of the divided social welfare state. I discuss how this study informs extant theories of American democracy, perceptions of class warfare, and our understanding of party politics. Next, I consider how the partisan patterns of the divided welfare state limit the extent of the government's redistributive efforts, provide ineffectual economic security, and distort the debate surrounding the national debt. Second, I discuss how the theoretical argument and statistical analysis in this book contributes to existing theories of social policy. The role of the Republican Party in social welfare policy challenges existing comparative welfare state theories, modifies theories of retrenchment, and adds a new dimension to existing critiques of public policy. Finally, I apply the partisan theory of the divided welfare state to understanding the politics surrounding the passage of the Affordable Care Act (ACA). My theory helps explain why Democrats fought for a public option and expanded Medicaid as a major component of the ACA. While the bill also contains a number of new social tax expenditures, these target lower-income workers and their employers as a means to level the health care playing field between low-income and high-income workers.

The Political and Policy Implications of the Divided Social Welfare State

One of the main goals of this book was to create and test a partisan theory of social policy that accounts for polarization and policy tools. The American public has long understood that a vote for the Democratic Party is a vote for increased government social spending targeted toward historically disadvantaged populations. However, a vote for the Republican Party is not necessarily a vote for smaller government. While the Republican Party has steadfastly over the years supported the private market, this support goes beyond cutting government spending and reducing income tax rates. The Republican Party actively promotes private market policy solutions through the use of tax subsidies and other forms of off-budget spending. These forms of spending have the same characteristics as public spending in that they change the incentives of private actors in the economy, result in the government picking winners and losers, and are paid for by increasing taxes, reducing spending, increasing borrowing, or higher deficits. Tax expenditures help the Republican Party solve an important puzzle for their particular form of distributive politics. In particular, Republicans can use tax expenditures to distribute federal money to unpopular but important constituencies such as large corporations and the rich. For example, the 529 college savings account is portrayed by some as an important tax expenditure program that helps middle-class families send their children to college. However, around 70 percent of the total benefits from this program are distributed to households making over $200,000 a year and will cost the federal government $1 billion over the next ten years. The coupling of a tax subsidy with the goal of financing college (both wildly popular with the public) hides the program's target group (rich families who are unpopular).

It is hard to overstate the importance of tax policy and tax expenditures to understanding Republican activism. The metrics used by political scientists and the media to gauge policy and government activism are a byproduct of the mid-twentieth century and narrowly focus on large, government-run social programs and appropriations spending. The policy activism of modern Republicans occurs on the revenue side of the budget process in the tax code. President George W. Bush along with a Republican Congress passed into law a number of tax bills that created tax expenditure programs for the following policy areas: economic development, natural disaster relief, energy production, national defense, unemployment, housing, education, and prescription drugs. The use of tax expenditures for private programs helps the Republican Party coordinate different factions within their coalition (such as small government conservatives, supporters who favor government support of religious activity, and businesses who want government assistance). For example, the Supreme Court's ruling in *Arizona Christian School Tuition Organization v. Winn et al.* claimed that tax expenditures are not a form of government spending and therefore could be used by governments to subsidize religious schools without violating the separation of church and state.

Next, the government's substantial financial commitment to subsidizing social insurance for the rich is another data point supporting the notion that economic elites hold sway over United States' politics (Bartels 2008, Gilens 2012). The result of more Republican power is less spending for the poor and increased benefits for the rich. In turn, the Democratic Party when in power increases the tax burden on the rich to pay for increased spending for its multiple constituencies. While any close observer of Washington politics understands these patterns of partisan distribution to be true, my examination here conceptualizes and demonstrates the spending mechanisms used by the two parties to alter the direction of income inequality. The influence of elite public opinion and business interest groups may help explain why the United States spends more on both social tax expenditures and private welfare than any other modern nation in the world. If policymakers give more weight to the policy preferences of the rich over the middle and working classes then we would expect social policy to move in the direction of increased tax subsidies at the expense of broad-based public programs. It could also be that as the U.S. Congress becomes comprised disproportionately of wealthy professionals then the social policy agenda tilts toward the preferences of economic elites (Carnes 2013). In addition, the creation of tax subsidies for private social welfare allows policymakers to cut banking, finance, and health care interest groups into the federal subsidy apparatus while being able to meet the mass public's demand for social insurance (Morgan and Campbell 2011). Finally, since tax expenditures offer more money to the rich they contribute to the public impression that both the tax system, specifically, and the federal government, more generally, are abused by the wealthiest Americans for their economic self-interests.

The divided social system distorts the national discussion about the relationship between class and public policy. The most visible aspects of the American public policy infrastructure are the progressive federal income tax system and regressive public social welfare programs such as welfare, and Medicaid. These two overemphasized features of the policy system result in the commonly held perception that the rich pay for government and the poor take from it. Yet this misguided view undercounts both how much the middle and working classes pay in federal taxes and how many benefits the rich receive as a result of federal tax expenditures and subsidies. The federal tax system is only slightly progressive (once payroll and other taxes are included) and social benefits are much less regressive once tax expenditures are included in calculating government welfare.

At the height of the 2012 Presidential election campaign, a video was released of Republican candidate Mitt Romney speaking at a private fundraising event in which Governor Romney said,

there are 47 percent who are with him (President Obama), who are dependent upon government, who believe that they are victims, who believe that government has a responsibility to care for them, who believe that they are entitled to health care, to food, to housing, to you name it . . . these are people who pay no income tax. Forty-seven percent of Americans pay no income tax. So our message of low taxes doesn't connect. *New York Times* 2012.

In 2013, 86 percent of the population paid federal taxes and the majority of these taxpayers paid more in payroll taxes than they did in income taxes (Williams 2013). Additionally, the vast majority of state governments have regressive tax systems so taking into account all taxes – federal, state, and local – paints a much different picture of which groups bear the burden of financing government programs. And not only does most of the population pay federal taxes, but 96 percent of the public has recently received some government benefit either through the use of public programs or federal tax expenditures (Mettler and Sides 2012). The reality is that everyone pays (through federal, state, and local taxes) and everyone takes in America, whether it is through a direct government check or a tax subsidy.

Relatedly, a social state that divides beneficiaries by socioeconomic class reinforces the inequities that exist in the private economy. As an example, the working class relies almost entirely on Social Security and Medicare for their retirement security while the wealthy use these public programs as supplements to their assets, capital income, private investments, 401ks, and employment-sponsored health insurance, all of which are subsidized by the federal government. So for wealthier retirees the progressive structure of public programs is integrated and offset with the regressive nature of social tax expenditures, while poorer retirees are wholly dependent upon the continued solvability and largesse of public programs. The hundreds of billions spent annually on providing economic security to the richest Americans could be better spent on national defense, tax cuts for the middle class, updating an outdated social safety net, or adding solvency to Social Security or Medicare. Not only are the distributional patterns of social tax expenditures illogical in an era of runaway inequality, many of these programs would never survive an open debate on the floor of the House of Representatives.

Consider the following example: a Congress member walks onto the floor of the House and offers the following proposal. The proposal is for a new retirement savings plan that would cost over $100 billion a year and allocate $80 billion of the program's benefits to families making more than $105,000 while the remaining $20 billion would be distributed among the middle class and no money from the program would be given to the poor. Even the casual student of American politics knows that this bill has no chance of passing into law. Yet this program already exists in the tax code in the form of a tax expenditure program that excludes contributions to employer-provided pension plans. And while most Americans are supportive of government funding for specific social programs, it is hard to envision a majority of the public favoring a government-run social welfare program that distributes more money to the wealthiest 20 percent of households than all other households combined. The ability of legislators to frame these programs as universal subsidies for popular social goals or tax relief hides the highly regressive distribution of federal dollars that we know from surveys is unpopular with the public. The cumulative result is that the media and public exaggerates the amount of taxes the wealthy pay and minimizes the amount of benefits the rich receive from the federal government. Overall, the mass public does not have an accurate picture of who pays and who benefits from the federal government.

There are also important policy effects that stem from the politics of the divided social system. First, the divided social welfare state is ineffective at assuaging the growth of income inequality. This ineffectiveness is because of both the limited impact of public social programs and the relative size of the private social system. Traditional welfare states produce large redistributive effects that reduce income inequality. And while many industrial nations have experienced sharp increases in national income inequality, no nation's social safety net has done less to stem the rising tide of income inequality than that of the United States. The public side of the social system is relatively small with limited benefits and therefore does not create much of an income floor for most Americans. The public system primarily assists the elderly, the unemployed, the poor, and veterans. In 2012, around 14 percent of the U.S. population was over 65 and an additional 14 percent was below the poverty line (and obviously there is some overlap). If we consider these two groups as the main beneficiaries of public social welfare then only a relatively small percentage of the U.S. population has access to public income assistance in any given year. In short, a mildly progressive federal income tax system combined with limited public benefits does not produce large enough income redistributive effects to counter the hypergrowth of rising inequality.

Next, the large U.S. private social system reinforces the inequities that exist in the private economy, where the quality of social benefits is often related to an individual's income. In addition, the number and value of social tax expenditures greatly reduce the progressivity of the federal tax system with the implication being that wealthier citizens have a lower effective tax rate in large part due to their use of all the deductions, exclusions, and exemptions available in the tax code. Therefore, the hundreds of tax expenditure programs in the tax code and the increased value of these programs have helped erode the progressive features of the income tax system, resulting in the federal government having a smaller impact on reducing post-tax and transfer income inequality over time. The result is that the federal government collects less revenue for public social programs (and everything else). In addition, the level of social tax expenditures in the United States negates a significant portion of the redistributive effects of public social spending. Historically, social spending has been disproportionately targeted at society's most vulnerable populations as a means to reduce inequality. However, I have shown here that an increase in tax expenditures at the expense of traditional social spending drives up income inequality. So not only do U.S. public social programs do less than those of most other countries to reduce market inequality, but the size and growth of social tax expenditures for private welfare increase inequality. This is increasingly not just an American story. The austerity movements in Europe and the increased use of tax expenditures by all types of governments have moved more welfare states toward reliance on private markets.

Next, for all the money both public and private that the country spends on social services and insurance, the government's financial commitment has not produced better outcomes for American citizens in reducing health risks, gaining access to high quality education, lowering poverty rates, or achieving a higher level of overall economic security. The divided social system creates a world-class health care, pension, and education system for the wealthy and a patchwork of public and private programs, with varying effectiveness, for the middle and working classes. In short, for a country that spends one out of every four dollars on social welfare programs, there is not a lot to show for it. The divided American welfare state just may be one of the most inefficient social systems in the world. In 2012, the federal government spent a combined (traditional spending plus tax expenditures) $1 trillion dollars on health care but according to the think tank Commonwealth Fund, the U.S. health system is one of the worst in the world in terms of efficiency and access. In fact, as the costs of employer-based health care and pension tax expenditures has gone up the percentage of workers covered under these programs have gone down and businesses have passed more of the risk to the individual worker

(Hacker 2004).[1] Proponents of social tax expenditures would argue that these programs are designed to encourage citizens to save and plan for their own economic security. However, the stagnation of wages, the rise of household debt, and the recent collapse of the housing market decimated the general public's ability to build up their savings and take advantage of these programs. As more individual tax expenditures have been added to the tax code; the savings rate in the United States has gone down. The federal tax code is comprised of programs that reward the rich for saving disposable income that they were already saving to begin with and these same programs have had no measurable effect on the behavior of the middle- and working-class citizens in saving for their own retirement, health care, and education.

Next, policymakers' utilization of "off-budget" subsidies distorts the politics surrounding national debates about the size of government and the national debt. During the Obama administration, there have been numerous partisan debates about whether or not to raise the country's debt ceiling, resulting in a federal government shutdown in 2013. The use of "off-budget" spending allows Republican legislators to call for cuts in government spending and deficit reduction (i.e., budgetary spending for the poor) without having to stop their distribution of federal funds to supporters through the tax code. Furthermore, the Republican pattern of increasing social tax expenditures while lowering discretionary social spending provides public credibility to Republicans' distorted claim that they are shrinking the size of government and taking action to address the national debt. A political strategy to control the national deficit that relies mainly on cuts in federal social spending disproportionately hits the poor since the majority of social programs aimed at the poor are part of the appropriations process. It is easier for Republicans to call for deficit reform and action on the national debt because their party's electoral coalition does not feel the pinch in their pocketbooks from cuts to discretionary spending. Since the Republican Party is considered to be more fiscally disciplined and better at reducing the national debt by the mass public, the party can run deficits through the tax code when they are in the majority and then turn around and call for deficit reduction when they are the minority party.

---

[1] If we include housing as part of social policy, the mortgage interest deduction costs the federal government hundreds of billions of dollars yet has been proven to incentivize families into buying larger homes, not first homes.

Democrats and Republicans are both responsible for adding to the size of the national debt. Since the Tax Reform Act of 1986, tax expenditures have grown in number and value every year and there has been no serious effort at tax reform. The most widely publicized effort at deficit reform came from The National Commission on Fiscal Responsibility and Reform, otherwise known as the Simpson-Bowles group. The Simpson-Bowles plan includes a "Zero Plan," which eliminated all tax expenditures except for the child tax credit and the EITC. The revenue generated from these cuts would be dedicated to deficit reduction and reductions in tax rates. In 2011, The Committee for a Responsible Federal Budget conducted a side-by-side analysis of thirty-two proposals for deficit and debt reduction. The only plans that did not call for a massive elimination or reduction of tax expenditures were Grover Norquist's Americans for Tax Reform, the National Taxpayers Union, Senator Rand Paul's 2011 Budget, the CATO Institute, and the highly conservative Republican Study Committee. Any political debate about reducing the national debt that does not address reducing and eliminating tax expenditures alongside entitlement reform is not a serious discussion about controlling the nation's debt.

Implications for Theories of the Welfare States and Public Policy

How does the analysis here contribute to existing theories of social welfare policy? The partisan division over public social spending and private subsidies has implications for understanding the U.S. welfare regime in a comparative perspective. In Esping-Andersen's seminal work (1990) he develops a typology of welfare states ranging from liberal to corporatist to social-democratic. The United States has long been considered a liberal welfare state that promotes individualism and where the social system is dominated by the free market. Liberal welfare states are known to provide minimal government-funded social benefits to citizens (especially the poor) and therefore produce small redistribution effects. The analysis here shows that the degree to which the U.S. is a liberal welfare regime at any one point in time is, in part, a function of political party power. Democrats and Republicans push and pull the social system toward more or less reliance on the state or the market. So while the U.S. welfare regime is liberal, the degree to which it is liberal ebbs and flows over time with changes in party control of government. However, Republicans have been more successful in pulling the divided social system toward the private sector than the Democrats have been with pushing it back toward the public side. This trend is in part a function of Republicans being more concerned with how benefits are delivered and Democrats being motivated by who benefits from social programs. The cumulative result has been a deepening of the liberal welfare regime over time punctuated by some efforts to extend popular public programs (i.e., the Medicaid expansion under the ACA).

Second, the liberal typology is defined by a government's lack of reliance on pubic programs, which restricts its ability to assist the poor. In the United States, the sharp increase in refundable tax credits has been a mechanism for policymakers to distribute federal money to the poor. The use of tax expenditures such as the EITC could make government assistance to the poor more palatable to the mass public and therefore politically sustainable over time. The bipartisan growth of the earned income tax credit (EITC) along with the Democrats' expansion of Medicaid as part of ACA has greatly expanded the role of the federal government in financially supporting poor families in America. The EITC is now one of the largest poverty assistance programs in the United States, costing around $60 billion in 2013. The EITC is credited with pulling over 6 million citizens out of poverty, half of whom are children (Jones 2014). And while the increased federal spending on the poor has not lowered the poverty level, it has softened the effects of stagnant income growth for working class families. While the two parties support the EITC program for different reasons, future expansions of the EITC seem to be the most likely federal effort at reducing poverty. The EITC has been and will continue to be the politically preferred mode of poverty assistance since the program includes work incentives and most of the spending for the programs occurs outside the budget. It is possible that the success of the EITC paves the way for a broader system of negative income taxes that would function as a basic guaranteed income in exchange for reforms or the elimination of Temporary Aid to Needy Families (TANF).

The analysis here also has implications for studies of welfare state retrenchment. The literature on social welfare retrenchment examines how high-profile, conservative efforts to reduce the welfare state largely failed (e.g., Pierson 1994, 1996). Pierson, for example, argues that the welfare's state resilience was primarily due to widespread public support for specific public social programs and institutional inertia. The cornerstones of the public American welfare state are undoubtedly popular with the general public. However, the inclusion of social tax expenditures changes some of the story surrounding welfare state retrenchment (see Hacker 2004). While the Republican Party was not successful in its attempts to scale back Social Security and Medicare, the analysis here shows that Republicans were able to expand large existing social tax expenditure programs and add new ones that grew the private social system while cutting discretionary social spending.

The government's role in subsidizing the growth of the private social state has a number of implications for retrenchment theories. First, while the popularity of public social programs has contributed to their resilience, so too has the popularity of social tax expenditure programs contributed to their protection and expansion. A majority of working-aged Americans today are enrolled in employment-based retirement and health care plans and the social tax expenditures that finance them are popular with the mass public (Faricy and Ellis 2014). These programs have grown substantially over time. The three main tax expenditure programs for employment-based benefits cost the U.S. government over $1.2 trillion dollars from 2010 to 2014. Moreover, the perception among policymakers is that certain social tax expenditure programs are politically untouchable, such as tax provisions for employment-based health care, 401ks, and charitable contributions. It is no coincidence that during the last major tax reform in 1986, many of the largest individual social tax expenditures were saved from the chopping block while business tax breaks were eliminated. Not only are the major social tax expenditures perceived as popular with the public, but they are also protected by powerful interests both within the industries they subsidize and by party leaders on the tax-writing committees. Finally, many of the same veto points that protect public programs protect social tax expenditures. Altogether, the tax expenditures that subsidize the private social state have been just as resilient as major public programs. The current divided social welfare state represents a stalemate between two retrenched and government supported systems that are popular for different reasons and with different constituencies.

Next, the increased "layering" of social tax expenditures onto the divided social system puts public social welfare programs at risk in the long run. First, the addition of tax expenditure programs for health care, pensions, and education reduces the demand for expansions to existing programs or new public social benefits. Studies have shown that passage of market-based social welfare reforms in health care and welfare reduced the saliency of these issues for the mass public, and therefore removed the possibility of expanding public welfare from the policy agenda (Morgan and Campbell 2011). Next, the addition of new tax expenditures for private programs expands the private social system and might one day make it easier to eliminate Social Security and Medicare. The stated goal of many conservative reformers is to use tax subsidies to transfer more public money to private programs so that the elimination of public benefits is politically possible. However, recent Republican attempts to use social tax expenditures as a way to convert Social Security and Medicare to more market-based programs have failed. Finally, increased tax expenditures permanently reduce federal revenues now and into the future, putting fiscal strain on public programs. This strategy is, in essence, the "starve the beast" theory in action. The purposeful creation of higher deficits and more debt allows the Republican Party to call for fiscal constraint and spending cuts when Democrats are in power. Therefore, as long as tax expenditures remain "hidden," any attempts at controlling the budget or calls to cut appropriations spending will fall disproportionately on public social programs.

Next, existing theories of public policy could be improved by including tax expenditures and other off-budget policy tools as part of the policy spectrum. As argued here and elsewhere (Bartels 2008, Grossmann and Hopkins 2014), Republicans and Democrats govern in different ways. In an excellent critique of existing policy theories Grossmann and Hopkins (2014) argue that the traditional theories of public policy either deemphasize the role of parties or treat party effects as symmetrical. These omissions are problematic given the rise of political polarization and especially the Republican Party's move to the far right (Grossmann and Hopkins 2014). The authors go on to claim, "Republicans view policy-making as a terrain for pursuing the broad goal of limiting government power – an objective shared in principle by most of the electorate – while Democrats champion particular government initiatives, programs, and regulations that also tend to command majority support among voters" (Grossmann and Hopkins 2014, p. 2). The authors show that the two political parties address the paradox of Ameican public opinion (a majority favoring small government and specific social spending) in different ways. Republicans united around small government conservatism try to thwart legislation and Democrats supported by a collection of interests deliver tangible benefits.

While I agree that extant public policy theories do not account for polarization and important changes to political parties in the American context, the Republican Party's conservatism does not stop their policy activism. I have argued here that Republicans and Democrats respond to calls for smaller government and increased spending by substituting one form of spending for another. In particular, Republicans thread their ideological needle by increasing the level of tax expenditures, which allows policymakers to claim that they are reducing federal revenues, while passing out federal subsidies to specialized interests. Second, the tools of public policy exist along an ideological spectrum and while traditional tools can be considered liberal since they expand the scope of government there is also a collection of conservative policy mechanisms. The exclusion of off-budget spending, grants, loans, and contingent liabilities neglects the main policy tools of the Republican Party. The fact is extant theories of political behavior and political institutions overrepresent liberal policymaking while ignoring the conservative side of the policy spectrum. Not only do public policy theories need to be updated to reflect important political changes, so too do conceptions of what is public policy. The Republican Party cannot hope to stay in power just by reducing the size of the federal government. While citizens may like the idea of smaller government in the abstract, the mass public (including a majority of Republicans) also demands government assistance, especially in the form of social benefits and services. Therefore, the Republican Party must balance reducing the size of government with other goals such as subsidizing business interests, providing tangible goods to their special interests, and implementing "conservative" policy solutions.

Finally, the partisan difference over public spending and tax subsidies for private welfare has implications for issue ownership. The two major political parties select different ratios of tax expenditures to public social spending in ways that reinforce each political party's comparative advantage. Petrocik (1996) presents a theory of issue ownership arguing that political parties in campaigns will emphasize issues on which they are advantaged and their opponents are disadvantaged. Egan (2013) has shown that a political party in power will create more ideologically extreme policies in areas that they "own" in the eyes of the mass public. The mass public has continually reported higher levels of trust for the Democratic Party in handling issues such as health care, Social Security, Medicare, education, and assistance to the poor (Egan 2013). In essence, the Democratic Party owns not only social policy but also the larger concept of using government power to address economic insecurity. While the public has accepted and supported Social Security and Medicare, the Democratic Party has had a harder time creating sustainable public programs in education, health care, and poverty assistance. The Democratic Party's challenge has been to increase federal spending for social welfare without expanding programs so much that they open themselves up to accusations of swelling the size of the federal government. The Democrats' focus has been more on creating and extending benefits to poorer populations through public means if they can, (e.g., Medicaid expansion, federalizing student loans) but also agreeing to tax expenditures during periods of divided government, especially for programs targeted at the working poor.

The Republican Party faces the challenge of having to create social policies in a political environment where Democrats own all the social policy areas. The Republican strategy has been to diminish the importance of social welfare issues by passing private alternatives so as to reduce the saliency of social policy to voters in future elections. The Republican Party will never be trusted more than Democrats to protect large government social programs. Therefore, the Republicans' best political option is to shift the conversation to issues areas they do own, such as taxes and controlling the deficit (Egan 2013). The ownership of these two issues fits well with the party's "starve the beast" strategy. The use of social tax expenditures combines popular policy goals (cheaper health care insurance, tuition support, etc.) with a popular policy tool, tax breaks. If government money for public programs is redirected to promote subsidies for private alternatives or expand the private sector (such as Medicare Part D), then the line that voters can draw between protecting public benefits and the Democratic Party may become weaker over time. As an example, Morgan and Campbell (2011) showed that while the passage of Medicare Part D did not hurt the Democrats' issue ownership of Medicare it did cause a decrease in public demand for a publicly administered prescription drug program. The political implications of Medicare Part D were that the Republican Party was able to create a popular government program that gave money to private pharmaceutical companies while taking away an issue that the Democrats may have used in the future to build their issue ownership advantage in Medicare.

Next, the Republicans' ownership of being trusted to lower the national deficit allows the party to call for cuts in social spending in the name of fiscal responsibility while increasing tax subsidies for private welfare. Since the public trusts the Republican Party to cut spending and keep a lid on the national debt, it allows Republicans to highlight their reductions to budgetary social spending, which assists Democratic constituencies, while their favored form of government patronage can be increased out of the spotlight. If the Republican Party cuts federal revenues through both marginal income rate cuts and more tax breaks without cutting social spending, then it allows their members to criticize the size of government during periods of Democratic control and try to force reductions in appropriations spending. In total, the Democratic

Party favors public social programs, in part, as a way to play to their issue advantages and Republicans promote the use of tax subsidies for private welfare for the same reasons.

The Partisan Theory of the Divided Social State and Health Care Reform

In 2010, President Obama and the Democrats in Congress passed sweeping health care reform formally known as the Patient Protection and Affordable Care Act (PPACA) and informally referred to it as Obamacare. The PPACA is a series of complex arrangements that attempts to reform the existing health care system through extending health care coverage to over 30 million Americans and decelerate health care costs. In this book, I've argued and demonstrated that Democrats, when in power, will alter the balance of power in the divided social system toward the public side as a means to target working-class voters and then pass on these new costs to wealthier voters. This theoretical argument captures the major elements of the Democratic Party's attempts to reform the national health care system. At the core of Obamacare is an effort to increase the number of poorer citizens with health care insurance by expanding Medicaid and revamping the private health insurance market while paying for it with tax increases on the rich and private health care organizations. Since over 80 percent of the country (mostly middle- and upper-income citizens) already had health care insurance in 2009, the federal government's efforts to finance increased health care insurance access disproportionately assisted uninsured groups – constituted mainly of working class citizens, minorities, young adults, and single-parent families (again, all groups that traditionally align with the Democratic Party). The increased costs that accompanied the ACA were targeted at wealthy families and businesses. In the following sections, I apply the partisan theory of the divided social state to the politics of health care reform, which shows the theory's explanatory power as well as revealing some of its limitations.

The Democratic Party's preference for using the public sector as a means to redistribute income and reduce inequality was evident in both its proposals and the final legislation. First, liberal Democrats pushed hard for the inclusion of a "public option" (a Medicare-type program for citizens under 65) that would have competed with private insurance plans. Progressive Democrats understood that their first preference of a single-payer government system would never pass through the legislature so they coalesced around the position of demanding a "public option."[2] While President Obama had campaigned on including a public option as part of health care reform, he realized soon after being elected that including this provision would alienate moderate Democrats and Republicans in the Senate and threaten the White House deals with the American Medical Association (AMA) and the pharmaceutical industry. Many of the Democrats who fought for the public option viewed the idea as much more than a legislative provision. The public option was part of a broader battle to demonstrate to the mass public that the federal government can be effective in assuaging economic insecurity, and, therefore, increase future confidence in the ability of the federal government through public programs to address societal problems. Congressional Republicans organized uniform opposition to the legislation in an effort to make Obamacare a national symbol of big government intrusion, which could be used against the Democrats in the 2010 midterm elections.

While much of the discussion around the health care debate focused on individual mandates, insurance exchanges, and even death panels, the federal government passed a massive expansion to Medicaid. The primary means through which the ACA increased access to health insurance was an expansion of the public health care program for the poor, Medicaid (16 out of the 30 million uninsured).[3] Prior to ACA, Medicaid was restricted to specific poor populations such as the elderly, disabled citizens, pregnant women, and some families with children. The ACA expanded health care access by standardizing and upping the income level to 138 percent of the federal poverty line ($24,344 for a family of three in 2012) and allowing childless adults and all families who means tested into the Medicaid program. In addition, PPACA closes the doughnut hole in Medicare Part D by helping seniors pay for their prescription drugs and this is partially offset by reducing the tax expenditures that go to private health care companies through the Medicare Advantage Plan. Young people, who overwhelmingly supported President Obama in the 2008 election, are allowed to stay on their parents' insurance until they are twenty-six and can qualify for Medicaid for the first time. The combined effect of these programs was to tilt the divided health care system a little more toward the public side.

---

[2] There were two public options: a strong version that would harness the power of Medicare pricing and a weak version that would just inject the government as an insurer in the private marketplace.

[3] Although Medicaid is not a purely public program since some administration is contracted out to private firms.

Not only did the ACA expand health care access to the working and middle classes, but it was paid for by eliminating tax deductions and raising taxes on the rich and businesses that profit from the health industry. The ACA included the following revenue-raising measures to help offset the increased cost of federally funded health care: an additional 0.9 percent tax increase on income over $250,000, capital gains tax increase, increased taxes on insurance companies, a new tax on the manufacturing of nongeneric drugs, a new tax on medical device manufacturers, large employers (over 50) being required to insure employees or pay a fee, tax increases on Blue Cross/Blue Shield, elimination of the tax expenditure for the Medicare Part D doughnut hole, a new tax on tanning salons, and establishment of a 40 percent excise tax on "Cadillac" health insurance plans. In addition, there were changes to medical deduction thresholds that limit the amount citizens may deduct from a number of health tax expenditure programs. Altogether, the Democratic Party used social policy as a means to allocate monetary and health benefits to demographic groups that are traditional party supporters at the expense of higher taxes to wealthier groups that vote for and support the Republican Party. Obamacare will allocate close to $900 billion dollars in direct spending and subsidies for the purpose of helping people and companies pay for new insurance; it tilts the balance of the insurance market in ways that equalize access between white-collar workers in large companies and blue-collar workers in smaller businesses and it constructs a federal regulatory scaffold that allows for the possibility of a more centralized health system in the future.

While Democrats did expand Medicaid and raised taxes on the rich, they also increased the number of tax expenditures for private health care. The ACA was designed to use the Medicaid expansion to provide health insurance to those families closest to the poverty line and then use tax subsidies for those families with income between 133 and 400 percent above the federal poverty line. A citizen or family that buys health insurance through the new exchanges will have a subsidy paid directly to their new provider so as to reduce their premium and out-of-pocket costs. The inclusion of subsidies for health care in the bill demonstrates that while Democrats may have a preference for public spending, it is a soft preference when tax expenditures can be used to assist working-class constituencies and gain some support from conservative interests.

There were a number of strategic reasons that President Obama and the Democrats used new tax expenditures for expanding access to the health care market. First, President Obama campaigned on bipartisan-ship and wanted to reach out to Republican legislators and conservative interests by designing a bill that heavily subsidized private health indus-tries. Second, the White House promised various health care lobbies that in exchange for tighter regulation, the industry would have access to new customers. Therefore, President Obama included the individual mandate along with substantial tax subsidies for employers, employees, and citi-zens buying on the individual market in the final bill. The support (or lack of a coordinated attack) for Obamacare from private health care organi-zations was gained, in part, through the promise that the federal reform would use the tax code to subsidize millions of new customers through the employment-based system and not move the divided health system too far in the public direction. Third, Democrats were very concerned about putting forth health care reform that could be directly attacked as a massive increase in the size and scope of government, especially coming after an $800 billion stimulus package passed one year earlier. The inclusion of tax expenditures guarded the President and Congres-sional Democrats against Republican attacks that they were drastically expanding the reach of government into the health care market or lay-ing a foundation for a single-payer system. Yet, the rise of the Tea Party movement showed that even the reliance on tax expenditures did not stop some groups from treating Obamacare as a massive increase in the pub-lic sector. Finally, President Obama and the Congressional Democrats also used new tax expenditure programs to increase low-income worker access to the health care system. As was discussed previously, prior to the individual mandate the workers who were most likely to be offered and enrolled in the employment-based plans were wealthier professionals in large companies. The extension of tax subsidies to both small businesses and the working poor was an effort by the federal government to level the private health insurance field between blue-collar and white-collar workers.

In 2011, the Republican Party offered a health care plan designed to counter the PPACA called the "Path to Prosperity," which was authored by Representative Paul Ryan. The Ryan Plan would reduce federal spend-ing on Medicare, Medicaid, and the State Children's Health Insurance Program (SCHIP) as a means to balance the budget by 2040. The biggest savings would come from changes to Medicare. First, the Ryan Plan changes the basic structure of Medicare from a defined benefits pro-gram to a federal subsidy system that would be used by the elderly to buy private health care insurance. Starting in 2022, new Medicare beneficiaries would have the federal government make direct payments to private health insurance companies for around $8,000 (this amount is capped over time and adjusted for age and income). These vouchers serve the same interests as tax expenditures, which is to use federal spending to support and subsidize the private market. The Congressional Budget Office (CBO) predicts that under the Ryan Plan the average out-of-pocket expenses for the elderly would more than double. For example, a current Medicare beneficiary pays about 22 percent of his or her Social Security income toward medical expenses; under the Ryan Plan the expectation is that a Medicare beneficiary would have to pay 49 percent of his or her Social Security income toward health care – a 27-point increase in personal costs for the elderly. In addition, the CBO estimates that under the Ryan Plan federal spending on Medicaid, SCHIP, and other federal medical subsidies would be cut by more than 75 percent relative to the current baseline projections (Congressional Budget Office 2011). Altogether, the Ryan Plan drastically reduces the direct role of the federal government in health care while using federal subsidies to grow the private health care market.

The current partisan politics of social policy are a result of both political parties having reached their long-term goals over taxes and social spending. Republicans want to lower federal taxes and Democrats want an American social welfare state. They both have won. The effective tax rate for the wealthiest Americans has never been so low and the level of social spending has never been so high. Democrats and Republicans have given the public what it has demanded for half of a century, which is more government spending and lower taxes. However, Republicans will not be able to substantially reduce federal taxes in the future unless there are major changes in the structure of Social Security, Medicare, and Medicaid. Similarly, Democrats will not be able to add programs to the social welfare state without serious changes to the federal tax system. The important issue going forward is not how to break the partisan stalemate or the degree to which the divided welfare state tilts toward the private versus the public sector, but whether the United States government can create a social safety net that meets the income security needs of its people in a modern and globalized economy.

The analysis here suggests a number of changes that would result in a more open policy process and potentially more representative social policy outcomes. First, one method for restraining federal government spending would be to formally place tax expenditures alongside direct spending in a portfolio for each policy area. This procedure would allow policymakers to identify redundancies and better evaluate the efficiency and efficacy of all government spending. Former Federal Reserve Chairman Alan Greenspan, representatives from the General Accounting Office (GAO), and representatives of the CBO have all appeared before Congress and requested that tax expenditures be included in the formal budgeting process as a way both to reduce government spending and to achieve more efficiency. There have been numerous legislative attempts to operationally equalize tax expenditures to direct spending measures in the budget process. Some examples include the Congressional Budget and Impoundment Act of 1974, which required the annual reporting of tax expenditures, and the Budget Enforcement Act of 1990 (BEA), which mandated that direct spending and tax expenditures be treated as equivalent for the purpose of setting spending limits under the pay-as-you-go requirement (PAYGO). If tax expenditures were placed alongside public spending in policy portfolios then when the federal government annually determined spending on old-age pensions, for example, policymakers would examine Social Security alongside the numerous tax expenditure programs for private pensions. If policymakers traded off expanded social tax expenditures at the expense of public social spending, at least in this system it would be in light of day.

Second, a proposal that has floated around think tanks for decades would have the federal government send each household each year an itemized list of their taxes paid and benefits received, including tax subsidies. We know that information can help people better understand their self-interests and therefore make better personal decisions. The American voter, armed with a household cost-benefit ratio of federal services and programs, would be more likely to connect his or her economic interests to candidates and policies. In short, a better conversation at the national level about the costs and benefits of public policy might start with a more honest accounting provided to voters about their real contributions to and benefits from the federal system. Finally, the U.S. federal government could reform the tax system so that there is a more visible line between the taxes that citizens pay and the goods and services they receive. The average voter suffers from myopia and misconceptions about the distributive effects of social policy and tax policy that at times result in perplexing policy outcomes, such as public support for eliminating the estate tax (Bartels 2008). If, for example, payroll taxes were tied to the costs of Medicare this policy arrangement would provide valuable information to voters about the relationship between health care costs and government revenue.[4] This type of tax system would not only help citizens learn about the workings of public policy but potentially control health care spending by making the costs of insurance visible to the average voter. Another alternative put forward by Robert Shiller is indexing income tax rates to the rate of income inequality so that when inequality rises so too would the top marginal income tax rates.

The pace and level of income inequality in the United States is at an all-time high. The rise of inequality is producing inequities in education levels, health outcomes, wages, and reducing the nation's economic growth. Therefore, the reduction of income inequality is increasingly becoming a public good in and of itself. And while the federal government is not able to stop globalization or stem the tide of technological advancement there are sensible steps that can be taken to reduce the amount of welfare given to the wealthy and provide a stronger safety net to America's most vulnerable populations.

[4] Len Burman of the Urban Institute's Tax Policy Center has proposed this idea.

References

Abramowitz, Alan I. and Kyle L. Saunders. 1998. "Ideological Realignment in the U.S. Electorate." *The Journal of Politics* 60(3): 634–652.

Abramowitz, Alan I. and Kyle L. Saunders. 2000. "Ideological realignment and US congressional elections." *Annual Meeting of the American Political Science Association*, Washington, DC.

Abramowitz, Alan I. and Kyle L. Saunders. 2006. "Exploring the Bases of Partisanship in the American Electorate: Social Identity vs. Ideology." *Political Research Quarterly* 59(2): 175–187.

Adema, William. 2010. *The Welfare State across Selected OECD Countries: How much does it really cost and how good is it in reducing poverty.* Organisation for Economic Co-operation and Development, Employment, Labour and Social Affairs Committee.

Adema, William, Pauline Fron, and Mexime Ladaique. 2011. *Is the European Welfare State Really More Expensive? Indicators on Social Spending, 1980–2012.* Organisation for Economic Co-operation and Development, Employment, Labour and Social Affairs Committee.

Alderson, A.S. and Nielsen, F. 2002. "Globalization and the Great U-Turn: Income Inequality Trends in 16 OECD Countries." *American Journal of Sociology* 107(5): 1244–1299.

Aldrich, John H. and David W. Rohde. 2000. "The Republican Revolution and the House Appropriations Committee." *The Journal of Politics* 62(1): 1–33.

Aldrich, John H., and David W. Rohde. 1998. "Measuring Conditional Party Government." Presented at the annual meeting of the Midwest Political Science Association.

Alt, James E. and Robert C. Lowry. 1994. "Divided Government, Fiscal Institutions, and Budget Deficits: Evidence from the States." *American Political Science Review* 88(4): 811–828.

Alvaredo, Facundo, Tony Atkinson, Thomas Piketty, and Emmanuel Saez. 2014. *The World Top Incomes Database.*

Autor, David H., Alan Manning, and Christopher L. Smith. 2010. "The Contribution of the Minimum Wage to U.S. Wage Inequality over Three Decades: A Reassessment." *National Bureau of Economics Research*, Working Paper No. 16533.

Bacon, Perry Jr. 2009. "Senate Republicans Send Obama Letter Opposing Public Health Plan." *Washington Post*, June 8, 2009.

Baicker, Katherine and Amitabh Chandra. 2006. "The Labor Market Effects of Rising Health Care Insurance Premiums." *Journal of Labor Economics* 24(3): 609–634.

Bartels, Larry M. 2005. "Homer Gets a Tax Cut: Inequality and Public Policy in the American Mind." *Perspectives on Politics* 3(1): 15–31.

Bartels, Larry M. 2008. *Unequal Democracy: The Political Economy of the New Gilded Age*. Princeton, NJ: Princeton University Press.

Baumgartner, F.R. and B.D. Jones. 1993. *Agendas and Instability in American Politics*. Chicago, IL: University of Chicago Press.

Bemelmans-Videc, M.L., R. Rist, E. Vedung (eds). 1998. *Carrots, Sticks and Sermons: Policy Instruments and Their Evaluation*. New Brunswick, NJ: Transaction Publishers.

Bhattacharya, J. and D. Lakdawalla. 2006. "Does Medicare Benefit the Poor?" *Journal of Public Economics* 90(1): 277–292.

Bickers, Kenneth N. and Robert M. Stein. 1996. "The Electoral Dynamics of the Federal Pork Barrel." *American Journal of Political Science* 40: 1300–1326.

Bickers, Kenneth N. and Robert M. Stein. 2000. "Congressional Pork Barrel in a Republican Era." *The Journal of Politics* 62: 1070–1086.

Bittker, Boris. 1968. "Comprehensive Income Taxation: A Response." Faculty Scholarship Series. Paper 2420. Yale Law School Legal Scholarship Repository.

Blais, André, Donald Blake and Stéphane Dion. 1993. "Do Parties Make a Difference? Parties and the Size of Government in Liberal Democracies." *American Journal of Political Science* 37(1): 40–62.

Blais, André, Donald Blake and Stéphane Dion. 1996. "Do Parties Make a Difference? A Reappraisal." *American Journal of Political Science* 40(2): 514–520.

Bosworth, Barry, Gary Burtless, and Eugene Steuerle. 1999. "Lifetime Earnings Patterns, the Distribution of Future Social Security Benefits, and the Impact of Pension Reform." Center for Retirement Research at Boston College.

Box-Steffensmeier, Janet M., Suzanne, De Boef, and T.M. Lin. 2004. "The Dynamics of the Partisan Gender Gap." *American Political Science Review* 98(3): 515–528.

Brady, David W., Hahrie Han, and Jeremy C. Pope. 2007. "Primary Elections and Candidate Ideology: Out of Step with the Primary Electorate?" *Legislative Studies Quarterly* 32(1): 79–105.

Brandolini, Andrea and Timothy M. Smeeding. 2006. "Patterns of Economic Inequality in Western Democracies: Some Facts on Levels and Trends." *PS: Political Science and Politics* 39(1): 21–26.

Brewer, Mark. 2005. "The Rise of Partisanship and the Expansion of Partisan Conflict within the American Electorate." *Political Research Quarterly* 58(2): 219–229.

Browning, Robert X. 1986. *Politics and Social Welfare Policy in the United States.* Knoxville, TN: University of Tennessee Press.

Bucks, Brian K., Arthur B. Kennickell, Traci L. Mach, and Kevin B. Moore. 2009. "Changes in U.S. Family Finances from 2004 to 2007: Evidence from the Survey of Consumer Finances." *Federal Reserve Board*, February 2009, p. A18, A19.

Bureau of Economic Analysis. 2010. *Industry Economic Accounts.*

Bureau of Labor and Statistics. 2011. *Annual Reports on Poverty and the Working Poor.* Washington, D.C.

Burman, Leonard E. 2003. Is the Tax Expenditure Concept Still Relevant? *National Tax Journal* 56: 613–27.

Burman, Leonard E., Christopher Geissler, and Eric J. Toder. 2008a. "How Big Are Total Individual Income Tax Expenditures, and Who Benefits from Them?" *American Economic Review* 98(2): 79–83.

Burman, Leonard, Christopher Geissler, and Eric Toder. 2008b. "The Growth, Distribution, and Opportunity Cost of Individual Income Tax Expenditures." American Social Science Associations Annual Meeting. New Orleans, LA.

Carmines, Edward G. and James A. Stimson. 1989. *Issue Evolution: Race and the Transformation of American Politics.* Princeton, NJ: Princeton University Press.

Carnes, Nicholas. 2013. *White-Collar Government: The Hidden Role of Class in Economic Policymaking.* Chicago, IL: University of Chicago Press.

Campbell, Andrea Louise. 2003. *How Policies Make Citizens: Senior Political Activism and the American Welfare State.* Princeton, NJ: Princeton University Press.

Carsey, Thomas M. and Barry Rundquist. 1999. "Party and Committee in Distributive Politics: Evidence from Defense Spending." *The Journal of Politics* 61(4): 1156–1169.

Cashell, B.W. 2009. "The Federal Government Debt: Its Size and Economic Significance," Congressional Research Service, CRS, Report for Congress.

Cogan, Marin and Jake Sherman. 2011. "Income gap slips into GOP talk." *Politico.* October 30, 2011.

Congressional Budget Office. 2011. *Long-Term Analysis of a Budget Proposal by Chairman Ryan.* Washington, DC: Government Printing Office.

Congressional Budget Office. 2012. *The Budget and Economic Outlook: Fiscal Years 2012 to 2022.* Washington, DC: Government Printing Office.

Cooper, Joseph and Gary Bombardier. 1968. "Presidential Leadership and Party Success." *The Journal of Politics* 30(4): 1012–1027.

Copeland, Craig. 2013. "Employment-Based Retirement Plan Participation: Geographic Differences and Trends, 2012."

Cox, Gary W. and Matthew D. McCubbins. 1986. "Electoral Politics as a Redistributive Game." *The Journal of Politics* 48(2): 370–389.

Cox, Gary W. and Matthew D. McCubbins. 1993. *Legislative Leviathan: Party Government in the House.* Berkeley: University of California Press.

De Boef, Suzanna, and Jim Granato. 1999. "Testing for Cointegrating Relationships with Near-Integrated Data." *Political Analysis* 8(1): 99–117.

De Boef, Suzanna and Luke Keele. 2008. "Taking Time Seriously." *American Journal of Political Science* 52(1): 184–200.

Edsall, Mary D. and Thomas B. Edsall. 1991. *Chain Reaction: The Impact of Race, Rights, and Taxes on American Politics*. New York: W.W. Norton & Company.

Egan, Patrick J. 2013. *Partisan Priorities: How Issue Ownership Drives and Distorts American Politics*. New York: Cambridge University Press.

Ellis, Christopher and Christopher Faricy. 2011. "Social Policy and Public Opinion: How the Ideological Direction of Spending Influences Public Mood." *The Journal of Politics* 73: 1095–1110.

Ellis, Christopher and James A. Stimson. 2012. *Ideology in America*. New York: Cambridge University Press.

Employee Benefit Research Institute. 2009. *The EBRI Databook on Employee Benefits*. Washington, DC: EBRI.

Employee Benefit Research Institute. 2010. *The EBRI Databook on Employee Benefits*. Washington, DC: EBRI.

Employee Benefit Research Institute. 2011. *The EBRI Databook on Employee Benefits*. Washington, DC: EBRI.

Employee Benefit Research Institute. 2012. *The EBRI Databook on Employee Benefits*. Washington, DC: EBRI.

Employee Benefit Research Institute. 2013. *The EBRI Databook on Employee Benefits*. Washington, DC: EBRI.

Engle, R.F. and Granger, C.W.J. 1987. "Co-integration and Error Correction: Representation, Estimation and Testing." *Econometrica* 55: 251–276.

Enthoven, Alain C. and Victor R. Fuchs. 2006. "Employment-Based Health Insurance: Past, Present, and Future." *Health Affairs* 25(6): 1538–1547.

Esping-Anderson, Gøsta. 1990. *The Three Worlds of Welfare Capitalism*. Princeton, NJ. Princeton University Press.

Faricy, Christopher. 2011. "The Politics of Social Policy in America: The Causes and Effects of Indirect versus Direct Social Spending." *Journal of Politics* 73: 74–83.

Faricy, Christopher, and Christopher Ellis. 2014. "Public Attitudes Toward Social Spending in the United States: The Differences Between Direct Spending and Tax Expenditures." *Political Behavior* 36: 53–76.

Feldman, Stanley. 1988. "Structure and Consistency in Public Opinion: The Role of Core Beliefs and Values." *American Journal of Political Science* 32: 416–40.

Fellowes, Matthew and Gretchen Rowe. 2004. "Politics and the New American Welfare States." *American Journal of Political Science* 48(2): 362–373.

Gelman, Andrew. 2008. *Red State, Blue State, Rich State, Poor State: Why Americans Vote the Way They Do*. Princeton, NJ: Princeton University Press.

Giertz, J. Fred and Dennis H. Sullivan. 1986. "Food Assistance Programs in the Reagan Administration." *Publius* 16(1): 133–148.

Gilens, Martin. 1999. *Why Americans Hate Welfare: Race, Media, and the Politics of Antipoverty Policy*. Chicago, IL: University of Chicago Press.

Gilens, Martin. 2012. *Affluence and Influence: Economic Inequality and Political Power in America*. Princeton, NJ: Princeton University Press.

Gilliam, Franklin D. Jr. 1999. "The 'Welfare Queen' Experiment." *Nieman Reports* 53(2): 49–53.

Gimpel, James G. and Jason E. Schuknecht. 2001. "Interstate Migration and Electoral Politics." *Journal of Politics* 63(1): 207–231.

Gitterman, D. 2010. *Boosting Paychecks: The Politics of Supporting America's Working Poor.* Washington, DC: Brookings Institution Press.

Goetz, Edward G. 1995. "Potential Effects of Federal Policy Devolution on Local Housing Expenditures." *Publius* 25(3): 99–116.

Golden, Miriam A. and Michael Wallerstein. 2011. "Domestic and International Causes for the Rise of Pay Inequality in OECD Nations Between 1980 and 2000," in David Brady (ed.), *Comparing European Workers Part A (Research in the Sociology of Work, Volume 22)*, Emerald Group Publishing Limited, 209–249.

Gottschalk, Marie. 2000. *The Shadow Welfare State: Labor, Business, and the Politics of Health-Care in the United States.* Ithaca, NY: Cornell University Press.

Government Accountability Office. 2005. "Tax Expenditures Represent a Substantial Federal Commitment and Need to Be Reexamined." GAO-05-690.

Groseclose, Tim, Steven D. Levitt, and James M. Synder, Jr. 1999. "Comparing Interest Group Scores across Time and Chambers: Adjusted ADA Scores for the U.S. Congress." *The American Political Science Review* 93(1): 33–50.

Grossmann, Matt and Casey B.K. Dominguez. 2009. "Party Coalitions and Interest Group Networks." *American Politics Research* 37(5): 767–800.

Grossmann, Matt and David A. Hopkins. 2014. "The Ideological Right vs. The Group Benefits Left: Asymmetric Politics in America." Presented at the Annual Meeting of the Midwest Political Science Association, Chicago.

Gruber, Jonathan. 1994. "The Incidence of Mandated Maternity Benefits." *American Economics Review* 84: 622–41.

Gruber, Jonathan. 2010. "The Tax Exclusion for Employer Sponsored Health Insurance." Working Paper 15766. National Bureau of Economic Research.

Gruber, Jonathan and Alan B. Krueger. 1991. *The Incidence of Mandated Employer-provided Insurance: Lessons from Workers' Compensation Insurance.* No. w3557. National Bureau of Economic Research.

Gustafsson, Bjorn and Mats Johansson. 1999. "In Search of Smoking Guns: What Makes Income Inequality Vary Over Time in Different Countries?" *American Sociological Review* 64: 585–605.

Hacker, Jacob S. 2002. *The Divided Welfare State: The Battle over Public and Private Social Benefits in the United States.* New York: Cambridge University Press.

Hacker, Jacob S. 2004. "Privatizing Risk without Privatizing the Welfare State: The Hidden Politics of Social Policy Retrenchment in the United States." *American Political Science Review* 98(2): 243–260.

Hacker, Jacob S. 2006. *The Great Risk Shift: The New Economic Insecurity and the Decline of the American Dream.* New York: Oxford University Press.

Hacker, J. and P. Pierson. 2010. *Winner-Take-All Politics: How Washington Made the Rich Richer – And Turned Its Back on the Middle Class.* New York: Simon and Schuster.

Haselswerdt, Jake and Brandon Bartels. 2013. "Citizen Perceptions of Tax Expenditures and Their Costs: Evidence From a Survey Experiment." A working paper.

Heaney, Michael T., Seth E. Masket, Joanne M. Miller, and Dara Strolovitch. 2012. "Polarized Networks: The Organizational Affiliations of National Party Convention Delegates." *American Behavioral Scientist* 56(12): 1654–1676.

Helderman, Rosalind and Paul Kane. 2011. "Debt-ceiling crisis still eludes compromise." *The Washington Post*, July 7, 2011.

Hetherington, Marc J. 2001. "Resurgent Mass Partisanship: The Role of Elite Polarization." *The American Political Science Review* 95(3): 619–631.

Hibbs, Douglas. 1987. *The American Political Economy: Macroeconomics and Electoral Politics in the United States*. Cambridge, MA: Harvard University Press.

Hodge, Scott A. 2011. "Distribution and Efficiency in the Tax Code." Hearing on the Distribution and Efficiency in the Tax Code Before the U.S. Senate Budget Committee. March 9, 2011.

House Report 112-058. 2011. *Concurrent Resolution on the Budget: Fiscal Year 2012*. April 11, 2011.

Howard, Christopher. 1997. *The Hidden Welfare State: Tax Expenditures and Social Policy in the United States*. Princeton, NJ: Princeton University Press.

Howard, Christopher. 2007. *The Welfare State Nobody Knows: Debunking Myths about U.S. Social Policy*. Princeton, NJ: Princeton University Press.

Huber, Evelyne and John D. Stephens. 2001. *Development and Crisis of the Welfare State: Parties and Policies in Global Markets*. Chicago, IL: University of Chicago Press.

Hungerford, Thomas L. 2008. *"Tax Expenditures and the Federal Budget."* Washington, DC: Congressional Research Service.

Hungerford, Thomas L. 2009. "The Redistributive Effect of Selected Federal Transfer and Tax Provisions." Washington, DC: Congressional Research Service.

Internal Revenue Service. 2003. *"SOI Bulletin: Selected Itemized Deductions."* Washington D.C.: Government Printing Office.

Jacobs, Lawrence and Theda Skocpol. 2005. *Inequality and American Democracy: What We Know and What We Need to Learn*. New York: Russell Sage Foundation.

Jacobson, Gary C. 2001. "A House and Senate Divided: The Clinton Legacy and the Congressional Elections of 2000." *Political Science Quarterly* 116(1): 5–27.

Jacobson, Gary C. 2005. "Polarized Politics and the 2004 Congressional and Presidential Elections." *Political Science Quarterly* 120(2): 199–218, 786–802.

Jacoby, William G. 2000. "Issue Framing and Public Opinion on Government Spending." *American Journal of Political Science* 44: 750–767.

Jacoby, William G. 2006. "Value Choices and American Public Opinion." *American Journal of Political Science* 50(3): 706–723.

Joint Committee on Taxation. 2007. *Estimates of Federal Tax Expenditures for Fiscal Years 2007–2011*. Washington, DC: Government Printing Office.

Joint Committee on Taxation. 2008a. *Estimates of Federal Tax Expenditures for Fiscal Years 2008–2012*. Washington, DC: Government Printing Office.

Joint Committee on Taxation. 2008b. "A Reconsideration of Tax Expenditure Analysis." JCX-37-08.

Joint Committee on Taxation. 2011. "Background Information on Tax Expenditure Analysis and Historical Survey of Tax Expenditure Estimates." Scheduled for a Public Hearing Before the Senate Finance Committee on Finance on March 1, 2011.

Joint Committee on Taxation. 2012. *Estimates of Federal Tax Expenditures for Fiscal Years 2011–2015*. Washington, DC: Government Printing Office.

Joint Committee on Taxation. 2013. *Estimates of Federal Tax Expenditures for Fiscal Years 2012–2017*. Washington, DC: Government Printing Office.

Jones, Bryan D. and Frank R. Baumgartner. 2005. *The Politics of Attention: How Government Prioritizes Problems*. Chicago, IL: University of Chicago Press.

Jones, Bryan D. and Frank R. Baumgartner. 2012. "From There to Here: Punctuated Equilibrium to the General Punctuation Thesis to a Theory of Government Information Processing." *Policy Studies Journal* 40(1): 1–20.

Jones, Bryan D., Frank R. Baumgartner, and James L. True. 1998. "Policy Punctuations: US Budget Authority, 1947–1995." *The Journal of Politics* 60(1): 1–33.

Jones, Byran D., Frank Baumgartner, and James L. True. 2008. "Historical Budget Records Converted to the Present Functional Categorization with Actual Results for FY 1947–2008." The Policy Agendas Project.

Jones, Maggie R. 2014. "Changes in EITC Eligibility and Participation, 2005–2009." Washington, DC: U.S. Census Bureau.

Judis, John B. and Ruy Teixeira. 2002. *The Emerging Democratic Majority*. New York: Scribner.

The Kaiser Family Foundation. 2010. *Employer Health Benefits: 2010 Summary of Findings*. Washington, DC: The Henry J. Kaiser Family Foundation.

The Kaiser Family Foundation. 2011. "Health Care Spending in the United States and Selected OECD Countries." April 2011. Washington, D.C: The Henry Kaiser Family Foundation.

Kellstedt, Paul M. 2000. "Media Framing and the Dynamics of Racial Policy Preferences." *American Journal of Political Science* 44: 239–255.

Kelly, Nathan J. 2009. *The Politics of Income Inequality in the United States*. New York: Cambridge University Press.

Kettl, Donald F. 1997. "The Global Revolution in Public Management: Driving Themes, Missing Links." *Journal of Policy Analysis and Management* 16(3): 446–462.

Kiewiet, D. Roderick and Mathew McCubbins. 1991. *The Logic of Delegation: Congressional Parties and the Appropriations Process*. Chicago, IL: University of Chicago Press.

Kleinbard, Edward. 2010a. "The Congress within the Congress: How Tax Expenditures Distort Our Budget and Our Political Processes." *Ohio Northern University Law Review* 36: 1–31.

Kleinbard, Edward. 2010b. "Tax Expenditure Framework Legislation." *National Tax Journal* 63: 353–382.

Knuckey, Jonathan. 2013. "The Survival of the Democratic Party Outside the South: An Update and Reassessment." *Party Politics* (2): 1–14.

Koger, Gregory, Seth Masket, and Hans Noel. 2009. "Partisan Webs: Information Exchange and Party Networks." *British Journal of Political Science* 39(03): 633–653.

Kristol, Bill. 1993. "Memorandum to Republican Leaders: Defeating President Clinton's Health Care Proposal."

Layman, Geoffrey C. and Thomas M. Carsey. 2002. "Party Polarization and 'Conflict Extension' in the American Electorate." *American Journal of Political Science* 46: 786–802.

Leachman, Michael, Dylan Grundman, and Nicholas Johnson. 2011. *Promoting State Budget Accountability Through Tax Expenditure Reporting*. Washington, DC: Center on Budget and Policy Priorities.

Lee, Frances E. 2000. "Senate Representation and Coalition Building in Distributive Politics." *The American Political Science Review* 94: 59–72.

Lee, Julie, Mark McClellan, and Jonathan Skinner. 1999. "The Distributional Effects of Medicare," in James M. Poterba (ed.), *Tax Policy and the Economy*, Cambridge, MA: MIT Press.

Leigh, Andrew. 2007. "How Closely Do Top Income Shares Track Other Measures of Inequality?" *The Economic Journal* 117: F619-F633.

Levitt, Steven D. and James M. Snyder, Jr. 1995. "Political Parties and the Distribution of Federal Outlays." *American Journal of Political Science*, 39: 958–980.

Levitt, Steven D. and James M. Snyder, Jr. 1997. "The Impact of Federal Spending on House Election Outcomes." *The Journal of Political Economy* 105: 3–53.

Levy, Frank and Richard J. Murnane. 2001. "Will Standards-Based Reforms Improve the Education of Students of Color?" *National Tax Journal* 54(2):401–415.

Lewis-Beck, Michael S., William Jacoby, Helmut Norpoth, and Herbert Weisberg. 2009. *The American Voter Revisited*. Ann Arbor: University of Michigan Press.

Liebman, Jeffrey. 2002. "Redistribution in the Current U.S. Social Security System," in *The Distributional Aspects of Social Security and Social Security Reform*. Chicago, IL: University of Chicago Press.

Lipsky, Michael and Steven Rathgeb Smith. 1989. "Nonprofit Organizations, Government, and the Welfare State." *Political Science Quarterly* 104(4): 625–648.

Lowi, Theodore. 1963. "Toward Functionalism in Political Science: The Case of Innovation in Party Systems." *The American Political Science Review* 57(3): 570–583.

Lowi, Theodore. 1969. *The End of Liberalism: Ideology, Policy, and the Crisis of Public Authority*. New York: WW Norton.

Lubove, Richard. 1968. *The Struggle for Social Security, 1900–1935*. Cambridge, MA: Harvard University Press.

Luxembourg Income Study. 2013. *LIS Cross-National Data Center*.

Mak, Tim. "Poll: Jobs priority over wealth gap." *Politico*. December 16, 2011.

Mann, Thomas E. and Norman J. Ornstein. 2012. *It's Even Worse Than It Looks: How the American Constitutional System Collided with the New Politics of Extremism*. New York: Basic Books.

Marmor, Theodore R. 2000. *The Politics of Medicare*. New Brunswick, NJ: Transaction Publishers.

Marr, Chuck and Brian Highsmith. 2011. "Reforming Tax Expenditures Can Reduce Deficits While Making the Tax Code More Efficient and Equitable." *Center on Budget and Policy Priorities.* Washington D.C.: CBPP.

Mayhew, David R. 1991. *Divided We Govern: Party Control, Lawmaking, and Investigations, 1946–1990.* New Haven, CT: Yale University Press.

McCall, Leslie. 2013. *The Undeserving Rich: American Beliefs about Inequality, Opportunity, and Redistribution.* New York: Cambridge University Press.

McCarty, Nolan, Keith T. Poole, and Howard Rosenthal. 1997. "The Realignment of National Politics and Income Distribution." *American Enterprise Institute Studies on Understanding Economic Inequality.*

McCarty, Nolan, Keith T. Poole, and Howard Rosenthal. 2000. "The Hunt for Party Discipline in Congress." *American Political Science Review* 95(3): 673–687.

McCarty, Nolan, Keith T. Poole, and Howard Rosenthal. 2006. *Polarized America: The Dance of Ideology and Unequal Riches.* Cambridge: MIT Press.

McCarty, Nolan, Keith T. Poole, and Howard Rosenthal. 2013. *Political Bubbles: financial crises and the failure of American democracy.*Princeton, NJ: Princeton University Press.

McClellan, M. and J. Skinner. 1999. "Medicare Reform: Who Pays, and Who Benefits?" *Health Affairs* 18(1): 48–62.

McClellan, Mark and Jonathan Skinner. 2006. "The Incidence of Medicare." *Journal of Public Economics,* 90(1–2): 257–276.

McGhee, Eric; Seth Masket, Boris Shor, Steven Rogers and Nolan McCarty. 2014. "A Primary Cause of Partisanship? Nomination Systems and Legislator Ideology." *American Journal of Political Science* 58(2): 337–351.

Mettler, Suzanne. 2007. "The Transformed Welfare State and the Redistribution of Political Voice." In Pierson, Paul and Theda Skocpol (eds.), *The Transformation of American Politics: Activist Government and the Rise of Conservatism,* Princeton, NJ: Princeton University Press, pp. 191–222.

Mettler, S. 2011. *The Submerged State: How Invisible Government Policies Undermine American Democracy.* Chicago, IL: University of Chicago Press.

Mettler, S. and John Sides. 2012. "We Are the 96 Percent." *New York Times,* September 25, 2012.

Mishel, Lawrence, Jared Bernstein, and Heather Boushey. 2003. *The State of Working America, 2002/2003.* Ithaca, NY: Cornell University Press.

Morgan, Kimberly J. and Andrea L. Campbell. 2011. *The Delegated Welfare State: Medicare, Markets, and the Governance of Social Policy.* New York: Oxford University Press.

Nadeau, Richard and Harold W. Stanley. 1993. "Class Polarization in Partisanship among Native Southern Whites, 1952–90." *American Journal of Political Science* 37(3): 900–919.

Nadeau, Richard, Richard G. Niemi, Harold W. Stanley, and Jean-Francois Godbout. 2004. "Class, Party, and South/Non-South Differences An Update." *American Politics Research* 32(1): 52–67.

Neckerman, Kathryn M. and Florencia Torche. 2007. "Inequality: Causes and Consequences." *Annual Review of Sociology* 33: 335–357.

New York Times. 2012. "Presidential Exit Polls."

New York Times Editorial Board. "Mitt Romney, Class Warrior." *New York Times.* September 19, 2012.

Nichter, Simeon. 2008. "Vote Buying or Turnout Buying? Machine Politics and the Secret Ballot." *American Political Science Review* 102(1): 19–31.

Obama, Barack. 2011a. *Speech on Deficit Cutting.* George Washington University, Washington, DC, April 13, 2011. Text accessible at: http://www.npr.org/2011/04/13/135383045/president-obamas-speech-on-deficit-cutting.

Obama, Barack. 2011b. *Speech on the Economy.* Osawatomie High School, Osawatomie, KS. December 6, 2011. Text accessible at: http://www.whitehouse.gov/the-press-office/2011/12/06/remarks-president-economy-osawatomie-kansas.

Obama, Barack. 2012. *State of the Union Address.* Text accessible at: http://www.whitehouse.gov/the-press-office/2012/01/24/remarks-president-state-union-address.

Oberlander, Jonathan. 2003. *The Political Life of Medicare.* Chicago, IL: University of Chicago Press.

Oberlander, Jonathan. 2007. "Learning from Failure in Health Care Reform." *New England Journal of Medicine* 357(17): 1677–1679.

Olson, Laura Katz. 2010. *The Politics of Medicaid.* New York: Columbia University Press.

Organisation for Economic Co-operation and Development. 2012. *OECD Social Expenditure Database, 1980–2012.* Paris.

Office of Management and Budget. *Budget of the US Government: 2011.* Washington, DC: Government Printing Office, 2011.

Office of Management and Budget. *Budget of the US Government: 2012.* Washington, DC: Government Printing Office, 2012.

Page, Benjamin I., and Lawrence R. Jacobs. 2009. *Class War? What Americans Really Think about Economic Inequality.* Chicago, IL: University of Chicago Press.

Pelosi, Nancy. Speech to the NAACP on July 17, 2009.

Petrocik, James R. 1996. "Issue Ownership in Presidential Elections, with a 1980 Case Study." *American Journal of Political Science* 40: 825–850.

Pew Research Center. 2014. "Most See Inequality Growing, but Partisans Differ Over Solutions." *Pew Research Center/USA Today Survey.* January 23, 2014.

Phelps, Charles E. 2002. *Health Economics.* Third Edition. New York: Pearson.

Pierson, Paul. 1994. *Dismantling the Welfare State? Reagan, Thatcher and the Politics of Retrenchment.* Cambridge: Cambridge University Press.

Pierson, Paul. 1996. "The New Politics of the Welfare State." *World Politics* 48(2): 143–179.

Piketty, Thomas. 2014. *Capital in the Twenty-First Century.* Cambridge, MA: Belknap Press.

Piketty, Thomas and Emmanuel Saez. 2003. "Income Inequality in the United States, 1913–1998." *The Quarterly Journal of Economics,* 118: 1–39.

Piketty, Thomas and Emmanuel Saez. 2006. "The Evolution of Top Incomes: A Historical and International Perspective." *The American Economic Review* 96: 200–205.

Pontusson, Jonas and Lane Kenworthy. 2005. "Rising Inequality and the Politics of Redistribution in Affluent Countries." *Perspectives on Politics* 3(3): 449–471.

Poole, Keith T. 1998. "Recovering a Basic Space From a Set of Issue Scales." *American Journal of Political Science* 42: 954–993.

Poole, Keith T. and Howard Rosenthal. 1984. "The Polarization of American Politics." *The Journal of Politics* 46(4): 1061–1079.

Poole, Keith T. and Howard Rosenthal. 1993. "Spatial Realignment and the Mapping of Issues in US History: The Evidence from Roll Call Voting." *Agenda Formation* 12: 13–39.

Poole, Keith and Howard Rosenthal. 1997. *Congress: A Political-Economic History of Roll-Call Voting*. New York: Oxford University Press.

Poole, Keith and Howard Rosenthal. 2001. "D-NOMINATE after 10 Years: A Comparative Update to Congress: A Political-Economic History of Roll-Call Voting." *Legislative Studies Quarterly* 26(1): 5–29.

Purcell, Patrick. 2008. "Pension Sponsorship and Participation: Summary of Recent Trends." *Federal Publications*: 543.

Rao, Nirmala. 1998. "Representation in Local Politics: A Reconsideration and Some New Evidence." *Political Studies* 46(1): 19–35.

Reno, Virginia and Elisa A. Walker. 2013. "Social Security Benefits, Finances, and Policy Options: A Primer." National Academy of Social Insurance.

Rohde, David W. 1991. *Parties and Leaders in the Postreform House*. Chicago, IL: University of Chicago Press.

Rosenberg, Joseph, Patrick Rooney, C. Eugene Steuerle, and Katherine Toran. 2011. "What's Been Happening to Charitable Giving Recently? A Look at the Data." Washington, DC: Urban Institute and Brookings Tax Policy Center.

Saez, Emmanuel and M.S. Veal. 2005. "The Evolution of High Incomes in Northern America: Lessons from Canadian Evidence." *National Bureau of Economic Research, Inc.*, NBER Working Papers: 2005.

Salamon, Lester, ed. 1989. *Beyond Privatisation, the Tools of Government Action*. Washington, DC: Urban Institute.

Salamon, Lester M. 2002. *The Tools of Government: A Guide to New Governance*. New York: Oxford University Press.

Schattscheidner, E.E. 1960. *The Semisovereign People: A Realist's View of Democracy in America*. Hinsdale, IL: The Dyrden Press.

Schneider, Anne, and Helen Ingram. 1993. "Social Construction of Target Populations: Implications for Politics and Policy." *American Political Science Review* 87(2): 334–347.

Skocpol, Theda. 1988. "The Limits of the New Deal System and the Roots of Contemporary Welfare Dilemmas." In Margaret Wier, Ann Shola Orloff, and Theda Skocpol (eds.) *The Politics of Social Policy in the United States*, Princeton, NJ: Princeton University Press, 293–311.

Skocpol, Theda. 1995. *Protecting Soldiers and Mothers: The Political Origins of Social Policy in the United States*. Cambridge, MA: Harvard University Press.

Slessarev, Helene. 1988. "Racial Tensions and Institutional Support: Social Programs During a Period of Retrenchment." In Margaret Wier, Ann Shola Orloff, and Theda Skocpol (eds.), *The Politics of Social Policy in the United States*, Princeton, NJ: Princeton University Press, 357–79.

Smith, Jessica C. and Carla Medalia. 2014. *Health Insurance Coverage in the United States: 2013*. Washington, DC: U.S. Census Bureau.

Smith, Mark A. 2000. *American Business and Political Power*. Chicago, IL: University of Chicago Press.

Smith, Mark A. 2007. *The Right Talk: How Conservatives transformed the Great Society into the Economic Society*. Princeton, NJ: Princeton University Press.

Social Security Administration. 2000. "Social Security Bulletin, Vol. 62 No. 4." *Social Security Administration*. Washington: Government Printing Office.

Social Security Administration. 2005. "Social Security Bulletin, Vol. 65 No. 4." *Social Security Administration*. Washington: Government Printing Office.

Social Security Administration. 2009. "Social Security Bulletin, Vol. 69 No. 1." *Social Security Administration*. Washington: Government Printing Office.

Sonmez, Felicia. 2011. "Tom Coburn unveils plan to achieve $9 trillion in deficit savings over next decade." *Washington Post*. July 18, 2011.

Soss, Joe. 1999. "Lessons of Welfare: Policy Design, Political Learning, and Political Action." *American Political Science Review* 93: 363–380.

Soss, Joe, Sanford F. Schram, Thomas P. Vartanian, and Erin O'Brien. 2003. "The Hard Line and the Color Line." *Race and the Politics of Welfare Reform*: 225–53.

Steuerle, Eugene and Adam Carasso. 2003. *Redistribution Under OASDI: How Much and to Whom?* Washington, DC: Urban-Brookings Tax Policy Center.

Stone, Chad, Hanhah Shaw, Danilo Trisi, and Arloc Sherman. 2012. *A Guide to Statistics on Historical Trends in Income Inequality*. Washington, DC: Center on Budget and Policy Priorities.

Stonecash, Jeffrey. 2000. *Class and Party in American Politics*. Boulder, CO: Westview Press.

Stonecash, Jeffrey M. and M.D. Mariani. 2000. "Republican Gains in the House in the 1994 Elections: Class Polarization in American Politics." *Political Science Quarterly* 115(1): 93–113.

Stonecash, Jeffrey M., Mark D. Brewer, and M.D. Mariani. 2003. *Diverging Parties: Social Change, Realignment, and Party Polarization*. Boulder, CO: Westview Press.

Surrey, Stanley S. 1974. *Pathways to Tax Reform: The Concept of Tax Expenditures*. Cambridge, MA: Harvard University Press.

Surrey, Stanely S. and Paul R. McDaniel. 1985. *Tax Expenditures*. Cambridge, MA: Harvard University Press.

Swindell, B., K. Schueler, and A. Bettelheim. 2004. *Bush's Domestic Vision: Help People Help Themselves*. Congressional Quarterly Weekly January 24, 2004.

Teles, Steven M. 2007. "Conservative Mobilization against Entrenched Liberalism." In Pierson, Paul and Theda Skocpol (eds.), *The Transformation of American Politics*. Princeton, NJ: Princeton University Press.

Theriault, Sean. 2008. *Party Polarization in Congress*. New York: Cambridge University Press.

Thomasson, Melissa. 2003. "The Importance of Group Coverage: How Tax Policy Shaped U.S Health Insurance." *The American Economic Review* 93(4): 1373–1384.

Titmuss, Richard M. 1965. "The Role of Redistribution in Social Policy," Social Security Bulletin, 28, 14–20.

Toder, Eric. 2005. "Tax Expenditures and Tax Reform: Issues and Analysis" Presented at the *National Tax Association Meetings*. Miami, FL.

Toder, E. J., Wasow, B., Ettlinger, M. P., and the Century Foundation. 2002. *Bad Breaks All Around: The Report of the Century Foundation Working Group on Tax Expenditures*. New York: Century Foundation Press.

Toder, Eric, Benjamin Harris, and Ketherine Lim. 2011. "Distributional Effects of Tax Expenditures." Washington, D.C: Tax Policy Center at the Urban Institute and Brookings Institution.

U.S. Census Bureau. 2011. Health Insurance Coverage in the United States: 2010

U.S. Department of Labor. 2010. *Women in the Labor Force: A Data Book*. Bureau of Labor Statistics. Washington, DC: Government Printing Office.

Verba, Sidney, Kay Lehman Schlozman, and Henry E. Brady. 1995. *Voice and Equality: Civic Voluntarism in American Politics*. Cambridge, MA: Harvard University Press.

Wanniski, Jude. 1976. "Taxes and a Two-Santa Theory." *National Observer* March 6, 1976.

Warshaw, Shirley Anne. 2009. *The Co-Presidency of Bush and Cheney*. Stanford, CA: Stanford University Press.

Weaver, R. K. 2000. *Ending Welfare as We Know It*. Washington, DC: Brookings Institution Press.

Weber, Mike. 2007. "2004 Public Use Tax File." Washington, DC: Individual Statistics Branch at the Internal Revenue Service.

Weir, Margaret, Ann Shola Orloff, and Theda Skocpol, eds. 1988. *The Politics of Social Policy in the United States*. Princeton, NJ: Princeton University Press.

Weisman, Jonathan. "Rejecting 'Buffett Rule,' House Passes Business Tax Cut." *New York Times*, April 19, 2012.

Williams, Roberton. 2013. *Fewer Americans Pay No Federal Income Tax*. Washington, D.C: The Tax Policy Center.

Wlezien, Christopher and Stuart N. Soroka. 2003. "Measures and Models of Budgetary Policy." *Policy Studies Journal* 31(2): 273–286.

Wong, Scott. "Dems: We'll Push the Buffett Rule 'All Year Long.'" *Politico*. April 5, 2012.

Woodbury, Stephen. 1983. "Substitution Between Wage and Nonwage Benefits." *The American Economic Review* 73: 166–182.

Zaller, John. 1992. *The Nature and Origins of Mass Opinion*. New York: Cambridge University Press.

Zingher, Joshua. 2014. "An Analysis of the Changing Social Bases of America's Political Parties: 1952–2008." *Electoral Studies* 35: 272–282.

Index

In page numbers so noted, fig, n, or t indicate figure, note, and table, respectively.

CPSIA information can be obtained
at www.ICGtesting.com
Printed in the USA
LVHW020322290721
693949LV00006B/559